THE WRONG END OF THE TABLE

THE WRONG END OF THE TABLE

A MOSTLY COMIC MEMOIR OF A MUSLIM ARAB AMERICAN WOMAN JUST TRYING TO FIT IN

AYSER SALMAN

FOREWORD BY REZA ASLAN

Skyhorse Publishing

Skyhorse Publishing books may be purchased in bulk at special discounts for sales promotion, corporate gifts, fund-raising, or educational purposes. Special editions can also be created to specifications. For details, contact the Special Sales Department, Skyhorse Publishing, 307 West 36th Street, 11th Floor, New York, NY 10018 or info@skyhorsepublishing.com.

Visit our website at www.skyhorsepublishing.com.

10 9 8 7 6 5 4 3 2 1

Library of Congress Cataloging-in-Publication Data is available on file.

Cover design by Erin Seaward-Hiatt
Cover photo credit: iStockphoto

Print ISBN: 978-1-5107-4207-9
Ebook ISBN: 978-1-5107-4208-6

Printed in the United States of America

For anyone who's ever been at the *wrong end*.

Contents

Foreword

Twenty years ago, you had to search for memoirs written by Middle Eastern Americans. That changed after 9/11, when anyone remotely reminiscent of anything Arabic was thrust into the spotlight. Social media came along, and with that, a whole new playing field where anyone from any background could tell their stories. It wasn't vanity; it was our duty. Middle Eastern Americans make up just over 3 percent of the nation's population. Muslim Americans (of all races) make up 1 percent. Yet you wouldn't realize it by how much we occupy the mainstream American psyche. We were compelled to correct the narrative.

Today, as the Trump Administration continues to push through an unprecedented degree of anti-Muslim measures, Islamophobia has grown. But so has the response from Muslim and Middle Eastern communities. In record numbers across the country, Muslims are registering to vote and taking to the streets in peaceful protest. Not only that, they're running for office, because the best protection under a democracy is to actually participate in it.

And yet despite all that, you still have to search to find meaningful stories that depict Muslims as anything other than potential terrorist threats. Even as civic engagement of Muslim Americans rises, the media itself has failed in keeping up. In both news and entertainment, Muslims are still presented as one-dimensional, rather than the complex and relatable characters that we really are.

Which brings us to Ayser Salman, a Muslim American who was born in Iraq, raised in Saudi Arabia and Kentucky, and has worked as a writer, producer, and editor in Hollywood for the past twenty years. If anyone represents the convergence of the issues going around Hollywood today, it would be her.

Pick up a Muslim American memoir these days, and you'll find that it typically tackles one of three subjects: political oppression in the Middle East, Islamophobia in the West, or renegotiating the East-West convergence of tradition and modernity. For many, faith is a core component of the writer's identity. But it's important to remember that Islam itself is not just merely a tradition; it's also a platform that helps us critically engage in the social issues that drive current events today.

And what of those stories where faith isn't as domineering? To be a secular Muslim is just as valid as being a religious one. And to find your identity more in your experience as an immigrant is just as compelling as finding it through spiritual awakening. To put it plainly, our stories should not be of Muslims who happen to live in America: they should be of Americans who happen to come from Muslim backgrounds.

Which is what makes *The Wrong End of the Table* such an insightful and enjoyable read. Through her own life story, Ayser Salman uses her experiences to distill not just Islam, but also the impact religion and culture have on how we interact and understand the world around us. What emerges is that rare voice that is both relatable and unafraid to examine the complexities of her American identity—as a minority, an immigrant, and a woman.

—REZA ASLAN, #1 *New York Times* bestselling author of
Zealot: The Life and Times of Jesus of Nazareth

All of the situations in this memoir are (mostly) true.
Some are ~~extremely~~ exaggerated (but I am honest when that happens).

All names have been changed to protect the innocent,
except for my immediate family and two of the men I dated.

THE WRONG END OF THE TABLE

Preface

With Thanks[1] & Apologies[2] to Mom

You know that feeling of being at the wrong end of the table? Like you're at a fabulous party but all the good stuff is happening just out of earshot? And you're there trying desperately to contribute and connect, but you're too far away? Nowadays they call it FOMO (Fear of Missing Out). But I've always known it as LAAI—Life as an Immigrant. It's why I wrote this book.

Like many immigrant stories, mine begins straightforwardly enough:

As you can see, I'm skeptical about these upcoming "amazing opportunities."

1. The **EMIGRATION** itself. That's when your father announces on the eve of your third birthday that your gift this year is the family moving from your comfy, cozy home in Baghdad, Iraq, with the huge backyard where you spent hours reading under the sun, to a tiny university apartment in the freezing-cold tundra of Columbus, Ohio. And though you don't get to bring with you

1 My mother has been telling me I'd be a great storyteller since I was a child. She's thrilled I'm finally listening to her after all these years and writing this book. I want to thank her for her support.

2 But there are also a few things in this book Mom might not be happy about . . .

the dollhouse you received from Aunt Reema, Dad promises you will have amazing opportunities, better than what would be possible if you stay in Baghdad. And so you embark on the journey. (Mainly because legal emancipation from your parents isn't an option in Iraq until the age of seventy-four, and even then only if you're married.[3])

2. Then comes the **EXCITEMENT**. That's when you and your baby brother, Zaid, discover the joys of hurling snowballs at each other and getting matching Star Wars footie pajamas. And later, when you move to Lexington, Kentucky, there's the joy of seeing horses close-up for the first time ever; and it's where, eight years later, you'll stand next to your father as he tearfully pledges allegiance to the flag of this country and becomes a naturalized citizen. As the song says, you're proud to be an American, where at least you know you're free.
3. But there's also the uncomfortable phase of **ASSIMILATION**. This is where they make you go to school and you have to stand in front of fifteen kindergartners and talk about where you came from and why you have such a weird name; then they make you go to speech therapy class to properly pronounce your *r*s the way Americans do. But while you're learning all this new stuff, you're also supposed to not forget the stuff from the "old country." This is especially important when Aunt Reema calls from Baghdad and you proudly answer the phone with an English "Hello," and she accuses you of turning your back on your native language and, of course, blames your mother.

It's bad enough being a kid who is trying to fit into mainstream America. But you have to do it on your own without much help from your parents because they're too busy trying to fit in as *adults*. And since

3 This might be a gross exaggeration.

they have to go to jobs so they can pay for your expanding Star Wars pajama addiction, you try not to burden them too much. Also, they're trying to calm Aunt Reema down, who by now assumes your father has bought himself a pair of leather pants and gotten a tattoo because somehow she obtained a bootlegged copy of the film *Easy Rider* and assumes all of America lives like that. So your mother makes you recite a few lines of Arabic nursery rhymes to Aunt Reema on the phone every damn week to prove you haven't gone rogue. When all you really wanna do is watch *Sesame Street*.[4]

My brother and I on the first day of school, two years into our American life. New haircuts. Matching Trapper Keepers. No sun protection for our eyes.

I was a kid, alone in a strange country, and I found solace in the things that typically keep you from feeling isolated when you're a kid alone in a strange country—books, magazines, TV, and movies. It was a way for me to connect with anyone who might remotely be like me. The book that resonated with me the *most* was the hilarious memoir *My Family and Other Animals* by Gerald Durrell. I instantly fell in love with it, mainly because it depicted the author's dysfunctional British family during their time living abroad in Corfu. In addition to the humor that naturally comes from "fish out of water" stories, it was the first time I'd read a literary account about a family as ~~batshit-crazy~~ ~~looney-tunes~~ *colorful* as mine. It encouraged me to view my family not as a source of annoyance, but as a source of entertainment. Of course, I didn't realize this fully until a few (million) hours of therapy and angst-filled journal entries later. That's when I thought, *If I'm an outsider, I, too, can write a book!*

4 My publisher just interrupted me to gently ask me to get to the point.

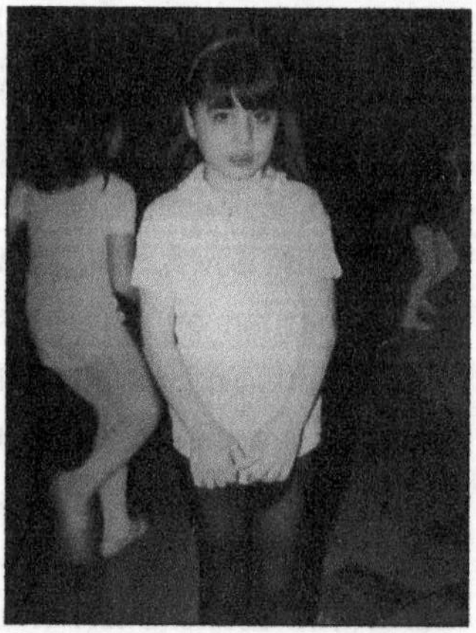

Not technically at the table, but definitely a fish out of water.

This book is meant to be entertaining and also educational: a how-to guide. Or, in my case, a how-*not*-to guide. The point is, you'll learn a lot of "Everything you ever wanted to know about Arabs but were afraid to ask" by turning the pages. For instance, Are Arabs dangerous? Answer: Yes, but not for reasons you would expect. You'll also get an insight into America from an outsider's lens. Why are American kids so obsessed with playing doctor? Answer: see Chapter 1, "'Playing Doctor'—Is This What Happens in Day Care?" It's also a book about a lot of the stuff Muslim girls are not supposed to talk about, e.g., dating and sex (Chapter 13, "Livin' on a Prayer: The Saudi Years, Final" and about ten other chapters).[5]

And it's a book for anyone who has ever felt like a fish out of water.

When I was a toddler, my parents moved my brother, Zaid, and me to the United States—to Lexington, Kentucky. It was the seventies, and Iraq wasn't the household name it is now. Whenever people asked, I told them I came from Ohio—which was *technically* true, since we landed in Columbus and stayed there for two years before settling in Lexington.

None of my blond-haired, blue-eyed counterparts at school in Kentucky seemed to be able to pronounce my name (AY-sir); and if they could, they'd tweak it with some clever play on words, such as "Ayser Eraser" or "Ayzur Razor Blade," as in, "Hey Ayzur Razor Blade, you gonna shave your mustache tonight?" This was before I turned eight,

5 My mother just interrupted me to express her concerns over how explicit I'm planning on being regarding dating and sex. I would like to assure my mother that whatever I say will not bring shame on the family, or at least upset Aunt Reema. Further, I would like to tell my mother that her nonrelevant interjections will be relegated to the footnotes section.

the age my mother deemed it acceptable to use cream bleach on my upper lip so the downy peach fuzz us dark-haired girls are cursed with wouldn't be noticeable. Bleaching your upper lip took care of *one* problem, but it created another once you went outside into direct sunlight. I can't tell you how many times during my second-grade career that I tried to join a game of four square at recess, only to hear, "Ayzur Razor, you have something shiny on your upper lip!" When they came up close enough to examine it, they screeched, "A yellow mustache! Ayzur Razor Mustard Face!"[6, 7] I began telling people at school that my real name was "Lisa" and that "Ayser" was some convoluted family name.[8]

My theory about being an immigrant is that it can go either of two ways:

---

6 I actually did take a razor to my mustard lip once. For two days, my life was blissfully free of ridicule at school. Then my mother discovered what I had done and screamed at me about how when you shave, the hair grows back thicker and now I was committed to a lifetime of hair removal if I didn't want to look like former Iraqi dictator Saddam Hussein. I didn't. The thought of her eight-year-old daughter wielding a blade repeatedly to fix the problem so horrified my mother that she allowed me to use Nair, under her close supervision. For those who don't know, Nair is a chemical cream you put on your face; it essentially *burns* the hair off, leaving a red mark over your upper lip. If you don't mind this, you're set. Until they start calling you "Ayzur Kool-Aid Mouth."

7 My mother wants to know whether I, as a strong Arab American woman, don't have better things to discuss than my hairy upper lip and reducing our people to a stereotype. Might my time be better used to discuss my life accomplishments as a demonstration of the "good side of Arabs"? She also suggests that since this happened some thirty years ago, perhaps I should simply "get over with it" (Mom has a habit of adding words where they shouldn't be and removing them when they should be there) because what I went through was nothing compared to her childhood. For example, no one threw *me* down into a dry well and dropped geckos on my head. I would like to express sorrow to my mother that she suffered this horror in her childhood and reiterate that it doesn't matter what culture it is—children can be assholes.

8 While we're on the subject of names: years later when I was working in TV news, a reporter affectionately called me "Eyesore." I was so impressed by the play on my name that I considered writing to those second-grade kids to say they'd missed a great taunt.

A) You find your groove, become part of the popular group at school, sit with Alice and Carla at lunch, and share Alice's mom's pork egg rolls and giggle about last night's episode of *Little House on the Prairie*, because: "How cuuuute is Albert?"

B) No *way* do you get invited to sit with Alice and Carla because they pull out adorable milk cartons from their lunch boxes, whereas you've got this liquid yogurt called *laban* that your dad packs because of its amazing health benefits—and let's not mention the taste. Okay, let's mention it. It tastes, and *smells*, like sour milk. Plus, Dad poured it into an old spaghetti sauce jar because he forgot to buy a proper thermos. Carla wrinkles her perfect button nose at your Ragu jar of smelly white liquid and declares, "Gross." You're told there's no room for you when you try to sit next to them, even though there are clearly *two* empty chairs.

I'll leave you to guess which category I fit into. Hint: I never got to share my views on Albert's adorable lisp with anyone except for my diary. And now here.[9]

No matter how I tried, I always seemed to end up at the wrong end. Literally and figuratively. I could've been at my own birthday party, where everyone was there to celebrate me, but it always seemed like something fun was happening at the other end of the crowd. Of course, this could've been partly due to my tiny, well-honed habit of being neurotic. It's a chicken or egg thing: which came first, my neuroses or my immigrantness?

Things did get better and the "table" got smaller when, in my early teens, we moved to Saudi Arabia for a few years. Finally, I met people

---

9 Due to copyright concerns, I can't show you a photo of Albert from *Little House on the Prairie*. But I will share that he is very cute. I kindly ask that you perform a web search.

like me—Middle Easterners who'd grown up in the States or England. I relaxed and embraced my ethnicity. I began answering to "Ayser" again and stopped wearing pink Izod shirts and plaid shorts—mainly because women aren't allowed to wear shorts in Saudi Arabia.[10, 11]

My one solace during these awkward years was to write down my thoughts and feelings to try to make sense of stuff. Much of my early entries were devoted to how unfair my parents were for not letting me do *anything* (more on that later). My journals became a place to vent about my overbearing family and all the cool things I would do once I broke free from their regime. I was an extremely ~~passionate~~ dramatic teenager, spending a lot of my adolescent years accusing them of ruining my life and then slamming doors.

When it was time for college, I shunned my parents' dream of me becoming a doctor in favor of journalism school. After graduation, I decided to move to Los Angeles to write and produce. I traded my diary for scripts and short films. After the twentieth revision of my pilot about two immigrant parents trying to fit in and balance the Old World with the New, I realized my *parents*, too, probably also felt like they were constantly at the wrong end of the table.

It's only now, as a grown woman in my forties, that I'm beginning to feel otherwise. This is partly because it's becoming increasingly common to turn on the news and see stories of ordinary Muslim Americans doing mundane things *not* involving explosives and actually contributing to society. But with America's growing openness and diversity also comes some backlash, and American Muslims are still targeted, privately and publicly. Hopefully, one day there will be a future young

---

10 My mother wants to make sure I'm not going to use this book to attack the religious customs of Arab countries. She also submits that not everyone can pull off plaid shorts. I want to assure my mother that I'm not planning on attacking any customs. And also, plaid shorts aren't much cuter than the banana-colored "high-waters" with red patches she made me wear. Further, I want to know whether she's going to keep interrupting me every time she reads something she doesn't like.

11 My father would also like me to give ample warning if a particular chapter contains "sensitive matter" that might be upsetting.

"Ayser" with my same background and experience for whom this book will be a quaint piece of history. But for now, dialogue and storytelling are important. Forty-something years is a long time for someone to feel like an outsider in a nation made up of immigrants. For that reason, I decided to share my story in the hopes that we can save America from an inevitable future population of forty-something-year-old outsiders—immigrant or not.[12, 13]

If you've ever felt like you've been at the wrong end of the table—whether you were born in an Iraqi dictatorship or hail from Lexington, Kentucky—this is for you. Though I can't speak for all of us, I can at least tell you *my* story.

---

12 I also thought I should hurry up and write this before President Trump kicks me out of the country. But then I realized that if that were to happen, I would be known as "exiled Iraqi American author Ayser Salman," which has a certain romance and is great for marketing.

13 My publisher would like me to know that while this is a noble aspiration, it's in everyone's interest that it not happen.

PART 1

THE KIDS' TABLE

1

"Playing Doctor"—Is This What Happens in Day Care?

When I was three years old, my parents moved my baby brother, Zaid, and me from Baghdad, Iraq, to Columbus, Ohio. Mom and Dad were looking for a place to emigrate with opportunities beyond what they found under the dictatorial regime of what was about to become Saddam Hussein's Iraq. Like many immigrants, they chose our new home based on where their Iraqi friends had settled—in our case, we had good friends in Ohio. We also moved for my father's new position at The Ohio State University. Dad was on sabbatical leave from Baghdad University as senior researcher in pharmacology.[1] As a pharmacologist, Dad studied the effects of drugs on the biological makeup of the body. My mother, who had also been a pharmacist back in Iraq, now worked as a research analyst. We migrated at the end of 1973, right before the dead of winter,[2] and spent five years learning the law of a new land before moving to Kentucky.

---

1 At the end of this sabbatical, my parents decided not to return to Iraq. Dad's funding was cut, which was a financial blow, but a fair trade-off for us to remain in the States and work to build on our American Dream.

2 Why do Arabs immigrate in the dead of winter? My research has uncovered that my family is not the only one to have done this—is it because flights are cheaper then?

My early immigrant experience in Ohio was colored by me attending various preschools and day-care centers—and then being taken out by my parents because of some "incident." Now before you get ready to call Retroactive Social Services or side with Donald Trump on the topic of troubled immigrants, let me explain. Nothing truly "terrible" happened to me, but, well, let's just say I won't ever be able to look at day-care center bathrooms in Ohio with unclouded eyes.

During lunchtime at one particular day-care facility, whose name I (conveniently) forget, as per the routine, the kids would line up to go to the bathroom before we trekked down to the lunch hall. That day, I didn't feel like participating in organized bathroom time. Maybe it was a small act of rebellion against the rules since I was "fresh off the boat" from a fascist regime; maybe I just didn't have to pee. The whole class lined up for the restrooms except me. Afterward, when we all went down to the lunch hall, suddenly I really, really, *really* had to pee. But I was too embarrassed to excuse myself.

So, I did what any kid would do—I peed right there.

In my pants.

While sitting at the lunch table.

Puddle city.

Here's where it could have gotten ugly. In the Hollywood version of my life, this is where some asshole kid named Keith screams, "SHE PEED!" and all the kids scatter like roaches when you suddenly turn the light on in the basement. You're branded the "Peeing Girl" or some other clever nomenclature given by five-year-olds. Then you'd have to change schools.[3]

But in this instance, I was spared the abuse with no one else the wiser. How? Through my strong aversion to milk. I loathed milk so much that I used to tell people I was allergic to it (even though there

3 Spoiler alert: you'll soon find out as you read this book that changing schools was a regular thing because my family moved a lot. Something about us being nomadic Arabs, or perhaps we just couldn't get comfortable. All I knew was that I would never be in one hell for long.

was no such thing as lactose intolerance in the seventies).[4] Even the school authorities knew I didn't drink milk, so instead of the cute milk carton the other kids got with their lunches, I got a cup of water. And on this "pee my pants" day, it came in handy. When one of the teachers approached and saw a puddle around my chair, she asked if I had spilled my water. Me, having not formulated a plan beyond the emptying of my bladder, froze like a deer in headlights and blankly nodded *yes*. Never mind that I didn't think to drink any of the contents of my still-full water cup. "It's okay!" the teacher sang sunnily. "We'll get you more, don't worry." It wasn't until later during naptime that someone noticed my wet clothes and later informed my mother that I had peed in my pink denim Garanimals.[5] Sure enough, not long afterward, we moved away, thus escaping any consequent horror. All because I didn't ask to use the restroom.

But here's the real deal: I actively avoided group restroom times because of this rather shocking fact—the kids at day care were constantly playing "doctor." Half the school population would lie facedown on the floor with their pants pulled down, while the other half sat next to them, lightly spanking them. I'm not saying it was like that damn scene from the movie *Eyes Wide Shut*, but to my shy, innocent, immigrant mind, it might as well have been an orgy. Naked butts everywhere! The ordeal seemed to last hours.[6]

In a continuation of the trend, at another day-care establishment, I witnessed for the very first time a *blow job*. Yep, you read correctly. Not something you'd expect of day care. Trust me, it wasn't something *I* expected to see, nor something my mother expected I would ever witness.

---

4 That's not true. It's probably just that it wasn't widely known. I totally exaggerated there.

5 History lesson: Garanimals was this awesome brand of kids' clothing that had animals as tags. To create a full outfit, you put the same animals together.

6 Actually, it was probably just two kids fooling around for five minutes or so. I'm sorry if my memory exaggerates reality.

Chrissie was, at nine years old, the mentor to my shy five-year-old self. She taught me necessary life skills, such as how to flip people off. While Chrissie pooped, under her orders, I would stand guard in front of the restroom entrance (the bathroom stalls in this school didn't have doors). If anyone tried to enter, I was to thrust my fist in their face with only the middle finger extended. Being an immigrant from a dictatorship, I was used to falling in line with authority figures and readily complied with Chrissie. When I went home that night, I practiced on my parents, who did a simultaneous spit take of their Sanka[7] and told me never to make that gesture again as it was very, *very* bad.[8]

Chrissie took me under her wing, protecting me from the rough-and-tumble kids who tried to limit my Tricycle Time. In return, I would do things for her. On that fateful day, I was riding my tricycle around the open hall during free-play, casually wiping my runny nose on my navy-blue wool sweater, when a member of Chrissie's posse approached and asked if I could come stand watch. I followed this kid to a make-shift tent made of blankets and chairs and stood outside, exactly as he instructed me. A few minutes later, he asked if I wanted to see, so I shrugged in agreement. He parted the blanket to reveal Chrissie kneeling in front of a slightly older boy of probably eleven years old *who had his penis in her mouth*. What was weird (and also sad) about the scene was the pure innocence with which I remember her engaging in the act; she might as well have been sucking on a lollipop.[9]

After about a couple of seconds of witnessing this, I think I had enough sense to declare "yuck" and walk away—coolly and calmly with an outward appearance of "I saw nothing," as I had often been instructed to exhibit in my home country, even though I was inwardly

---

7 An instant decaf coffee brand popular in American households in the seventies.

8 Ah, the innocence of the seventies. My father has since learned variations on this gesture, which he employs frequently when talking to customer service representatives on the phone. Luckily, they don't see what he's doing.

9 Why did she do it? On hindsight, I wonder if she might have been acting out due to a horrific situation in her life. I'm not sure what became of Chrissie, but I do hope she made it out okay.

panicking and trying to make sense of it all. My daze was broken when a tomboy girl named Leslie rode by on a Big Wheel bike and yelled, "ARE THEY SUCKING DICKS IN THERE AGAIN?" Apparently, it was not a one-time occurrence.

I didn't tell my mother until a week later as we were driving to school.

I can still hear the deafening screech of tires as she pulled the car over. She was so angry that she drove me all the way home, dropped me off with the babysitter, drove back to that facility, and tore into them for allowing this to happen on their watch. Since it had technically happened at the end of the day during free play, the head of the school claimed that they had done whatever they could to rein kids in but that they couldn't control all of them. And furthermore, "What can you do? Kids are curious."

When we got home, my mother sat me down. She told me that in this country I would encounter things I wouldn't be able to understand, but that I could (and should) always talk to her so she could try to make sense of whatever troubled me. I nodded. But I already had a theory: my thought was that American kids were obsessed with playing doctor because they were always getting a shot in the butt whenever they visited a real doctor.[10] I don't recall going to the doctor in Iraq as much as I did in America. But according to my mom, I just didn't remember Iraqi doctor visits because I was three years old. I'm sure this was her way of making up "Mom Lies" to shut me up.[11]

And again, we moved not long after that.

---

10 I would be interested in knowing if the percentage of kids playing doctor has decreased in this modern time of the antivaccine movement. People with kids, please let me know.

11 Like the time she told me that the yellow flowers outside my bedroom window wouldn't bloom if I cried. I held in my tears until I saw the movie *Bambi* and bawled for hours. Immediately, I felt guilty that the flowers would not bloom because of me. Of course, a week later they did anyway. And it was then that I started to suspect most of the things my mother told me . . .

My experiences in day-care centers might be why I never really took to Columbus, Ohio. I apologize to the residents of what I'm sure is a fine town. I do have fond memories of driving along the Olentangy River—though that was probably because we were by then heading out of the state into our new home of Kentucky. I don't really miss Columbus, except for its awesome Center of Science and Industry (COSI) and The Ohio State University (OSU), where the buckeye trees are worth a visit.

But don't go near any day-care centers, just in case.

2

My Trouble with Men

My trouble with men began at an early age—six years old, to be exact, when I was still in kindergarten in Ohio.

I know what you're thinking: *Six is too old for me to be in kindergarten.*

Well, I had come to the States when I was three years old and only spoke Arabic. Having to learn English later in life put me behind, and I started school later than most kids. This might also have been due to the fact that I'd fainted at my kindergarten entrance exam, which prompted the counselor to tell my parents that I wasn't emotionally ready for school.[1]

You may now be wondering exactly what kind of kindergarten this was if it had an entrance exam. Well, perhaps it was less of an entrance exam and more of an emotional readiness placement test, during which I remember being unable to correctly identify some letters of the English alphabet in lowercase. The Arabic alphabet doesn't distinguish between upper- and lowercase letters, so you can imagine the stress this caused me when I encountered English—*q* totally looks like a *g*, by the way. Plus, I was still learning how to read from left to right instead

---

1 Okay, I might be being a little dramatic. It could also have been simply because my birthday fell in December, which meant I would have been too young to start within that school year.

of Arabic's right to left.[2] On top of that, when it came to the drawing exercise, I added too many birds in the sky, which is apparently a sign of emotional disturbance in children. For all the reasons above, the counselor decided I wasn't emotionally ready and recommended I wait a year before starting school.[3]

So there I was in kindergarten, six years old and way taller than everyone else. In our school photo, I'm standing at the back with all the other awkward fast-growers instead of seated at the floor with the normal-sized kids. But the memory that stood out the most was my very first "fail" with the opposite sex.

I was sitting politely at my desk when a kid with a big shock of curly red hair ran up to me. His name was Adam.

> **ADAM:** Hi, Ayser (*pronounced correctly, by the way*).
>
> *He awkwardly held out a wad of paper.*
>
> **ADAM:** I got you something. Uh . . . it's from my collection. It's brand new.

He stood there long enough to watch me unwrap the paper—it was a gleaming, shiny, brand new quarter from 1975 in perfect condition. Then he promptly ran away. I spent the rest of the day admiring the quarter, which found a prominent place on my desk and in my daydreaming. I wondered about its significance. Could this have been my first experience pondering about the concept of things happening exactly as they are supposed to? Had I not been held back from starting kindergarten, I wouldn't have met Adam, which meant I wouldn't have experienced my very first romantic gesture. Life had a way of working

---

2 I feel I was at a cultural disadvantage doing this test (yes, I'm pulling out the race card).

3 In a few chapters, you'll discover that I ended up skipping from fourth to fifth grade, so this age thing eventually evens out.

itself out. Life was glorious. I was feeling great . . . until I proudly showed the quarter to my mother.

Now, I'd like you to picture the most heinous atrocity you could ever imagine. So heinous, it's unspeakable. Got an image? Feeling pretty icky about it? Okay. Keep that in mind, because that's how my mother reacted.

MOM: You can *not* take this!

Disgustedly, she holds the quarter between her thumb and forefinger as far away from her body as she can.

MOM: This is how it starts. Next thing he's going to think he owns you!

My father walks in and Mom shoves the quarter in his face.

MOM: Talk to your daughter. A boy gave her this!

Dad takes a moment to put on his bifocals and studies the offending item.

DAD: Does he think you're cheap?

My mother looks at me, satisfied.

DAD: He should have given you a silver dollar!

Now, Mom is disgusted with me, the quarter, and Dad.

MOM: This is how you set an example?!

She snatches the quarter from him and turns to me.

MOM: Never, ever let a man buy you with gifts, Ayser. Give this back to him and tell him you are not for sale! That is how you get a man to respect you.

The next day, I saw Adam. We stood face-to-face, or, in our case, his face to my second shirt button. I can only imagine what disadvantage this put him in as I delivered the following news:

"Adam, I can't take this money from you because you're a boy and I'm not for sale!"

Adam looked as if he were about to say something, decided against it, and ran away—but not before bursting into tears.

This would set the tone for my relationship with the opposite sex for much of my life. It also shaped my relationship with coins. For some reason, four quarters is worth more to me than ten dimes. Years later, when I did get engaged, and having previously told my fiancé, John, that story, he gave me a newly minted quarter to "make up for the years I had to do without it." It remains one of the most romantic things anyone has ever done for me.

3

Land of the Free, Home of the McMuffin

I'd like to apologize to the city of Columbus, Ohio, for unfairly attacking it in the very first chapter. It's not the city's fault that some weird shit happened to me while I was there. A lot of good stuff also happened: Columbus is where I learned English, specifically how to properly say my *r*s so it didn't sound like I had a speech impediment. Columbus is also where I learned to ride a bike without training wheels, though that experience was marred by the fact that as soon as I got five feet away from the house feeling proud of myself, I vividly remember turning into the path of a figure of a soldier who was pointing a gun at me, causing me to drop my bike and rush home in a panic. Once I was safely inside our apartment, my parents managed to calm me down enough to get me to describe the suspect. Crouching down low, I peered outside our living room window and pointed him out to my father. After a quick investigation—which involved Dad glancing outside for fifteen seconds—it was determined that the dangerous and cunning sniper was actually my shy six-year-old neighbor, Sreekanth, wielding a neon-yellow plastic toy water machine gun. My parents made me go back outside.

In retrospect, this might have been the first instance of my own prejudice and racism—I had gut-reacted to a vision of Sreekanth as a dangerous, murdering soldier, when in reality he was a sweet

Atari aficionado from India who loved rabbits. I want to apologize to Sreekanth, especially since the following week he dumped ice-cold lemonade down my back because he thought a spider was crawling on me and he had heard that spiders hate lemon-scented stuff. What a romantic gesture that was! It was the first time in this strange land that anyone had ever tried to protect me from a blood-sucking daddy longlegs.

While I'm sure my parents didn't fully grasp the romance of Sreekanth's gesture (probably because we were both only six), they did understand the value of my having another friend who was also an immigrant in hopes that I wouldn't feel so isolated. So, the next morning they invited him to McDonald's for breakfast with us. Which brings me to one of my best memories of Columbus, Ohio.

Columbus was where I, along with my family, developed a love for the McDonald's Egg McMuffin. We consumed so many of those perfectly fluffy breakfast sandwiches that I now associate the city with them. When we moved to Lexington, Kentucky, we stopped eating McMuffins, which could have had something to do with the fact that someone (Dad) discovered that McMuffins contained ham, a food my Muslim family couldn't eat. *Sausage* McMuffins were okay, though, because Muslims "know" that's not really pork.[1]

During those first years in the States, we enjoyed many similar culinary delights, such as bologna boats, which were hamburgers with Wonder Bread instead of buns so that when you put ketchup on and smashed the two slices together it looked like the bread was bleeding. We also ate liver, lots of liver. I'm not sure why.[2] And we consumed a ton of fast food. McDonald's was my favorite, and Arby's came in a close

1 This is not an attack on McDonald's. I'm just clarifying that some Muslims won't eat pork but let sausage—and pepperoni—slide. Our fridge was always stocked with pepperoni. To this day, when I choose my pizza topping, it is a *no* to ham and a *yes* to pepperoni.

2 My mother would like my readers to know that she served liver because it's the most nutrient-dense food around. Also, it was the seventies.

second. Then there was Dairy Queen, because you could clip coupons out of the back of cereal boxes and get a free Dilly Bar.

I think I, along with Sreekanth, enjoyed our fast food probably even more than nonimmigrants did. Sure, any six-year-old who's given the chance to go for a cheeseburger and hot, salty fries will jump at that. But when you're a six-year-old immigrant whose parents have moved you across the globe and you can't process that it's for your greater good and all you know is that your world is weird and you don't have any friends and everyone speaks funny but they look at *you* like you're the one speaking funny—it gets scary. But then you get to go to McDonald's and order a cheeseburger and hot, salty fries and everything seems fine. At least for a moment.

It wasn't just us kids who had a fast food love affair. My mother soon realized that she could go half and half for dinner—buying fast food items and giving them her Iraqi twist. We would go to KFC (back when it was only known by its full name, Kentucky Fried Chicken) and buy a bucket of chicken and sides. She'd save half the chicken and we'd eat the rest of the meal. The next day, we'd find an Arabic meal made up of the Colonel's chicken doctored with Za'atar spices and with a side of saffron rice and tabbouleh salad. It was delightful. That was the summer when she and Sreekanth's mom shared a subscription to *Better Homes and Gardens* magazine and they tried out all sorts of recipes. On the weekends, when she had the time, she also made various Middle Eastern delicacies and American fare—pineapple upside-down cake and ice cream sheet cake were my favorites.

To this day, whenever I'm in a strange land or city and I'm feeling out of sorts, I look for the familiar yellow arches of McDonald's, or the white-and-green mermaid logo of Starbucks—and, as silly as it seems, I find it comforting.

I also sometimes wonder what Sreekanth is up to . . .

4

Eh-French Eh-Fries

There's an inconvenience to hailing from a country that boasts a dictatorship. I'm not talking about the obvious reasons:

1. That you live under an oppressive regime.
2. That even when you leave the country, you may have relatives who still live under said oppressive regime.
3. That you have to think twice about pulling any shenanigans, such as speaking out against said oppressive regime, lest said regime takes an unwanted interest in any of your relatives who may still live there.

Those are very important reasons, but when you're six and eight, you couldn't care less. Because at that age, there's only one takeaway from the whole "being from a fascist country" scenario:

You can't ever complain to your parents. About. Anything.

Any discomfort you feel in your new country doesn't even come close to what you would have experienced had you still been living in Iraq. My brother and I (and later on my sister, too) endured this to an excruciating degree as kids.

Let's say you want to go to McDonald's (see previous chapter). You state your desire (you whine). Mom refuses. You insist (you whine louder). This is what you'll get:

"Mac-Do-Nalds! You want to go to Mac-Do-Nalds! And eat eh-French eh-fries?[1] Don't you think your cousin Dahlia would love to eat eh-French eh-fries?! But she can't, because they don't have Mac-Do-Nalds in Iraq! They don't have eh-French eh-fries! They have one potato to share between the five of them! And they are happy!"

Or maybe you utter the phrase beginning with "But all the other kids . . ." Such as:

"But all the other kids are going to Disneyland on their Christmas break!"

"But all the other kids get to stay up late and watch *Dukes of Hazzard*!"

"But all the other kids get to sleep over at Mindy's house!"

You'll get the following earful:

"Other kids? What other kids?! The ones back home who wish they could just have enough money to go to the su-par-mar-ket? Or maybe you mean the kids who don't have a television to watch and have to listen to cats fighting in the streets at night for entertainment? And what do you mean you want to sleep at Mindy's house? You have a perfectly fine house! You could be like your Aunt Nabeela who used to share a room with seven sisters. She dreamed of having her own bed. You have your own room!"

Should you then offer the rebuttal of "Well, I didn't ask you to bring me to this country," you can then expect a diatribe about how *un-a-grate-fool* you are:

"I can't believe I raised such an un-a-grate-fool daughter. What did I do wrong?"

God forbid Mom should ever hear you utter the words, "I'm bored." When that happens, it's GAME. OVER.

"Bored?! You better thank God you have the luxury to be bored! Your cousin Hisham carries bags of rice on his back every day after school to help his parents make money. Last year, he fainted in the

---

1 Mom tends to add extra syllables to words.

street because of heat stroke and hit his head on a rock! I am sure he would be very happy to be bored . . . *Bored!*"

This will go on and on until you've not only given up from sheer exhaustion, but you're now pleading with her to let you do the chores. Or you're feigning interest in Dad's pharmacotherapy book while your brother tries to hold his breath on the other side of the room and not move, so maybe she'll forget she even has children until the storm blows over . . .

Eventually, Zaid and I got hip to it. We came up with code words like CIA operatives in order to communicate our true feelings freely.

So bored became *so grateful*.

"Hey, I'm *so grateful*!" we'd say to each other, collapsing into peals of laughter at our inside joke. We'd spend hours coming up with new words in case our code got cracked. But as this went on, our code making become so intricate we got confused. Was *happy* the code word for *stupid* or *tired*? Then we'd have to start over with a new system. The good news was we got so caught up in inventing code words that there was little time to be bored.

. . . Maybe Mom was onto something.

5
Fuck Off, Ian

My trouble with men continued into second grade, this time taking the form of unrequited love—an agony I would be dealing with in some form or other for most of my life. Even as a kid, I'd harbored secret crushes on boys, never letting on that I liked them because I had been taught that I shouldn't chase anyone. If a boy liked me, he would let me know. Well, no one ever let me know. At least not in a manner I understood (see below, re: Ian). So I had no recourse but to keep my crushes to myself.

But before I launch into my dating life, let me backtrack and paint you a picture of my grade school existence.

For one, there was my "unpronounceable" name, which resulted in a growing list of creative nicknames, such as "Ayser Eraser," "Ayser Razor Blade," and "Ayser Razor Mustard Face." To keep the insults at bay, I went by "Lisa," with minimal effect. And like many other immigrants, I also learned in an excruciatingly hard way the importance of only packing lunches that were familiar to the standard American elementary school cafeteria, circa 1970s—i.e., bologna sandwiches, PB&J with the crusts cut off, nicely sliced carrot sticks, and red apples. Poor Agnes Jones was shunned for half a year just because she brought rice cakes for lunch.[1]

1 A visionary.

After Dad packed me the sour-milk-smelling laban in an old Ragu jar for lunch once, and I was punished for it, I had the street smarts to, a few weeks later, check my food before I walked through the school doors. I discovered my mother had packed me the dolma (stuffed grape leaves) along with beef kebab, both of which were delicious but had the unfortunate characteristic of resembling poop to average second graders. I didn't even want to think of the potential horror I'd managed to avoid as I chucked my meal in the trash before walking into the building.[2] I was so hungry that I ate a Snickers bar I'd kept in my desk and then felt so nauseated that, by the time I got home, I couldn't even stomach the buttered toast that was waiting for me.

In conclusion, I was awkward and I hated school—but there *was* one bright spot in my day: Theodore.

Shy little Theodore wore glasses and a blue fur coat that made him look like Cookie Monster. He was also the cutest boy I'd ever seen. What girl doesn't like Cookie Monster?[3] Theodore was adorable and quiet, and I pined for him in the way you do when you're an immigrant girl from Iraq whose first language was not English—you know, from your seat at the back of the school bus, while you practiced saying your *r*s in order to sound like a real American.[4] I did this for weeks. Finally, one day I decided I had gathered enough courage to go up to talk to him. I was going to say his name properly. The night before I planned to make my move, I practiced in my bedroom after dinner.

"Hello, Thee-o-dorrrr . . . hi, Theo-dorrrr . . . errr. Orrr. Theo-dorr."[5]

Mom heard this and rushed in without knocking, worried that I was feeling ill because of all the "horrible noises"! I decided I'd had enough practice. It was time to get a good night's sleep before tomorrow's performance. The next day, I ate my Cream of Wheat, drank my juice, and

---

2 Sorry, Mom, but it really was a matter of life and death!

3 Disclaimer: I do not have some weird plushy fetish involving blue puppets.

4 The key is to touch your tongue to the roof of your mouth.

5 In hindsight, I should have shortened his name to *Theo*. It would have been cute and sassy. But, at the time, I wasn't cute and sassy.

took my vitamins. I asked Mom to put my hair up in a high ponytail instead of the low braid I usually wore. At the time it seemed like an innocent choice, but looking back it might have been because I thought a high pony would make me look more feminine and therefore more approachable to my beloved.[6]

So there I was, ready for my moment. During free play, I walked up to Theodore's desk—and just as I opened my mouth, this punk-ass kid named Ian interrupted us. Ian had shaggy red hair and freckles, and he carried around a pencil that he would kiss during recess—and tell everyone it was me. I hated it; what eight-year-old wants to be referred to as a pencil? In hindsight, perhaps this was his second-grade version of flirting, and I'd missed the signs.[7] Also, he shouldn't have been so pushy and weird. Did he think the pencil was capable of giving consent?!

Before I could say hi to Theodore using my newly practiced diction, Ian came running up, screeching about how I'd told him to *fuck off.* He thrust a sheet of paper in my face with the scrawled-out words, *FUCK OFF IAN. SINCERELY, AYSER SALEM.*

I was shocked. For the record, I had *not* told Ian to fuck off. In fact, I didn't even know what that F-word was. True, I'd already learned the middle finger gesture, but no one had told me that a verbal equivalent existed, so I can promise that no such profanity was spouted from me to him. Furthermore, the truth was I was simply an eight-year-old immigrant who had come to America to escape a fascist regime during a time of a hostage crisis instigated by a neighboring country's regime. I wasn't in a position or mindset to make any waves in this new country. I just wanted to keep my head down, learn English, and maybe be invited to play four square with the other kids during recess. I wasn't about to use a swear word on anyone, let alone write one down on a piece of paper

---

6 I know, this sounds antifeminist in this modern age. To any young ladies reading this, take my eight-year-old self with a grain of salt—it was the seventies, and women were just beginning to burn their bras. We still had a long way to go.

7 To be honest, I've missed tons of similar signs since then. But that's another story. For later chapters.

that could be later used as evidence. Plus, I was a sweet, shy kid who wouldn't hurt a fly.

The more I analyzed Ian's idiotic note, the more ludicrous I found it. Not only was I being accused of execrating[8] another student with big, bold letters from a #2 pencil on a lined sheet of paper, but apparently I had also been proud enough of my work to sign my first name to it. The best part: I had misspelled my last name, purportedly to maintain the mystery of the letter writer's identity. *Salem*? Who's that?! Had Ian been reading about witch trials in Salem, Massachusetts? Or did his parents smoke Salem cigarettes? A misspelling is not much of a stretch to camouflage my tracks, Ian!

The most devastating part of this was that Theodore had witnessed Ian's outburst, killing the big moment I'd been working myself up to. Theodore now thought I'd done this horrible thing. I'm not sure Theodore believed him—he'd just stared blankly and chewed on the writing end of his pencil. Sometimes, I wonder how this experience came to shape Theodore's view on Arab immigrants, since I was probably the only one he'd met at that young age. Did it plant a seed of the stereotype that Arabs are vindictive and angry? Or was he smart enough to recognize that I, the innocent victim, was dealing with a language barrier, subjected to Ian's maniacal machinations? Or perhaps Theodore was only interested in eating lead? Who knows?

Shortly after the incident, my family moved (again), and I never got a second chance with Theodore.

Theodore, if you're reading this, I want to let you know that Ian was a ~~jealous spurned~~ dumb kid, and though I never told him to fuck off in the second grade, I certainly would today if I could.

Then perhaps you and I could have the conversation we missed out on all those years ago . . .

8 An old "SAT" word for *defaming*—I've always wanted to use it in a sentence.

6
Star-Spangled Rodeo

Whenever I reminisce about my early childhood days, I notice a pattern. Almost all my memories revolve around music (and that's why many of the chapters in this book are named after song titles). Ask me about any time in my life, and I'll be able to tell you which songs are most representative of that period—for example, my time in Ohio is defined by the singers Ronnie Milsap and Glen Campbell, while my later years in Saudi Arabia call forth the Carpenters and Olivia Newton-John. I discovered the Beatles in high school and lived by their credo, "Let it be." And college was my heavy metal and goth music phase (short-lived) with a heaping side of R.E.M. and Echo & the Bunnymen.

My love for music came from my mother. When I was little, she often told me that if I was feeling sad or depressed, putting on music would instantly brighten my mood and transport me to a magical place. One of my earliest memories from Ohio is Mom preparing a hybrid Middle Eastern–American feast while her small FM radio played pop music in the background. I would sit at the very small table in the corner of our very small kitchen and "help" her shape rice into balls for kibbe and squeeze lemon juice into tabbouleh and various other side dishes. As we worked, Mom would buzz around the kitchen, humming happily to whatever tune was on the radio. Every now and then, she would repeat the words from the commercials, her way of strengthening her fledgling English.[1] On rare occasions, a song would come on that would make us go into all-out performance mode. We'd dance out into the living room, Mom holding the spatula as a microphone while Zaid played air guitar. One of our favorite songs was Glen Campbell's "Rhinestone Cowboy." Zaid especially would get so excited that, even after the song was over, he would rush into our bedroom and continue his own a cappella performance while jumping up and down on his bed. To this day, hearing it brings back a flood of memories for all of us.

Whenever Dad came home from work and tried to switch the radio to the news—probably a continuation of whatever he was listening to in the car—Mom would shut him down. "My kitchen, *my* music," she'd say and shoo him out. There were times, especially during the Iran hostage crisis of the late seventies, when Dad would sit in our blue Mercury Montego parked on the street below our nondescript brick apartment building for a half-hour and listen to the radio to soak up the information he craved. Eventually, this ended when a neighbor complained about a "suspicious Mexican man loitering in a blue car for long periods of time." With his mustache, and the fact that Middle-Easterners weren't common in Columbus, people often mistook our family for Mexicans—and we didn't correct them. It was safer to let them believe we were part of a more familiar ethnicity than to tell them we were Arabs, which at the time was a largely misunderstood group. Plus, "Iraq" sounded like "Iran," which, because of the hostage crisis, was seen as the enemy. You can imagine the crisis of identity this environment created. I never wanted to leave our apartment.

Music became the thing that soothed me in a hostile, new world. Having been uprooted from Baghdad to Columbus at a young age, leaving behind our large house with my toys and a backyard swing for a cold and snowy land where I had to share a bedroom with my kid brother as creaky radiator pipes pinged loudly during the night, I needed some grounding. My favorite songs had the ability to root me,

1 I should clarify that while Dad had gone to college in the States and spoke perfect English, Mom hadn't and was learning the language around the same time I was.

giving me something familiar to hold onto like a comfortable, audible security blanket, as I learned to live in a foreign world with its foreign, impenetrable language.

In second grade, I hated that I wasn't learning English quickly enough. Worse, I had an annoying speech impediment that required me to attend a special class to practice saying my *r*s properly. The class started fifteen minutes into the last period of school, which meant that while other students quietly practiced cursive writing at their desks while dreaming of the afterschool snacks their moms had prepared, I had to pack up my belongings and walk out of the classroom, calling attention to myself. During those early days in America, my only goal at school was to disappear and be invisible until the bell rang at the end of the day, signaling the time for my escape. One particular day when I tried to make my invisible exit, I tripped and fell in the doorway, causing my skirt to flip up, exposing my turquoise undies. I didn't even need to look back at the class to know that it was Ian who was snickering—I will never forget that stupid hyena laugh of his.[2]

This was not my first embarrassment at that school. A few weeks prior, we were rehearsing our class play about Native Americans, and to my horror I was cast to say the line "We bring them iron and ore." First, what a nightmare for a person who has trouble pronouncing the letter *r*. Second, since I was learning English from my parents at home who had strong accents, I naturally pronounced *iron* as "eye-run."

"Eye-run," I said. "Eye-urn," the teacher repeated.

So I said it the way I *thought* she was saying it, but what came out of my mouth were still the sounds I had learned from my parents. I could tell she was being patient, but you just know when everyone else thinks you're being annoying. They were sick of me, and I was sick of the whole experience.

I trudged home that day, ignoring Mom's sing-songy greeting and going into my room and shutting the door. Trouble was, I shared it with

---

2 That's right—fuck off, Ian.

my brother. When he came home, he flopped on the bed and started jumping up and down, singing a random pop song. I wished he would go away. For some reason, Zaid had an easier time making friends at school, perhaps because he was more mellow than I.[3] Annoyed, I was forced to leave my room and went into the kitchen.

Mom could tell I didn't want to talk about it, so she didn't press. She placed some cheese and saltine crackers in front of me, turned on the radio, and went about her business stirring a pot on the stove. When Glen Campbell's "Rhinestone Cowboy" came on, she began humming. Still moping, I pretended to be impervious to the song's beat. But then it got to the chorus, and Mom belted out loud, "Like a Rhinestone Cowboy! Nah nah nah nah . . . Star Spangled Rodeo!"—she didn't know all the words. Her exaggerated dance made me chuckle. When she noticed her ploy was working, she emphasized her movements until I was laughing out loud. Soon, Zaid had joined us and was dancing away on the coffee table.

By the time Dad came home, we had exhausted ourselves and were lying in a circle on the area rug in the living room. We didn't need to tell him about our little secret afternoon dance party.

That's how I learned you don't always need to talk about your problems. You just need music.

---

3 Though earlier that week he did cut a big chunk out of Kit's bangs (one of his many young girlfriends) as they played barber shop. Kit's mother was understandably concerned and thought maybe the two of them should not hang around each other anymore. When Kit smiled, you could see a gap where her two front teeth were supposed to be, mirroring the gap in her bangs. Personally, I appreciated the symmetry of my brother's work.

7
"Hate Crime" or Random Bee-Stinging Incident? You Decide

When I was eight, the Salman family left Ohio and migrated south to Lexington, Kentucky, which would become our new home—though we would only live there for the next year and a half before temporarily moving to Saudi Arabia for my parents' teaching jobs at the local universities. We would always return to Lexington during the summer—mainly because the sun in Saudi Arabia in July would literally burn you to a crisp.[1] Because of my long history here, I consider Lexington my second hometown—the first, obviously, being Baghdad.

We moved from Ohio to Lexington for my father's new job as senior researcher at the University of Kentucky's college of pharmacy and medicine. Mom got a job as a research analyst there. My parents also had Iraqi friends in Lexington, one of their important prerequisites for moving to a new place. Once again, we traveled in the dead of winter, as Arab immigrants are wont to do.[2] And once again, I mostly holed up at home, watching TV, reading books, and eating buttered toast.

---

1 I apologize for using the word *literally*—this sentence is hyperbolic. As you can tell, I like to exaggerate.

2 See Chapter 1, "'Playing Doctor'—Is This What Happens in Day Care?"

Soon enough, spring came around, and my mother made me go outside because I was starting to develop a pale-green pallor.[3] At first, I confined myself to the yard of our duplex, too scared to venture out and befriend the group of kids playing across the street who looked to be my age. Eventually, Mom got tired of peering out the window daily to see me examining the same weed patch where the yard met the sidewalk (I was "gardening," okay?). She thrust a plunger into my hand and made me return it to our neighbors across the street, the Packers.[4] And that's where I met my first Kentucky friends.

It's also where I might have encountered my first hate crime. Here's the story.

The Packers were a wonderful Mormon family who had regular family dinners every night. Their daughter, Cara, was allowed to invite her friends to dinner, and I attended one such meal along with Cara's other bestie, Debbie, who lived down the street. Debbie, the only child of atheists, was so enamored of Cara's close-knit religious family that she convinced the Packers to agree to unofficially adopt her. I, too, attempted to request for adoption, so taken was I with their kindness.[5] I almost convinced them that I was already an honorary Mormon, since both our religions shared a common belief of abstaining from alcohol, but Debbie argued that there was no such thing as an honorary Mormon and accused me of being jealous that *she* got to have homemade chicken and dumplings at the Packers' that one time during Eid.[6] To Debbie, I already had my own religion with its own "dinners and stuff." Why couldn't I just stop being a "dumb copycat" and go back to my family *where I belonged*?

---

3 As an Arab, you're supposed to be somewhat beige; though I'm more of a khaki color to begin with.

4 Yes, we didn't have our own plunger and had to borrow it—kinda like borrowing someone's toothbrush or razor.

5 They'd lent us a *plunger.*

6 Eid is the festival after the Muslim month of Ramadan, which is commemorated by community celebrations. My parents had made me stay home for a party they were hosting for the small contingent of Arabs we knew in town.

When someone tells you to go back to a place where you belong, they are insinuating that you don't belong with everyone else. The anti-immigrant sentiment is pretty clear. If Debbie wanted to explore different traditions outside of her own family, why couldn't I? It was my first experience of direct racism.

The "hate crime" part then came a few months later when Debbie pushed me into a swarm of poisonous bees, causing me to get stung. Well, according to me, at least. My mother disagrees. While I'm convinced that incident qualifies for the notoriety of being Lexington, Kentucky's first documented case of a Muslim hate crime, Mom argues that you can't accuse someone of a hate crime just because they were awful to you forty years ago. Maybe Debbie wasn't any more of a racist than she was just a *mean girl*. Furthermore, Mom would like to remind me that I wasn't actually pushed into the bees; I'd tripped on cracked concrete by the dumpsters and fell on my own. If I had heeded her repeated warnings to stay away from that area, this "hate crime" wouldn't have happened at all. I'll leave it to you to decide.[7]

Anyway, at some point, Debbie found out that my parents drank coffee, while Mormons are supposed to abstain from the beverage. She raised such a fuss that the Packers, who were quiet and peace-loving people, decided they didn't want the drama of having an honorary Muslim Mormon daughter along with an unofficially adopted atheist Mormon daughter. Respectfully, they declined both our offers. Debbie was so pissed off at me that we stopped being friends. But the truth was I knew our friendship was already doomed once I realized she was simply mean-spirited. And it didn't help that Debbie's (real) mother felt I was a bad influence and disallowed her from playing with me—not because I came from a Muslim family of coffee drinkers, but rather because Debbie and I had picked on Debbie's cousin, Julie, making her

7 My editor wants me to clarify that this is an example of hyperbole, which I'm fond of. She wants to make it clear to readers that no one seriously thinks this was a hate crime. But in my view, bees could be considered tiny weapons. . . . I still think we should let the readers decide.

cry. Technically, Debbie had led the charge and I just chimed in, hoping to fit in. But, as my mother later explained to me, you can call one another names within the family, but it's unforgiveable if someone *outside* the family does it.[8]

It was just another life lesson in America.

8 My mother is relieved I'm finally acknowledging that I learned some good things from her instead of simply using her as comedic fodder.

8

Sibling Rivalry, or: How to Stop Your Sister from Getting the Western Name

When I was nine and finally assimilating to life in Lexington, my baby sister, Lameace, was born. Above is a photo from when she was about three years old.

It's a hilarious photo: her complete frown, the superimposition of a bike wheel near her head. The latter was the result of our brother experimenting with one of those camera lenses so popular in the early eighties that allowed you to do in-camera effects. Zaid was trying to frame her face inside the wheel but missed the mark by several inches. But her frown, spanning almost to the edges of her face like a cartoon, takes the cake.

According to Zaid, she'd frowned because she was annoyed that he had forced her to be the subject of his photo experiment. According to Lameace, I had been positioned behind her and was pinching her to make her frown. I find the latter hard to believe as I consider myself a protective older sister who would never do such a thing. Plus, the way it usually works is the older sibling is mean to the *next* younger sibling in line, which explains why my brother has countless scars from the many stitches he's received whenever I chased him into a sharp corner or dared him to slide down the windshield of our Mercury Montego or threw a record horizontally at his neck.[1] And that's why with Lameace, it was his turn.

Zaid took the baton willingly, if not unorthodoxly. A science nerd, he was studying the concepts of DNA around the time Lameace was three years old. He would come home, get really close to her face, and whisper quietly but sternly, "Deoxy-ribo-nucleic ACID." She'd burst into tears and run to my mother, because who wouldn't if someone got in their face, spouting that vulgarity?[2]

When our baby sister was born, Zaid and I were super excited and we fought over who got to hold her. She was an adorable baby.[3] My brother had already picked out a name, "Leonard," even though he knew full well that the baby was going to be a she.[4] I was fine with this name. Leonard Kadhim Salman had a certain ring to it. It's customary in our culture for the family's patriarchal name, in our case *Kadhim*, to be used as every child's middle name, as it had been for Zaid and me.

1 Before you start thinking I was the devil child, let me clarify that these games were experiments often instigated by Zaid himself. Or at least he never protested much.

2 When it came to disciplining Zaid, my mother would tell him calmly to stop whatever he was doing. No threats of grounding, no rescinded TV privileges, like I'd endured. Sure, I had inflicted physical harm on Zaid, but everyone knows *emotional* wounds are the ones that don't heal. The oldest child always gets the short end of the stick.

3 She's since grown up to be an adorable adult.

4 Maybe he was just ahead of his time and keen to break gender-conforming boundaries.

But then Mom went rogue. Out of the blue, she announced that maybe she would break with tradition and not use Kadhim as a middle name. Maybe she wouldn't even give Leonard a middle name. I didn't like where she was going with this. Wasn't it bad enough that she was having the hippie seventies pregnancy, complete with T-shirts featuring an arrow pointing downward to signify that a baby was indeed growing in her stomach (in case the giant baby bump didn't translate)? I began worrying that Mom had been abducted and brainwashed by aliens. That, or she still had a severe case of pregnancy brain,[5] which had made her forget everything she'd ever stood for.

And then it got worse.

Mom decided she wanted to name the baby *Amanda-Cheyenne*.

What. The. Fuuuuuuck?!

Amanda. *Cheyenne?* My brother and I had weird names that caused us to get picked on by the kids in school, names that were butchered by even the most well-meaning of folks. It was a rite of passage for us Salman kids. But now this new one was coming along, already born into privilege by the fact that she would be delivered on US soil, making her the only member in our family who could run for president. Not that my brother or I had political aspirations, but it would have been nice to have *had* the option. Plus, she was about to get a nice, normal, feminine-sounding name that was accessible to non-Arabs as well as Arabs.

I wasn't having it. I presented my case to my mother. First, I wanted to know what her reasoning was in choosing this name.

"*Amanda* is very feminine name, and *Cheyenne* reminds me of the Western frontier" was her response. "It's very American."

When I pressed further, it turns out there was a deeper story to this: before Mom was pregnant with my sister, we had all taken a family trip in early spring, driving from Kentucky to California. One day, we got stuck in a blizzard right outside of Cheyenne, Wyoming. It was apparently so bad that Dad, normally the optimist, didn't know if we

5 Also called *Momnesia*.

would make it out alive. But he persevered, continuing to drive slowly and steadily ahead until eventually the snow cleared and visibility was restored. Mom recounts that the first thing she saw was a sign for the town Cheyenne. And she vowed right then and there that if she had another child, he or she would be named after the sign.

Powerful and poetic, right? Sure. But do you think that mattered at all to a nine-year-old? That's a big fat no.

I demanded to know why the baby would get two names when I only had one. I was informed that nothing else worked with *Ayser*. "Your name stands alone," Mom quickly added.

Throughout my upbringing, my mother always instilled in me the value of being mature. Sometimes this meant I had to keep a stiff upper lip when I wanted nothing more than to throw a temper tantrum. As the eldest child, it was my responsibility to set a good example for my younger siblings, and this was a responsibility I did not take lightly. So, in this particular case, I attempted to be mature and poised. I decided I would present a logical and rational argument for why baby Leonard should have an Arabic name instead of a Western name to be consistent with the rest of our family nomenclature, so dear baby sister wouldn't feel like an outsider. It was for *her* sake.

That's how I wanted it to go down. It's what I *thought* I would say. What I actually blurted out was:

"It's not fair that she gets two American names and I have to be *Ayser Razor Blade, MUSTARD FACE*!"

Then I stormed out of the room, accidentally knocking another family portrait off the wall, cracking the frame.

Whatever fuss I made must have done the trick (or the aliens returned Mom's real soul to her body), because the next day, my parents sent out birth announcements proudly welcoming baby Lameace Kadhim Salman into the world. I took it as a sign that Mom had listened to me and not my brother, as there wasn't any mention of *Leonard* anywhere.

My sister and I are very close now. I always feel that relationships are honed through time and/or conflict. In this case, we had both. It was not too long ago when she and I got into hair-pulling fights in the back of my parents' car[6]—or last year at my parents' house when, during an argument with her, I smashed my mother's favorite teacup. But as they say, no one pushes your buttons more than family. And I consider myself blessed to have this opportunity.

6 And when I say not too long ago, I mean within the last ten years. I'm not proud of this.

9

The Saudi Years: Pt. 1 ("Xanadu," a Place Nobody Dared to Go)

As if my young immigrant life weren't awkward enough, when I was ten, my parents announced they were moving us to Riyadh, Saudi Arabia. They'd both acquired fantastic teaching jobs at the university and thought it would be a great opportunity for the whole family, both financially and also as a way of getting back in touch with our Middle Eastern roots. The latter might have been sparked by my then-recent confession to Mom about the underground sex ring I was involved with, which was organized by the neighborhood kids . . .

Okay, it wasn't so much a sex ring as it was a dirty "Truth or Dare" game that my friend Gretchen and her older sister, Maggie, made up. It took place weekly and was only comprised of four girls until Cara brought in her boy crush, William.

Basically, I was the narc who busted up the ~~sex ring~~ innocent kid's game and cockblocked Cara from William when I snitched to my mother that I had just experienced my first kiss—with another girl.[1] I'd spilled the beans because I was ~~a dutiful and honest girl~~ feeling

1 The dare was to touch tongues with Gretchen, so I'm not even sure it qualifies as a kiss.

guilty about hiding secrets. Additionally, I was also proud about how I'd exhibited sexual self-restraint by kissing a girl instead of a *boy*—in my mind, it "didn't really count" if two girls were just being curious and experimenting.[2] This of course led Mom to have "words" with the parents of Cara and Gretchen, and my friends suddenly found themselves assigned more household chores since they clearly had too much time on their hands. I can see why I had no friends.

Luckily, we found ourselves preparing for yet another move—and this time I wasn't upset. Much of my neighborhood had shunned me following my Eliot Ness–style shutdown of their afterschool games. They had stopped inviting me on their weekly bike rides to Begley's Drugs for candy wax lips and Big Chew gum, and if I ever saw them and jumped on my bike to breathlessly catch up, one of them would suddenly "remember they had to go to do that thing," leaving me alone.

Another reason I was happy to leave Lexington was that one of the parents in the neighborhood had called us dirty immigrants who belonged back in our country. Well, he didn't actually say those words, but he had mentioned to my father that we might now be more comfortable in our own climate, with our own language.[3]

All this to say I was actually looking forward to the change.

A month before our departure, my time was divided between carefully removing my Scotch-taped Ziggy posters from the wall and packing them so they would survive the transatlantic journey, and visiting various doctors' offices to receive the excessive amount of vaccines needed to travel to that area. By my ninety-eighth injection, I began to question whether this was indeed a good move for our family. What country required this much immunization?! Unless they weren't

2 This excuse has actually been used many a time. My friend Susie declared to her college boyfriend, who'd caught her making out with Pam, that she was just "experimenting." Of course, she's now married to Pam and living in Colorado, along with their two pugs, McNulty and Bunk (named after the two main characters on the best television show ever, *The Wire*).

3 My father cautions me against projecting racist undertones onto this perfectly innocent conversation he had had with our neighbor.

immunizations at all, but some sort of serum to turn us kids into mutants . . . ? As part of my new lifestyle as neighborhood outcast, I had spent much of my time indoors, buried in my brother's comic books; I was currently perusing the X-Men series. I brought up these concerns to my parents, who told me to stop being so nervous and finish my packing.

One day, Dad gave me an encyclopedia in hopes of educating me on my soon-to-be new country of residence. This gesture did nothing to assuage my nerves; in fact, it had the opposite effect as I began reading about the strictly religious country we were heading to. Saudi women were required to wear a black, silky robe-cape thing called an *abaya* while in public. They were also expected to cover their faces with a veil that only revealed their eyes, called a *niqab*. They had to wear this even in the dead of summer. As a preteen with a propensity toward sweating and frizzy hair, I wasn't thrilled about the requirement of being enshrouded head to toe in black silk in 700-degree heat,[4] though I did like the idea of being able to hide my curly hair under a scarf. But I told myself it would be a worthwhile trade-off to have new friends who didn't think I was weird. Wouldn't it be amazing to finally fit in somewhere and maybe even be one of the—dare I say it—Cool Kids? A girl can dream!

I kept on reading the encyclopedia and studying up on my new home, until I came across the part that described the public square in Riyadh, which was a site for Friday prayers—and public executions. Public. *Executions*.

Holy. Fucking. Hell.

I slammed the book shut and threw it across the room as if that would somehow erase this new information from existence. Public executions!? I wasn't ready for this. I hated horror films, and ghost stories gave me nightmares—in particular, "The Legend of Sleepy Hollow," where the horseman gets his head blown off in battle and whose ghost comes back every night searching for his missing body part.

4 Pure hyperbole. It rarely gets hotter than 650 degrees.

Completely freaked out and suddenly worried for my baby sister, who was much more helpless than I, I burst into my parents' room, certain that once I delivered this knowledge, they would cancel the trip. Sure, it would mean a ton of wasted vaccinations, but perhaps we could go to nearby Africa or something so they wouldn't have been in vain.

My parents were as sympathetic as anyone would be when jolted out of a deep sleep at 3 a.m. by a nine-year-old crying hysterically about the safety of the baby. I've seen my mother *really angry* only a handful of times in my life—this was one of them. She shot out of bed to the baby's rescue, tripping and stubbing her toe (and breaking it) on the bed-post. When it was revealed that Lameace was okay, Mom was overcome with a mixture of relief, then happiness, then sadness, then anger in one awesome gale force of emotions. She screamed at me and hobbled to the bathroom. She didn't speak to me for an entire day.

Dad was a bit more philosophical about the whole thing. Realizing that I was genuinely scared, he told me not to worry, saying that the square was far away from where we would be living. I didn't like Dad's casual response. What if we took a trip to one of the souks[5] to buy shoes or a new dress and kept wandering through the aisles until—*bam!*—we stumbled upon a beheading? I was reassured that this would not happen, that the government was aware that families and kids would be roaming around nearby, and that they had the appropriate protections in place.

I tried to do what my favorite Ziggy poster said: "Be Positive." But I was not consoled. By the time I accompanied Mom to the doctor so he could drill a hole into the nail of her jammed toe to relieve pressure on the blood blister,[6] I had begun to think that this long-term Saudi Arabia trip was a horrible idea. Suddenly, being a nerd kid with no friends in comfortable, cozy Lexington, Kentucky, seemed like a better proposition than whatever awaited me in this scary new country.

5 A marketplace or bazaar.
6 . . . and also to get my final set of vaccines.

The day of our dreaded departure came. After a long flight with multiple layovers in Europe, we arrived at Riyadh Airport, which was crowded, less modern, and less clean than what I was used to. I saw women in abayas and niqabs, just like I had read about. Men wore the traditional long, white gown or *thawb* with a red-checkered headdress called the *kafiyah*. There were screaming children and very few chairs to sit on. It might have been my jet lag, but it didn't seem like a very inviting place.

Still, I tried to remain optimistic.

We put our bags through the X-ray machine, and they were transported to a separate table where airport officials opened and searched them. This was before the age of prohibited liquids, so I couldn't imagine what they would find that the X-ray hadn't detected. A man wearing the traditional thawb and an official airport worker jacket reached into my bag, grabbed my *Teen Beat* magazine, and began combing through. Then, with a flick of his wrist, he tossed it in the trash behind him.

"Wait!" I protested as my mother nudged me to be quiet. The man shook his head and said, "Haram."

Next, he found the loose magazine photos I had saved of Valerie Bertinelli lounging by a pool—I liked her hair in that picture and wanted to get mine styled in the same way. Nope. "Haram," he said as he crumpled it up and tossed it aside.

Finally, he got to my prized diary, a small pink book with a lock secured on it to hide all my nine-year-old secrets. On the cover was a picture of a cartoon boy and girl smooching, similar to what you'd find on a Hallmark card. Mr. Haram studied it for a few minutes as if he were debating asking me to unlock it.

In Arabic, my mother said, "For children. She's just a child." That seemed to appease him. He put my diary back into my bag, but not before taking a sharpie and scribbling out the image of the boy and girl kissing on the cover.[7]

---

7 NO JOKE. He actually did this.

"Hey!" I protested. Mom tugged at me harder to shut me up. "Haram," he said one last time before returning my backpack, unzipped, and turning his attention to the next hapless passenger's bag.

As we walked away, my mother said, "*Haram* in Arabic means *forbidden*. Never argue. There are going to be things you can't do here. They have strict rules."

And she wasn't exaggerating. I would soon discover there were a ton of rules in Saudi Arabia:[8]

- No pointing.
- No taking pictures of people in public.
- No laughing loudly if you're a female.
- No going outside without a scarf on your head as well as an abaya obscuring your body if you're a female
- No bacon (which I wasn't too bothered about).
- No alcohol (which didn't bother me yet).
- No driving for women (which also didn't bother me yet).
- No suggestive images in magazines—they would be scribbled out with a sharpie.
- No suggestive images in movies and TV—they would be ungracefully edited out.
- No traveling as a woman without a male companion—usually a brother or husband.
- No expression of freedom of religion. If you were Christian, you kept it to yourself.
- No movie theaters.
- No concert halls.
- No social mixing—at the malls there were "women only" and "men only" sections. Schools were also segregated into "boy only" and "girl only" institutions.

8 These were real rules in the eighties—for once, I'm not exaggerating.

- During the month of Ramadan, no eating, drinking, or smoking outside during daylight hours, even if you were not fasting.

In addition to these rules, Saudi Arabia also had a religious police called *Mutawwi'un* (moo-taw-ah-oon), *Mutawwi'* in the singular form. They would go around enforcing the above rules usually by fining offenders. They had very little patience and often weren't polite about it. For example, if you smoked during Ramadan, they'd write you a ticket, but not before smacking the cigarette out of your hand. At least, this happened to my brother's math teacher. I'm sure it didn't help that he was a Middle Easterner; the Mutawwi'un are known to be nicer to Westerners, and they are also supposed to be nicer to women.

We finally left the airport, hailed a taxi, and drove into town, deciding to stop at a fast food restaurant for dinner before heading to our new empty apartment. The thought of a hamburger, fries, and an ice-cold Coke helped ease the sting of the confiscation of half the contents of my backpack, and I cheered up. But when we asked the driver to take us to McDonald's, we were told there was *no* McDonald's.[9]

What kind of country didn't have a McDonald's? I hated this place!

The driver, seeing my discontentment, helpfully declared, "Beed Zahoot! I take you there! Beed Zahoot. You like!" My brother, who had been stoic and restrained during the entire airport experience, had suddenly had enough. "I DON'T WANT ZAHOOT!" he yelled. "I WANT SOMETHING AMERICAN!" Little baby Lameace, who had been sleeping quietly up until this point, woke up and joined his cause, wailing loudly. Mom tried to console her while Dad conferred with the driver in Arabic to find out what he meant by *Beed Zahoot*.

It turned out he was actually saying *Pizza Hut*. The Arabic language doesn't contain the letter "p," which makes for some translation modifications. It's not Pepsi but *Bebsi*. On that subject, if you wanted a soda in Riyadh back then, you could only get a Bebsi. Coke products were banned

9 The first McDonald's in Riyadh didn't open until 1993.

for the longest time because of a boycott by the Arab League as punishment for Coke being sold in Israel. To my ten-year-old brain, which didn't quite understand political sacrifices, this was a huge inconvenience. Thank god Dr. Pepper, my second favorite drink, was not a Coke product and available in Riyadh, though it was hard to get unless you made a long weekend trek to a huge grocery store called Euro Marché.

We sat at Beed Zahoot and ate our American fare. Bebsi was available, as was a weird root beer/red soda combo called Vimto. The latter was too sweet, but at least it had bubbles, so I drank it. Then we got back into the taxi and drove away from the city and into the deep desert for what seemed like an hour, seeing nothing but sand, sand, and more sand. Back in the eighties, Saudi Arabia was not as fully developed as it is today, and there was a lot of empty desert space. It was beyond anything I'd ever seen. From what I remembered about Iraq, the country was half sand, half greenery. But Saudi Arabia was all beige. And yes, I actually saw a Bedouin tent with a camel tied up next to it. Further ahead, we saw a huge complex of apartment towers, sprawled like an oasis in the distance. That was our new home.

We arrived at our relatively modern apartment. It looked pretty normal for the eighties—yellow velour couches, brown paneling. The main bathroom had a bidet installed in the toilet, but the bathroom right off from the entrance was less conventional—instead of the regular American toilet, it featured a squatting toilet called a *mirhad*.[10] I didn't quite know what to make of this. After staring at this "toilet" for a few minutes, I shut the door and walked away. That bathroom soon became our storage room for bikes and for cleaning the mud off our shoes . . . and occasionally for actual toilet usage if the other two in the house were occupied.

Over the next week, I stayed in my bedroom (which I claimed first, using my eldest sibling privilege), uninterested in leaving our apartment,

10 It's been said that using squatting toilets makes for a healthier bathroom-going experience. Do a web search.

so overwhelmed was I by this country's rules. What if I inadvertently did something *haram* and got carted away to jail—or worse, this public execution square? Come to think of it, how far away was this square, and what if their ghosts came wandering into our subdivision? I also had incredible jet lag, which really does a number on a person. I would lie awake night after night, thinking I saw weird shapes in the corners of my room and hoping no giant headless horseman (or camelman) would walk by my bedroom window. It was during this time that I began having a recurring dream that I still have to this day. In it, I've committed some crime and am awaiting my punishment, but I'm regretful and wish I could go back in time to undo the thing I did. During those first weeks, my wish was to go back in time to my simple little life in Lexington, Kentucky, where I was a quiet, nerdy kid who didn't get picked to play dodgeball.[11] My old life seemed friendlier and less hostile than this new environment.

The mirhad or squat toilet, popular in the Middle East. Author: Scottperry

Over the next few days, I was too afraid to leave the apartment. But I couldn't admit this to any members of my family. If you can recall,[12] my young fears of being attacked by a random soldier had been callously dismissed, so I'd learned to keep any concerns to myself. My family thought I had developed an intense fascination with Saudi TV programming, which consisted of only two state-run channels, an English and Arabic one (the latter mainly played Japanese anime cartoons dubbed over in Arabic). During the day, Zaid would go outside, and I would watch him from the window like the shut-in I had become, ready to ask him questions when he returned. I was always curious about how

11 I was fine with *not* playing dodgeball.

12 Chapter 3, "Land of the Free, Home of the McMuffin."

the guys who wore those Arab man-gowns were able to ride bikes; I couldn't see the road well from my window. Eventually, my brother got tired of being my eyes and ears on the ground and snapped, "Why dontcha stop being a scaredy-cat and just go outside!" At the same time, Mom, who was tired of me sitting on the couch watching the adventures of Kimba the White Lion, gave me a scarf and abaya to put on and sent me outside.

I decided to take it slow. I literally counted the steps from our front door.

On day one, I took thirty steps before heading back inside.

On day two, I took forty steps and then went back inside.

By day three, I had begun counting in feet; and on day five, I used landmarks: "I will go to the swing set in front of the next building and then stop."

On day six, I met Amirah, who lived in the building next to ours.

I heard her before I saw her. She was swinging in the playground, happily singing an off-key rendition of a new song I was currently obsessed with: Olivia Newton-John's "Xanadu" from the soon-to-be-released movie by the same name about a roller-skating magical muse. The movie was coming out in the States in a few months, but it would be forever before it would arrive on Saudi soil—on VHS tape, since movie theaters were banned at the time. I hoped sincerely that the VHS would show the actual movie; sometimes, movies were bootlegged wherein an individual would sneak a video camera into a theater and tape the movie along with the backs of the heads of the audience.[13] Regardless, I had already seen the trailers and couldn't wait. I'd played the song every night on my Walkman in my attempts to soothe myself to sleep. And now I had come across someone else who knew the song—someone else who lived in Saudi Arabia who was like me!

13 It was either that or a government-sanctioned version touched by a censor's heavy hand.

I slowly approached Amirah. She seemed so free. So happy. So uninhibited. I was fascinated, if not nervous—she was *singing in public*! When the song ended, she began singing "Summer Nights," the duet between Olivia Newton-John and John Travolta from the movie *Grease*. That got me out of my shell. I marched over and joined her in a duet, graciously taking the male part with my deep alto voice. She offered me the left ear on her headphone, and we put our heads together and sang loudly and proudly . . . until a stern-looking woman shushed us as she walked by.[14]

For some reason, the whole incident made me start laughing. It was the first time I'd done so since arriving two weeks before. My hysterical laughter made Amirah laugh too, and we fell down on the sand and lay on our backs laughing until we couldn't breathe—which only made us laugh more to the point of actually crying. Honestly, I'm not sure if I was crying because I was laughing so hard or because I had been overwhelmed by a flood of emotional relief. The ice was definitely broken—between me and my new friend, and also between me and my new home.

Soon, the lady in the niqab came by again.[15] Lady Niqab said something in Arabic about proper ladies not rolling around in the sand and told us to get up or she would call our parents. So, we did.

When I got home, I took off my jacket and dumped sand onto the floor that Mom had just vacuumed, causing her to force me into the mirhad room to take a shower.

In spite of the fact that I felt like a horse being washed in a stable, I felt happy and hopeful.

Maybe this place wasn't so bad.

Maybe I could grow to actually like it.

---

14 I couldn't actually tell if she was stern-looking—she was in full niqab with her face covered.

15 At least I think it was her. Her face *was* covered after all (though Amirah noticed that she was wearing the same red Adidas sneakers).

10

The Saudi Years: Pt. 2 ("We Go Together")

I was happier than I had been in a long time. I had a new pal, who was rapidly becoming my very first real Best Friend. I was on my best behavior and tried to keep a lid on my inner nerd for as long as I could; I didn't want to do anything to send her running for the ~~hills~~ sand dunes.

Once, I had a close call when I accidentally dripped spaghetti sauce on a Judy Blume book she'd lent me. I tried to wipe it off with a wet napkin, but that only made the problem worse, spreading the stain and blurring the words on the page. I panicked and spent two hours debating what was better, telling her the truth or saying that the book was stolen by a *Mutawwi'* when my family was out on a Friday morning.[1] While I was agonizing over this, my doorbell rang and Amirah entered, bringing some dolmah her mom had made. I awkwardly blurted out my confession and told her I would pay to have the book replaced. She laughed at me until she realized I was serious, then waved it off with a flick of her hand. "I get chocolate milk on my books all the time. Spaghetti sauce will be a nice change." That's when I realized I might have found my soul sister.

1 Back then, Saudi Arabia was on a Saturday-to-Wednesday business schedule. Weekends were Thursdays and Fridays.

We spent hours practicing how to ride bikes without getting our abayas caught in the spokes. We would eventually perfect our technique three months later, but not before a minor trip to the ER to stitch up her eye, which had split open when Amirah took a fall.[2] Those few weeks we practically lived at each other's houses, singing duets from *Grease* and by ABBA. Amirah also introduced me to the movie *Bugsy Malone*, a gangster musical starring a young Scott Baio and Jodie Foster. We watched that film so many times and sang its songs with such ferocity that it led to the one and only time in my life I've ever seen Dad lose his shit.

On our 453rd viewing, he flung open the TV room door and bellowed:

"WHAT IS WITH YOU AND THAT MOVIE?! WATCH SOMETHING ELSE!"

When Dad realized I had a guest, he quickly retreated, embarrassed to have made a scene in front of a non-family member. But that was the thing about Amirah—she was like family. And I was grateful for her.

I wished this could have been my life indefinitely, but I knew it had to end. It was still the holidays, and school would begin soon. Once again, I would be the weird new kid. Furthermore, I was about to enter fourth grade and Amirah was in fifth grade, so we wouldn't be in classes together. She promised this would not come between us, but I knew better. I hoped she would at least be on the bus ride to school so I wouldn't have to walk into the schoolyard alone, but on the first day of classes, she had to get her stitches removed.

As I sat on the bus by myself, I felt incredibly self-conscious. I was the only kid not wearing the school uniform of a white shirt and a long plaid skirt. My mother hadn't known where to get the uniform in time. Instead, I wore pants under an abaya because I didn't own any long skirts.

---

2 Amirah's dad was just being cautious; she didn't actually have a concussion. I knew because right after she fell, I made her sing the theme song from *Grease*, and she knew all the words.

I hoped my abaya would provide the uniformity that I needed to fit in. I braced myself for what was becoming typical first-day anxiety and awkwardness: having to explain my name to dozens of curious and judgmental eyes and elaborating on where I had come from, why I was here, etc.

I certainly wasn't prepared for what I actually experienced—a warm and welcoming air from the girls in the class. "HEH-LOW AY-SIR SEL-MAHN!" they chanted in sing-songy unison, at the teacher's request, putting the emphasis on the second syllable of my last name, which is how it's pronounced in Arabic. They seemed genuinely happy to see me. Perhaps my relieved mind was playing tricks on me, but I was also pretty sure I heard a quiet cheer coming from the back of the class. What? Surely there was some catch here. Were they zombie alien kids, like in that movie *Village of the Damned* (except none of them were blonde)? This was too suspicious!

Afterward at recess, the girls gathered around and we traded stories of where I had come from and the countries the other girls called home. Many of them were from Pakistan, and a few had grown up in England or Wales. One lucky girl had been living in San Diego, California, before her family moved here. They still had a house there, which they visited during the summers.[3] I envied all these girls who would return to "exotic" places like San Diego or London, while I most likely would be spending my summer in Kentucky. And since I was newly arrived from America, a couple of the Pakistani girls wanted to know if I had ever met Olivia Newton-John herself, who was becoming all the rage. I told them that this possibility was unlikely for me, being from Kentucky, but that my new friend from San Diego had a better chance.

It was the best first day of school I'd ever experienced. I was actually enjoying myself. No one asked why I wasn't wearing a uniform; no one told me to bleach my mustache. No one commented on how my deodorant didn't work, and no one suggested that maybe I should try

3 That's the Saudi Arabia I knew—most of us were only there for the school year, and we would travel with our families back overseas during the summer.

putting perfume in my hair to make it smell better.[4] *Who were these girls?* If not zombie alien kids, could they be regular, awkward preteen girls like me?

Had I finally found *my people*?!

I didn't have long to ponder this. Soon after recess, the headmistress pulled me out of class. At first I thought it was because I refused to take off my abaya, but apparently I wasn't registered as a student in the English section of the school. There were two divisions, an English-speaking section and another that taught the same curriculum completely in Arabic. The headmistress stated that since both my parents were Arabs, the assumption was that I spoke fluent Arabic and should be learning in Arabic, unlike many of the girls in the English section who had Western mothers. This was their logic.

I panicked. I didn't speak any Arabic, apart from understanding my parents whenever they spoke it at home. Furthermore, each country's dialect is different, and Iraqi Arabic sounds vastly different from Saudi Arabic; it's like Gaelic compared to Bostonian English. I could barely understand the Saudi dialect, let alone try to speak it, and I was so upset about this turn of events that I almost burst into tears right then and there, but years of tough school experiences had taught me to be stoic. So I packed up my book bag and trudged over to the Arabic section. Once again, I was faced with Mean Girls and Cool Girls and Wannabees, just as I had in America—but this time with a language barrier. Once again, I found myself longing for the good old days of just being the nerd girl who was shunned from sitting with Alice and Carla at lunch. This time, I was sitting in math class not understanding a damn thing and trying to hold back tears of frustration and anxiety.

Mercifully, the day ended. I told my mother what had happened, and she got pissed. Clearly this was a mistake. She asked me why I hadn't

---

4 In fact, later on in the bathroom, I witnessed one girl casually insert a paper towel into her shirt under her armpit as she openly told me that she sweated so badly she needed to apply a protective barrier. She wasn't even embarrassed.

called her earlier, then jumped up as if she were going to get into the car to drive to the school to speak to the headmistress—but then remembered she wasn't allowed to drive. Also, it was after hours and the school was closed. So, she did the next best thing. She wrote a strongly worded letter, crumpled it up, and then wrote a *less* strongly worded one.[5] The next day, Mom came to school, had a meeting with the headmistress, and the whole thing was resolved. I returned to the English school.

Apart from my nightmarish first day, there was a relaxed air about the school that I appreciated. I attributed this to the fact that it was an all-girls school. In addition to the nationwide practice of gender segregation in schools, colleges, and workplaces, the idea here was also for students to focus and study without the distraction of the opposite sex. I would find this segregation annoying once I went through puberty and developed a stronger interest in boys; but for now it was perfect. I didn't have to worry about boys pulling my hair or yanking up my skirt to expose my underwear. I didn't have to be concerned about a boy pulling a toy gun on me or telling another student that I'd told him to "fuck off."

For the first time in a long while, I didn't feel a sense of dread about going to school. I found the space to just be myself, or at least to figure out what *that* was, especially since I had spent the last few years hiding the real me or molding myself to what I thought I had to be. Except for the few times I encountered the Mean Girls from the Arabic section who taunted me about forgetting my mother tongue and being relegated to the "lower class" English section, I actually enjoyed myself. I had friends; I fit in. I came out of my shell. In fact, I became quite gregarious. The word we used back in the eighties was *spaz*, actually. Now that I had the freedom to be myself, I became the *loudest* version of myself. It's a good thing there were no boys to distract me. I could go full Spaz.

5 The two letters were identical except for the amount of curse words in the first one.

In the middle of fourth grade, I took some exams and skipped into the fifth grade. Mom must have felt guilty about me starting kindergarten a year later and constantly being the oldest kid in class. When the opportunity came and my teachers told her I wasn't being challenged enough, she told them to skip me a grade.

As part of my transfer, I literally moved my desk out of the fourth-grade room and into the fifth-grade room. I'll never forget that day. The students applauded me. And there was Amirah in the front row, with an empty space next to her that she'd prepared so we could sit together. I'd never felt so welcomed in my life. My new friends and I had the time of our lives. We were a weird group; but I was a weirdo surrounded by weirdos, which made me normal. In our little bubble of innocence, we bonded over all the repressions and rules we were subjected to. We pretended we were rebels or suffragettes, though of course we only rebelled within the confines of our homes or classrooms. There was no real rebellion here, unless of course you count the weird trend of wetting toilet paper and throwing it up to the ceiling to make it stick. For two months, you couldn't walk into a room without looking up to see a white mound of congealed paper hanging from the ceiling. When we weren't "rebelling," we were making up our own plays or acting out scenes from movies like *Grease* and *Xanadu*. I always played the John Travolta part because of my thick eyebrows and short hair.

Me, second from the left, looking cool in my fingerless mesh gloves.

I was surrounded by so much friendship and goodwill that it took the sting off when Amirah moved back to Egypt at the end of the year. We kept in touch for a few years before falling off the grid. But I will always be forever grateful to Amirah for being my very first real best friend. And I'm so appreciative of that time in my life when I made lifelong friends who allowed me the space to reset myself.

During those years, I didn't have to *try* to be one of the cool kids. I *was* a cool kid.

11
The Saudi Years: Continued ("Close to You")

I have a fantastic relationship with my father. I feel fortunate to have inherited many of his good qualities—intelligence, sense of humor, compassion, optimism, and a huge curiosity about life. He is the real deal. Not a fake bone in his body, and he lives life fully. Anyone who meets my father loves him.

Dad has a PhD in pharmacology and has worked his entire life. Today, even in his late eighties, though he's not practicing his trade anymore, he constantly reads and enriches himself. We talk every evening, and almost always he shares something he's learned from the "Yoo-Tyoob" or the "Goo-Gul." Five years ago, he decided he wanted to teach himself to draw, so he bought the supplies he needed and set about diligently and painstakingly working on sketches. And he was very good. Dad is also a whiz at technology, much better than I am.[1] But he also holds firm to old-school habits, such as falling asleep while listening to news on the radio through earphones. Inevitably, he absorbs the reports of horrific news into his dreams and will often startle Mom when he loudly comes out of a nightmare. When he realizes it was just

1 Unlike me, he has an iPad. I'm a complete Luddite, which is ironic considering I work as an editor, a job that's completely software-based.

a dream, he promptly falls back asleep like a baby, leaving Mom wide awake and trying to calm *her* nerves.

But growing up, my dynamic with my father was a little different. While I respected and loved him, our interactions were almost always at arm's length. He was a brilliant genius whose mind never stopped, and the flip side of that was his perpetual workaholic nature, both at work and at home. As children, we hardly saw him—he was either working far away or in the next room, engaged in something that required his attention. There was no time for deep conversations. He was such a hard worker that, even on family vacations, you would find him alone with a textbook, reading about pharmacology.

But I never questioned or doubted his love. He was a great provider, a good role model, and the strong, silent type. He was just *Dad*, albeit a dad who was always slightly removed.[2] And so it was a special blessing that our relationship changed briefly when I was twelve years old, during a memorable period when we would spend hours of quality time together, just me and him, without any familial obligations or work distractions—not even a pharmacology book! It happened by accident . . . well, actually *because* of an accident.

It was a weekend afternoon. My brother and I were fighting over what to watch on TV. I wanted to watch Peter Sellers's *The Party* for the hundredth time,[3] and he wanted to watch *Godzilla and Godzuki*.[4] As is often the case with siblings, the winner is the one who snatches the remote and runs into the bathroom. In this case, he snatched it first, but being a competitive person (and a sore loser, apparently), I chased after him and tried to wrestle the remote away. We both reached the bathroom at the same time, and, unbeknownst to Zaid, my hand was in the door hinge when he slammed the door shut, smashing my left pinky.

---

2 Side note: I'm aware of the theory that people who grow up with an absent father tend to seek out unavailable men. Well, that would be future Ayser's problem . . .

3 I still love this film, even though I know I shouldn't because of the unfortunately cartoonish depiction of an Indian man.

4 An animated series from the seventies created by Hanna-Barbera.

The next few moments felt surreal. I tried pulling my finger out, even though the door was firmly closed on it. The doors in our house were heavy, and I was in a dire situation. My biggest fear during those days was losing a limb, and this image was fresh in my mind as I desperately tried to extricate my finger. Then, I came out of my shock and began screaming, and Zaid realized what was going on. He opened the door and I freed my pinky, bracing myself for whatever mangled mess I would find. But there was no horror-movie gore. No blood at all. Somehow the impact had split my finger in the middle but missed a major artery. I must have gone back into shock, because the next thing I did was ask for a Band-Aid so I could return to the living room to watch TV, as if this were a minor paper cut.

By this time, my mother, who had been taking a nap, appeared and sprang into Mom Crisis Mode. In one motion, she grabbed my hand, wrapped it in a clean towel, shoved it into a bag of ice, and scooped me away into a cab, once again cursing the city for not allowing women to drive.[5] On the way to the ER, my shock wore off, and I became slightly hysterical. "I don't wanna lose my finger! I don't want it to be cut off!" I kept crying over and over, as if saying it would ensure it wouldn't happen. We arrived at the hospital, where I received stitches and was promised that my finger would be saved. It was wrapped up in a bandage, and I was free to go home.

The whole experience was traumatic for all of us, but buried under the trauma was a silver lining. My injury required repeated visits to the hospital, to cleanse and redress the wound and eventually get the stitches taken out. All told, Dad and I made about five trips back and forth during a two-month period, just him and me.

Each week, I would get into the backseat of Dad's dusty blue Mazda[6] for the forty-minute ride to the hospital. We developed a routine. Dad would turn on Saudi radio to listen to the news, and I would daydream

5 Dad was at work at this time.

6 Dusty, because of the Saudi sand. The car was originally a vibrant navy.

about the rock band I was going to start and wonder if my as-yet-unbegun career as a keyboardist would be hindered by my injury. Our doctor sometimes worked on weekends, so depending on the day of the week, we would change up the itinerary. If it was a school day, we would stop for fast food at the Saudi version of Dairy Queen after the doctor's visit. On weekends, we'd make multiple stops. I never thought I'd have so much fun, running errands with Dad.[7]

Dad in front of our trusty dusty Mazda.

Sometimes Dad stopped at the electronics store either to buy replacement earphones for his transistor radio that he kept losing[8] or to bring in his prized short-wave radio for repair, telling the shop attendant it wasn't picking up the Voice of America radio program as well as it had the week before. The shop owners all knew Dad by name and would greet him enthusiastically. "Doc-toor Selmahhn!" they exclaimed and offered us tea, because that's what they do in the Middle East (the hype is real, y'all). Dad would sit and drink with them while conversing about their families, about whom he seemed to know a lot. I began to wonder whether he was actually running some kind of transistor radio ring instead of working at the university. He would try to engage me in their conversation, asking the men if they had daughters my age. They all did, and most of their daughters loved reading the Enid Blyton

7 My mother wonders why I didn't react with a similar enthusiasm back in Lexington when she took me along on her trips to Kmart or Hobby Lobby to get supplies for her macramé pot hanger projects. It's not that I didn't enjoy time with Mom; I loved walking down the aisles and making pyramids out of the colored blocks of modeling clay. It's just that those outings took place in Lexington, where there was more I could have done, like watching TV, going to the movies, or riding bikes wearing shorts . . .

8 Don't tell him, but Mom hid them in an effort to reduce his radio-induced nightly terrors.

books my friends and I were obsessed with.[9] I would politely engage, but truth be told, I wanted to hurry up and get on to our next destination—because I knew the next stop was the best stop.

After the electronics store, we would make our way to a huge bookstore downtown. It stocked everything: literary hardcovers, pulp fiction paperbacks, textbooks, school supplies, and comic books from all countries. But the best thing they sold by far were the uncensored magazines! For real. It was hard enough in Saudi Arabia to get a Western magazine, let alone one that didn't have its pages ripped out for being too racy or having bikinis, miniskirts, and bare arms scribbled out with black marker. To have an establishment that carried untouched magazines was my heaven![10] The shop owner kept them behind a desk, out of plain view, and you had to ask for them. It was so secret and exhilarating!

I made this discovery during our first visit to the bookstore, when the shopkeeper noticed the fancy red Mary Janes I'd scored the previous summer on a trip to Austria. Having a daughter himself, he understood my devotion to fashion. Perhaps he'd also seen my bandaged hand and, in sympathy, whipped out a magazine from behind his desk. It was an issue of *Seventeen* magazine that featured an article on Lynda Carter, a.k.a. Wonder Woman[11]—specifically Lynda's Los Angeles home, as described by a niece who had been visiting her. I still remember the short skirt and tall boot combo Lynda wore in the feature photograph within the magazine's pages, an outfit I tried emulating in my own fashion over the next two years. I saved this issue[12] for many years after, only because it was one of my few Saudi-bought periodicals still in pristine condition. You know what I'm talking about—the feeling you get

9 Our favorite Enid Blyton book series was the one about girls at a British boarding school, which offered us a sense of escape and adventure.

10 To this day, even though most of my magazines now come in the mail by subscription, I still get a rush whenever I buy one off the rack.

11 The OG Wonder Woman, the one on TV with the invisible plane and the seventies sound effects.

12 I would show you the cover of the issue, but legal issues prevent me from doing so.

when you open a new magazine that is still flat and crisp, complete with the smell of new paper.

I was so excited about receiving the magazine that day, more so than any average person should ever be about a teen fashion mag. But it wasn't just a magazine to me. Those papers and images represented a pipeline to America. In Riyadh, I only had access to mainly British or European products, and so on the rare occasion that I found something American, I treasured it.

Dad and I would make two more stops after the bookstore. First, we'd visit the nearby bakery. As soon as we arrived, Dad would hold up three fingers, and a guy would pull out three *huge*, round sheets[13] of hot Arabic bread straight from a pit-fire oven and bag them up for us. They smelled *amazing*, and it took too much of our resolve to wait until we got home, so we'd tear into half of one sheet on the car ride back. Finally, we'd stop at our favorite street food vendor for shawarma and falafel, which we wouldn't even touch until we got home despite how amazing *that* smelled because we now felt guilty for eating all the bread.

The thing I remember most about this time with Dad was the music we listened to in the car. Dad had a cassette tape of the Carpenters' greatest hits, and instead of listening to the radio on our way back home, he'd pop that tape in. I thought those songs were incredibly sappy and sad at the time, but in hindsight, the nostalgia that Karen Carpenter's melodic voice conveys when I hear her sing snaps me back every time. There I am again in the backseat of that little blue car, wrapped up in my daydreams of future greatness as we drove along the dusty, not-yet-developed highways in and out of town, very much content to be hanging out with Dad—just the two of us, sharing our secret bread fresh from the oven.

---

13 I say *sheet* because these were gigantic versions of the smaller round-shaped pita bread you might be familiar with.

There is a saying in the Quran that my mother always recites to me in Arabic.[14] It translates to "And maybe you hate something that is good for you, and maybe you love something that is bad for you." It's the perfect description for that time during my preteens when a disaster turned into an amazing connection with my father. Though I don't like to remember the accident, I wouldn't change the part that came afterward for anything.

From then on, I also began looking for the silver lining in seemingly negative events. There wasn't always one—sometimes bad things just happen—but whenever there was, I was glad I'd looked.

14 Usually when she doesn't want me to do something, such as being interested in whichever boy I'm into at the time.

12
How to Be a Rock Star

When I was thirteen, I wanted to be a rock star.

Mind you, I had no particular musical aspirations nor was I musically inclined. I was simply intrigued by the mystique of a rock star, and I wanted in. So, I declared that this would be my chosen profession when I grew up and diligently penned down my "Rules for Success," which I read every day to make sure I followed said rules.

I found the list recently and thought I'd share some of the original text.

Goals for the Future (with God's Help)

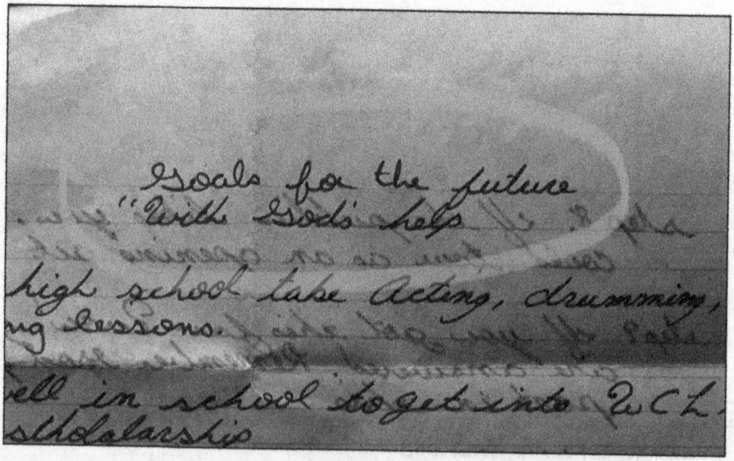

Step 1:
In high school, take acting, drumming & singing lessons.

Step 2:
Do well in school to get into UCLA on a scholarship.[1]

Step 3:
During college, try to find some people with talent. If you do, form a band. It's better to have one person in the band who you know well. If you don't form a band during this time, keep looking & studying & practicing.

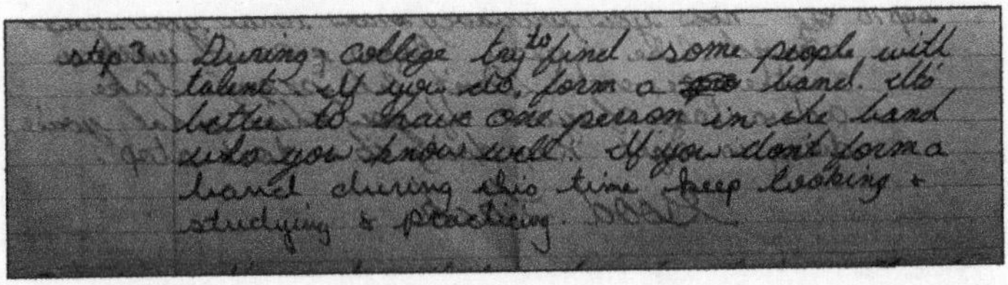
step 3. During college try to find some people with talent. If you do, form a band. It's better to have one person in the band who you know well. If you don't form a band during this time keep looking + studying & practicing.

Step 5:
This is the hard part! This calls for a lot of luck & hard work. If you play pretty good music (& original) it will be easier getting a record company. Get a manager first.

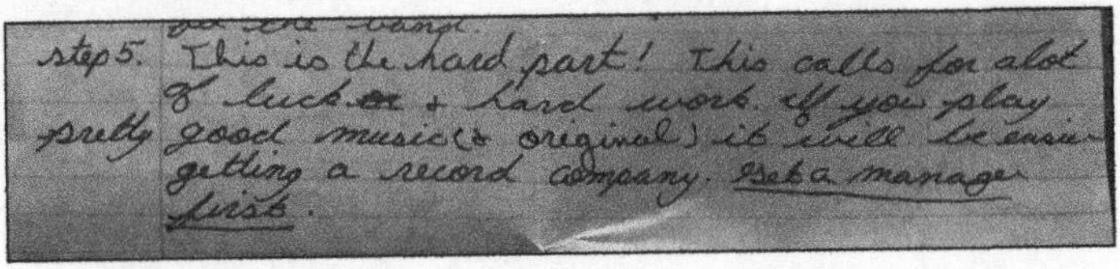
step 5. This is the hard part! This calls for alot of luck + hard work. If you play pretty good music (& original) it will be easier getting a record company. Get a manager first.

Step 7:
Probably you now have at least a pretty good company and a reliable manager. Now you have to get the public to like you. Don't be discouraged—Loverboy[2] *was booed twice as opening acts. You're lucky to make it to this point. Practice, practice & be persistent.*

---

1 Mom had told me that I could indeed become a rock star after I'd completed the requisite college degree that was expected of me. So, I dutifully incorporated it into my plan.

2 My favorite band at the time.

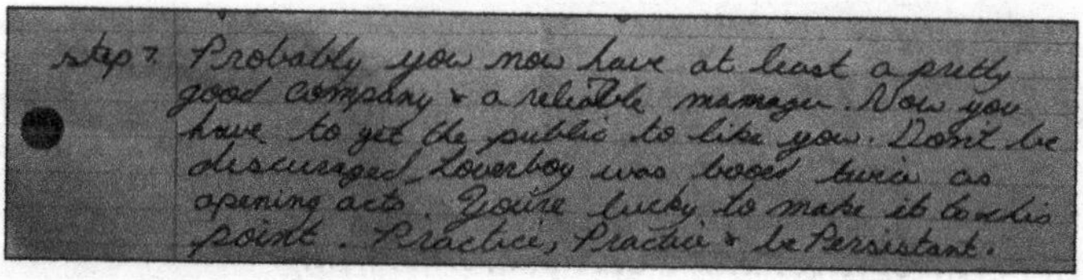
step 7. Probably you now have at least a pretty good company & a reliable manager. Now you have to get the public to like you. Don't be discouraged, Loverboy was booed twice as opening acts. You're lucky to make it to this point. Practice, Practice & be Persistant.

Side note: I didn't actually become a rock star or even join a band in college, but I maintained my earlier philosophy of practice, practice, practice—and being persistent. And, of course, the importance of getting a good manager/agent/representative.

13

The Saudi Years: Final ("Livin' on a Prayer")

The summer before tenth grade, my classmates and I underwent an awakening. For the past year, we had been on a collective "Period Watch" as we each eagerly awaited the rite of passage to womanhood. We had all read the Judy Blume book *Are You There God? It's Me, Margaret* and were excited to begin our lives as women.

I got my period earlier that spring. Over the summer, I exchanged letters with my best friends, Sara and Rania, sharing my experiences about mundane things that somehow felt different now. Even ice cream tasted different "now that I was a woman." To be honest, I probably needed to cool it on my daily double scoop; changing hormones meant a change in metabolism.

I was fourteen. My hormones were percolating, my body was transforming, and I felt alive and awake in a way that I hadn't before. If this was puberty, I loved it! Forget all those horror stories about mood swings and zits and greasy hair and awful cramps. Perhaps, I thought in those early days, I would be the outlier, enjoying a perfectly smooth transition through my adolescence.

Well, of course, it all soon went south. I got zits, had awful cramps, and those mood swings? Holy hell! I want to apologize to my parents for this dark period. Luckily, I was living in the safe confines of Saudi

Arabia where I couldn't really hang out with the bad crowd or pick up any bad habits—unless you count toilet papering the teachers' lounge.

My personality changed as well. I turned inward and wasn't interested in participating in the reality around me. All I wanted to do was read, listen to music, and daydream—disappearing into future, fanciful worlds where I would be rich, successful, and famous. People my own age scared me to death, especially boys. If I was walking down the street and saw more than two boys, I would literally change my course and walk the other way.

That summer, when we were spending our holidays back in Lexington, it took me literally six days to purchase a record album at Sam Goody, the music store at the mall. The ordeal began on a Tuesday. I entered with the intention of buying *Synchronicity* by The Police. I'd just come from the bookstore next door where I had purchased the latest V.C. Andrews novel. I set my bag down on the floor, found the album, and then continued to rifle through the stacks, looking for anything else interesting. This was in the days before iTunes, Napster, Shazam, and all the other digital music platforms where you could choose what you wanted to buy by actually *listening* to it; back then, you chose your music based on how cool the album cover was.

As I stood there trying to decide whether I wanted *Pyromania* by Def Leppard, which was new to me at the time, three goons ambushed me from behind and grabbed my bag. They tossed it back and forth to one another while I watched helplessly, unsure of whether I should try to snatch it back and run or just save myself and take off . . .

Let's rewind. Okay, that's *not* what happened. I was fresh from reading a bunch of bad Harlequin romance novels where the heroine gets kidnapped, and my teenage imagination was in overdrive.[1] What *actually* happened was three skinny guys in jeans and baseball caps walked

1 For some reason, the hero in those books would always be captured by pirates and tortured—usually involving some awful maiming of his manhood. WTF message were authors trying to send to readers . . . ?

up, and one of them saw my bag on the floor and wanted to know what was in it. In hindsight, maybe he was flirting,[2] but Awkward Teenage Me missed that. Goon #1 asked what was inside the bag, so I told him it was a book. "What kind of book?" he queried and tried to pick up my bag to see for himself, which freaked me out. I snatched it back and gave the only response I could—which was in the moment motivated by panic and awkwardness but also a pretty clever shutdown of the harassment, if I do say so myself—"THE KIND YOU *READ*!" I yelled as I ran out the door, stopping only when I barged into a women's lingerie store. I stayed there until it was time for Mom to pick me up—forty minutes later. I wonder what the sales clerk thought of the awkward teenager who still needed a training bra but who was painstakingly scrutinizing every item in the maternity section.

The next day, I went back to Sam Goody but got ten feet from the front door before I spotted some male youths "lurking" inside. I changed course and went to the Hallmark store, where I spent thirty-five minutes browsing the card selection. By day three, Mom had become so annoyed that I wanted to spend so much time at the mall that she refused to take me. Day four was spent at the movies—*Ghostbusters*!—and on day five, we had to visit some friends of Dad's, which took all day.

On day six, Dad had errands to run by the mall, so I convinced him to drop me off. It was morning and blissfully quiet, with only elderly mall walkers doing their laps. I was there the minute the clerk unlocked and raised the metal gate. I strode in with purpose, found the album, paid for it, and left, within fifteen minutes. No unwanted encounters with any males—or any other human, come to think of it. It was *Synchronicity*! The album, but also literally my experience.[3]

The events of that week alone made me look forward to August, when we would return to Saudi Arabia and I could go back to my simple boy-free life in my all-girl classrooms, engaging in wacky antics like

---

2 Unrelated: I *was* wearing my cute plaid shorts and white high-top Reeboks.

3 I still have that album—a memento of my teenage struggles.

hiding the chalkboard before the teacher came in so we couldn't have class. It was ironic—I was excited to return to the sheltered confines and comfort of the rules I had come to know so well.

But things were changing, and once again I was the last to embrace the change. Whereas I had previously felt like I was at the wrong end of the table, now it seemed like I was the last one to leave the party, which had long died down. While most of my friends and classmates were welcoming their changing bodies and minds and discovering boys, I was still in the blissful tween phase—goofy young girl, not yet a serious woman. My epic summer tale of going out in public to buy music albums and avoiding boys paled in comparison to those of my friends, who'd returned to Saudi with adventure stories of first loves and first kisses that had happened on *their* summer vacations. Unlike me, many of my friends did not appreciate being back in Saudi. They were now restless women who wished to take on the world but were relegated to studying for physics exams and memorizing passages of the Quran for religion class. And they were *bored*. Bored, teenage girls who, without the distraction of boys in the classroom, *wanted* the distraction of boys.

If there was one thing that unified us all, it was that hormone-driven emotion: we were pissed off. I was pissed off that I had spent the summer recording hours of American sitcoms on VHS only to find that the format was not compatible with the type of VCR we had in Riyadh (#NerdProblems). Sara was pissed that she had to leave her summer "boyfriend" back in Michigan. Rania was pissed that now that she had gotten her period, her mother wouldn't let her play soccer with her brother and his friends because it "wasn't something a respectable Muslim lady did." Rania was a kickass soccer player, and she craved the challenge of playing with the boys, who took the game more seriously than most girls did. The last thing on her mind was boys. But rules are rules.

Meanwhile, I was also annoyed because I felt like Sara and Rania had left me behind with their "developing-before-me" selves. I remember crying a lot during this time. Actually, we all cried a lot—or, to use the more refined term, we unabashedly and freely "shared our emotions." To this day, I trace my ability to freely discuss my insecurities and feelings back to that year in Saudi when I inadvertently became part of my first Women's Circle. Each Wednesday before we went off for the Thursday-Friday weekend, a group of at least ten of us would gather in the schoolyard, sit cross-legged on the ground, and vent. About anything. It was usually about our feelings and how we were upset about something one of the other girls had said. The gathering was a public forum to air our grievances, and it often degenerated into hysterical tears. Yep, it basically became a Cry Circle. As I'm sure you're aware, emotions are contagious and we hadn't yet learned the art of moderating these sessions, so the floor usually went to whoever cried the loudest tears. And if you've ever seen a teenage girl cry . . . well, you'll know that this is one *tough* competition. Soon, what began as an attempt for catharsis and bonding degenerated into bad feelings and silent treatment. We would leave for the weekend upset, spend two days complaining on the phone to our best friend about what had transpired *within* the Cry Circle instead of outside of it, but then quickly get over it by the time we returned to class on Saturday.

While I'd spent my years prior to Saudi trying to be invisible or at least fit in, my time in the country had turned me into a social chameleon. I'd become everyone's friend. However, I had become so good at staying out of everyone's drama that I was more of a spectator to, instead of a participant in, much of my friends' lives. For starters, it seemed that everyone except for Rania and me had now acquired a "boyfriend."

Now, this was a country with gender segregation in schools, malls, and pretty much anywhere else, save the random family house party. So, you can imagine the creativity it took for a girl and a guy to actually meet up. But never underestimate the power of a hormonal teenage girl frustrated with life in a dusty desert town and looking for something to while away her "sentence." To be clear, having a boyfriend in Saudi Arabia wasn't what you'd think it was. Having a boyfriend simply meant you and the guy both knew you liked each other. Seeing each other was another thing entirely. And forget speaking. This was all before texting, email, Facebook, and cell phones—the dark ages even for those of us who lived in the Western world. Now, try living in Saudi Arabia, a strictly religious country where women could hardly do anything.

A girl and boy who liked each other would spend weeks making eyes at one another as they were getting into their respective cars to go home from school. I was too shy and anxious to even attempt this, so worried was I about Mom's warning that "people would talk," thus ruining my reputation (which at the time was *so* crucial for a female). As a dutiful Muslim daughter, I would not even dare to flirt. But more important, I had no idea *how* to flirt. And God forbid a boy would express interest in me; I would shut it down in an instant.[4] But many of my friends, who were braver than I, threw caution to the wind and "dated" boys.

Here's how they did it: if the girl was lucky, the boy she liked was the brother of her friend, thereby allowing her to actually have face-to-face time with him under the guise of going to her friend's house to hang out. But if the girl was not blessed with any connections with the boy, she would have to rely on extreme measures. In this case, the hapless couple would communicate via paper notes or secret phone calls. In the latter scenario, the boy would call his paramour's house, posing as a girl if her parents picked up first.

Let's examine the case of my friend Deena. Deena liked Shareef. Since they couldn't date openly, they would proceed as such:

- Shareef's sister would call Deena. If Deena answered, great—his sister would hand the phone to Shareef, and they could steal a few moments of conversation.
- If Deena *didn't* answer, Shareef's sister would have to greet Deena's mom or her nosy younger brother and make small talk. After about a minute, Deena would get on the line as well and start talking to Shareef's sister about girl stuff like periods

4 As we've seen from the earlier record store fiasco.

or cramps, until Deena's mom or brother got bored and hung up. Then and only then could Shareef pick up.

Sometimes Deena's dad would pick up in the middle of the phone call and wonder who the male voice was on the other line. That's when Deena would tell him that he was hearing sounds from the TV (she had a TV and VCR in her bedroom), and she and Shareef would quickly hang up. When the couple wanted to see each other, they would use the excuse of parties at friends' homes. But those were usually chaperoned by adults, and it would be suspicious if Shareef was seen hanging out constantly with a bunch of teenage girls. When things got desperate and the couple got tired of sneaking around, the male would put on a niqab and abaya in order to walk freely beside his girlfriend in public.

One time, Shareef and Deena got into a really close call at the mall. They had wound up in a dressing room to make out, when they were busted by a sales clerk. Luckily, it was hard to identify two black-clad silhouettes that had taken off running—except that Deena had been wearing a very distinctive pair of jelly shoes that she'd gotten in London over the summer. She was forced to dispose of them in the trash can in the ladies' room so she wouldn't be identified.[5] Shareef gave her his white Adidas sneakers, threw away his abaya and niqab, and walked barefoot to the drugstore, where he bought a pair of flip-flops, avoiding as best as he could having to explain what had happened to his shoes.

That day, Deena slept over at my house. She spent the whole night crying, shaken with fear. We had all heard enough horror stories and urban legends of prominent Saudi figures, such as Saudi princesses, who were stoned to death after they were caught messing around with men they weren't married to.[6] It was a sobering reminder for Deena and a caution to me that it wasn't worth risking my life for the temporary thrill of walking next to my crush at the mall for twenty minutes.

5 The things you do for love.

6 And let's not forget the execution square I'd read about in the encyclopedia.

The incident made Deena vow to never have a boyfriend again while she was living in Saudi. Luckily for her, she ended up moving back to Wales at the end of the year, where she met her now-husband.[7]

Sadly, we also remember the harrowing stories of the ones who were not so lucky. The consequences were not as extreme as things like honor killings, which still take place in parts of the stricter Muslim regions. Thankfully, I don't personally know anyone to whom this has happened. But there were a few instances in my school of girls being roughed up by members of their family. Suhad, a girl who had gorgeous, black, silken hair down to her breastbone, was corresponding with a boy when she was found out by her father. He did the unthinkable. He dragged her downstairs by her lovely hair, pulled her into the kitchen, grabbed a pair of shears, and cut it all off. Suhad was absent from school for a week before she returned, bruised and with a spiky haircut. It was probably the most horrific thing I'd ever witnessed. But given the reality of honor killings elsewhere in the country, Suhad was lucky that the only thing she'd lost was her hair. It's awful to say, but that was the cold reality in which we lived.

That year in Saudi, I was also involved in my one big adventure. Well, okay, it was not firsthand; it happened to one of my good friends, and I played a part in it, somewhat. We dubbed it "the Great Jordanian Escape."

Magda, one of our friends, had been sent to Riyadh by her mother in Texas to live with her father and his new young Jordanian wife. Magda had apparently been showing signs of a wild life in her hometown of Houston, and her mother wanted her to have some structure and discipline. The problem was Magda's new stepmom wanted her father all to herself and was constantly trying to drive a wedge between Magda and her dad. It wasn't uncommon for Magda to talk about how "The Bitch" would lock her out of her house for hours; but when Magda's father came home, she was wide-eyed in her explanation that she had

7 They are happily married with three handsome boys.

been napping because of the hot Saudi heat and hadn't heard her stepdaughter knock or ring the doorbell. I felt bad for Magda, but she was a tough cookie. She wasn't afraid of authority like I was and clearly wasn't as sheltered as me. I envied her ability to stand up to anyone, even the headmistress. She always had an air of being unbothered by anything, while I always sweated the small stuff.[8]

After two years of living in Saudi, Magda's mom decided she wanted her daughter back home in Houston, but Magda's dad refused. As far as he was concerned, Magda was benefiting from the strict Saudi life, and he didn't want her to return to the den of corruption that was her Texas high school. He forbade her to leave. In Saudi, women need a male companion whenever they travel; plus, a father has rights over the mother—especially one living in the United States. So, Magda took matters into her own hands. With the help of her friends, she planned an escape. Leading up to the escape, Magda stayed the night at Sara's house each weekend, where she could call her mother in Houston and talk freely about their plan without worrying about Magda's evil stepmother eavesdropping. But Sara's mom, Rose, wasn't supposed to know about the plan, either. When Rose found out one evening, Sara implored, "Please don't tell Dad anything!" Rose, an American, was sympathetic; but she didn't like the idea of lying to her husband. She made a deal with Sara. "Don't tell me anything, and consider yourselves free to go about your business." Apart from Rose, none of our other parents could know about the escape. We couldn't risk them meddling and messing things up.

One hurdle down.

Since Magda couldn't ask her father for her passport without arousing all manners of suspicion, she worked out a plan to get a new replacement passport issued by telling the embassy she'd lost hers. When it was ready, Magda collected it from the US embassy in Riyadh. Then

8 Actually, I pretty much sweated, period.

she gave it to Sara, who mailed it to Magda's mother in Houston for safekeeping.[9]

Two hurdles down. It was *go time*.

Magda planned to meet her mother in Jordan, after convincing her dad to let her visit an aunt who lived there. Upon their reunion, they would fly back to America together. We all said several prayers for Magda, crossed our fingers, wished upon all the stars in the sky. Then we left it to God.

A week before my own family was scheduled to fly back to the United States—for good this time—Magda left for her "vacation" in Jordan, where she would meet her mom. As we hugged good-bye, I felt excited that she, too, would soon be getting the hell out. I was shocked when, five days later, I got a call from Magda saying she was back in Saudi. Apparently one of our friends, Hiba, the goody-two-shoes member of the group, had told *her* father about the plan, who then told Magda's father, who shut it all down. Magda's dad had the Jordanian government refuse her entry at the airport in Jordan. They turned her away without even allowing her to see her mom and sent her back to Saudi.

We were devastated and scared for Magda. I remember the feeling of guilt that nestled in my chest as I boarded my plane out of Saudi for my new life in Kentucky. I was getting out, while Magda was left behind. Though there was nothing I could have done, I felt like I had failed my friend.

When she returned to Saudi, Magda's life became hell. Her father transformed into a prison guard and put her on complete lockdown. She wasn't allowed to talk to her mother and couldn't visit friends or have them over. If she was alone in the house, her father locked her in. She was trapped.

Over the next two and half years that she was in Saudi, Magda tried two more times to flee. The following summer, I heard that she had tried to escape to the American embassy in Greece, but her plan fell

9 Magda's stepmom had an annoying habit of going through Magda's drawers.

through because of poor planning. Luckily, her father didn't find out about that attempt.

The third time was the charm. That summer, Magda's dad had finally relented and allowed her mother to visit her in the West Bank for a family trip. Magda and her mother took a year to plan the escape. She even sent me letters that were written in code in case they were intercepted. Her mother arranged for Magda to receive an American passport at the American Embassy in Riyadh, and she snuck out of school to pick it up. We were all worried, if the plan didn't work, that this time Magda's father wouldn't be as "understanding" as the last failed attempt.

But when the time came, all the pieces finally fell into place. Magda escaped successfully, nearly three years after she'd first begun planning it. Her father disowned her, and in the last twenty-nine years, she's only spoken to him once, for fifteen minutes.

I will always remember Magda as my bravest, fiercest friend. She was a fan of the rock band Bon Jovi, and their song "Livin' on a Prayer" became a sort of anthem for all us girls during that difficult time in Saudi.

To this day, whenever I hear the guitar chords of that song, I get emotional as I think of how my time in Saudi was at once good and also bad. Good because it gave me stronger ties to my roots, a deeper appreciation for other cultures, amazing lifelong friendships, and the discovery of my voice for the first time in my life; and bad when I think about all the oppression and restrictions we faced even as we battled against our teenage angst.

We really were living on a prayer back then.

14

Then There Was the Time I (Unknowingly) Became a Lesbian

After five years of attending an all-girls school in Saudi Arabia (and essentially having no contact with boys), my family moved back to Lexington just in time for my junior year of high school—a time of proms, underage drinking, and lots of teenage hormones. My mother, especially concerned about the latter two things, liked the idea of me attending the small private Catholic school[1] within walking distance from our house. As she saw it, the discipline would be good for me since I had just spent five years in a similarly regulated environment. Plus, she felt I would be less intimidated and would have an easier time fitting in at the Catholic school, which had a smaller student count of six hundred students in total, compared to the thousands typical of a high school population. Ultimately, she said it was my decision.

I'd seen enough high school movies to know that I didn't want the daily intimidation of being lost at a large public school with kids openly

1 She wasn't concerned about the different religion and actually loved the promise of structure offered by a religiously run school.

drinking, shooting up drugs, and having sex under the bleachers.[2] I wanted a pleasant high school experience. And I wanted to study a lot. So, I chose Lexington Catholic High School. Little did I or Mom know that attending a private school didn't mean the absence of drugs, drinking, and sex—it just meant it was all done on the sly, unless you count the occasional high school dance when a freshman girl would drink too much, pass out in the school yard, and need to have the paramedics pump her stomach.[3] Also, just as my parents had wanted me to have structure and discipline, so did the parents of half of the other students. This meant that there were many young men and women at Lexington Catholic High (LCH) who had previously been expelled from their county schools for bad behavior—LCH was their path toward the straight and narrow. Meanwhile, the other half of the school population was made up of kids who had grown up together in the private school system and had known one another since kindergarten. Talk about an ironclad clique.

Had I known this before I'd made my decision, I might have chosen differently. But it was too late. There I was, odd girl with a weird name, newly arrived from a foreign country, *again*. Only this time with added teenage hormones, awkwardness, and years of baggage of being the uncool girl at school in America. That made it so much worse.

This time, however, I was prepared. Having spent the past five years of my life completely fitting in and being my unabashed, free-spirited, spazzy self, I did not relish the idea of potentially being an outcast again. I took matters into my own hands and decided that people couldn't make fun of me if I made fun of *myself*. Everything became a joke, especially when it was about me. If my lunch consisted of pickled turnips—which Katie Smith thought smelled putrid, malodorous, and abominable[4]—I pretended I was grossed out too, rolling my eyes and

2 Okay, this is probably a slightly exaggerated account of public high school debauchery.
3 This actually happened.
4 We were studying for the SATs, and these were some of the words we had to learn.

groaning that my overbearing Aunt Reema had pushed them on me when she was in town and that I had to be polite because she was old.[5]

And if I couldn't dress up according to our fifties-themed junior dance, I rolled with it. While all the girls were psyched to wear poodle skirts and saddle shoes, Mom made me a skirt that looked suspiciously like a seventies hippie peasant skirt, even though she insisted it's what *they* wore in Baghdad during the fifties. I wore it but slapped a name tag on my chest that said "1950s Has-Been." Don't worry if you don't understand—none of them did, either.[6]

And if my Halloween costume didn't go according to plan, I took it in my stride, too. My idea that year of dressing up as the green clay animation character Gumby was thwarted by Mom, who forbade me from cutting up our old green blanket because "No child of mine is destroying family property for some silly dressup" (even though the blanket was sitting in the back of a closet and had a huge burn hole in it that would make a perfect face hole). Instead, she handed me an abaya and hijab and told me to go as an Arabian princess. I complied out of laziness, and when Will Roth bumped into me in the school hallway and demanded to know, "How is that a costume when that's what your people wear anyway?" I replied lamely, "Well, of course that's what *your* people would think!" Unfortunately, I didn't have a clever comeback ready.[7]

My protective shield of sarcasm during high school probably made me come off as a self-loathing, inauthentic jerk. But it was a necessary survival tactic in ~~prison~~ high school. My tendency to hide my true

---

5 The truth was I *loved* pickled turnips and had packed these myself. They are amazing when eaten with a tuna sandwich. I could only have wished that Aunt Reema would bring them over from Iraq as they were hard to get in 1980s Lexington, Kentucky.

6 I'm not even sure I understood my own logic. But I knew what I was going for.

7 Our encounter was interesting for two reasons. First, Will was Jewish, so when I used the "your people" phrase, I was perhaps inadvertently committing my first (and since then only) verbal act of anti-Semitism. Even if he had started it by stereotyping Arabs. Second, he was, incidentally, dressed as Gumby himself. I guess it all worked out—his Gumby costume was much better than mine would have been.

feelings behind jokes served to protect me from being hurt—but it in turn also prevented me from forming deep connections.

On the very first day of junior year at my new school, I forced myself to get out of Dad's Oldsmobile Cutlass Ciera and trudged into the sea of students pouring into the school building. The first thing I noticed was that I was the only one not in uniform. My parents had told me that the students didn't wear them on the first day of school—and I believed them. But here they all were, the girls in navy skirts and white button-down shirts and the boys in khaki pants and blue button-downs. I was wearing black pants and a glitter-splattered long shirt, which was popular in the late eighties. This was the second time my parents had failed me on the issue of school uniforms.

You never forget your first time walking through the crowds of a new school. I remember mine vividly. No one was particularly mean to me; they all seemed very polite, the result of years of education in the private school system. I simply felt like I was invisible. One girl did say, "Nice shirt!"—in a way that wasn't complimentary or mocking. I was just another fish in the sea. I felt lonely and ostracized. To be safe, I went to the restroom and turned my shirt inside out so it wasn't so in-your-face with glitter. Then I put on my black cardigan in an attempt to cover up the fact that I was wearing my shirt inside-out.

When I emerged from the restroom, a bell rang, and everyone filed out of the school. Unsure of what was happening, I quietly followed along. We walked across the street to the Catholic church for the first-day-of-school mass. Since I wasn't familiar with any Catholic customs, I did whatever everyone else did. I tried to recite what they recited. I stood up when they stood up. I sat down when they sat down. After forty-five minutes of this, everyone got up. I got up too, thinking we were done. But instead of exiting the church, the students lined up facing the front of the church. I watched as, one by one, they went up to the altar, opened their mouths, and allowed a priest to place a cracker on their tongues. This ritual fascinated me. How had I never heard of this before? Someone tapped me on the shoulder—I realized I had left a huge gap between myself and the person in front of me. I quickly walked ahead. But now I felt uneasy. I didn't feel right participating in this ceremony. I wasn't sure if it was for everyone or just Catholics. And even though I'd worked to harden myself on the outside, on the inside I was still a sensitive person. I didn't want to intrude on this ceremony. I didn't want to be shamed for taking advantage of a religion and customs I knew nothing about. On the other hand, to get out of the line now would be to attract attention to myself. These were the thoughts racing through my mind as I kept moving along with everyone else.

I carefully watched what the students did when they got to the altar and craned my ear to listen in case there was something I needed to recite to the priest. I gleaned no information from my surroundings. Meanwhile, the line was inching forward, putting me closer to my moment. By the time I got up to the altar, my cheeks were flushed and my hair was matted to my face with nervous sweat. I was so intent on not fucking up that I immediately opened my mouth and stuck my tongue out, the way you do at the doctor's office when he wants to look down your throat.[8] The priest looked at me kindly and said, "Body of Christ," before placing the rice-cracker-type thing in my mouth. I tried to focus on the fact that it was actually a cracker and not in fact made up of Christ's body, but I was getting a little freaked out. Did this act mean I had somehow inadvertently converted to Catholicism? I couldn't afford to take any more chances.

When the line continued down to the chalice of wine station, I somehow managed to turn away and stumble back to my pew, to my own embarrassment. My fear of burning in both a Muslim and Catholic hell for religious impersonation and for not standing firm in my convictions propelled me forward. I cursed myself for making the wrong decision about attending a Catholic school. I couldn't handle rituals like these daily or weekly—or *ever again*. For the rest of mass, I stayed

8 My memory isn't clear on this, but I'm pretty sure I actually said, "Ahh," which elicited a chuckle from behind me.

in my seat and pretended to be overly concerned with my shoelace, while repeating my mantra, "Be cool, Ayser. Be cool."

Unsurprisingly, I soon developed a reputation at LCH of being a snob. Not only that—I also became known as a lesbian. A lesbian snob.

A week later in the school cafeteria (this was two months before the Gumby–Arabian Princess Halloween showdown), Will Roth, who was standing behind me in the cafeteria line, overheard me asking the lunch lady if the tuna sandwich contained mayonnaise. When he wanted to know why I'd asked, I told him magnanimously that my mother had always told me never to eat anything made with mayo, as it might cause salmonella. At home, we substituted mustard for mayo. Will answered, "But your name is *Salman*, so shouldn't you be immune to Salman-ella?" That cracked him up.

Dumbfounded, I simply turned back to the lunch lady and asked if she could arrange for a mustard replacement. She didn't seem keen on indulging my culinary quirks and slapped a scoop of tuna on my plate, along with two slices of bread. Behind me, Will made a second attempt. "When you were in Saudi Arabia, did you ride a camel?" I turned back and politely told him I had not but internally kicked myself for not actively trying to ride a camel after having lived there all those years.[9] What a wasted opportunity! That's like living in Kentucky and not riding a horse.

At this point, Will was joined by some members of his soccer team, and his attention was off me. Thank God! I quickly sped through the line, choosing vegetable soup and some green beans. I pitched my tuna Salmonella sandwich in the trash.[10]

I was done with Will—until biology class, where he was my lab partner. Throughout our human anatomy class, he cracked topical jokes, such as, "Is there a big difference between male and female anatomy? Yes,

---

9 Though I *have* tasted camel meat, and that's a memory I'd like to have erased.

10 By the way, Tuna Salmonella would be a fun children's book character. She would be an exotic bacterium who goes around making kids sick if they don't wash their hands or avoid room-temperature mayonnaise.

a vas deferens." I laughed politely and wondered what his deal was. Was he an aspiring comedian who wanted to test his material out on me?[11]

The next week, I was eating my pickled turnips in the restroom stall (they were particularly pungent this week) when I heard two girls come in. I stopped crunching and eavesdropped.

"Are you asking Will to the Sadie Hawkins dance?"

"I would, but he's so up the ass of that new girl."

"The one from Saudi Arabia? Have you noticed her eyelashes? They're so long. I gotta ask her what kind of mascara she uses."

"She's so odd. Katie said she drinks pickle juice."

"Gawd. Maybe she's pregnant!"[12]

"Does he know he has no chance with her?"

"Will's a dumbass. He doesn't understand that there are women out there who aren't into men, and specifically not him."

"I hope he does ask her out just so I can watch that train wreck. I've never seen a lesbian shutdown before."

I was a very stylish lesbian.

I heard them walk out, leaving me to process what I'd just heard. Did they really think I was a lesbian? I'd be lying if I said that didn't annoy me. In today's society, there's nothing cooler than a lesbian who doesn't give a damn; but back in late-eighties Kentucky, that wasn't the case, nor was it common. More important, I was annoyed that I had been, once again, misunderstood.

I was still an outsider. If I wanted to fit in, I had a lot of work to do.

---

11 Yes, I was *that* ignorant when it came to knowing if I was being hit on.

12 See? This is how rumors get started in high school.

15

"Let It Be": the High School Years, Continued

There I was, a weird Middle Eastern lesbian who may or may not have been pregnant but who had amazing lashes (which, by the way, were real, Megan, and not the result of mascara—I didn't know how to wear makeup yet). I was off to a bad start in my American high school career.

All of this might have been easier to deal with had I not been the only Muslim kid within a fifty-mile radius.

. . . Okay, that's a gross exaggeration. I did know other Muslims, if you counted the kids of my parents' friends. Almost every week, there would be a new Iraqi family moving into town, and almost every week Dad would volunteer me to hang out with their daughters and show them around. I would take them to the mall, mainly because I was in search of the perfect pair of acid-wash jeans for myself, but also because I wanted to casually walk by the Christian bookstore where my latest crush, Daniel, was working. In high school, I was an expert in the art of walking casually past boys I liked and ignoring them. But mainly, hanging out with these girls was super boring because they only ever wanted to talk about makeup and the boys they were betrothed to, most of whom were back in the Middle East, though one lucky girl had a guy waiting for her in Orange County, California. This pissed me off because getting a California dude was *my* dream. It should have been *me*, not her. At least *I* knew not to wear opaque white tights if I hadn't shaved my legs . . . I guess my hostility explains why I didn't have any Arab or Muslim friends, either. I was too busy trying to fit in when they weren't.

So, what does any gal do if she wants to fit in with the cool crowd? Honestly, I still don't know the answer to that. But I'll tell you what she *shouldn't* do: she should *not* opt to join the choir or try out for solo roles in talent shows. I'm pretty sure this is a surefire high-school-career killer. Well, that's exactly what *this* gal did!

Seth Howard[1] was a great guitar player, and he was really cute. I liked him, and he liked me back—for a minute. By this time, my hair had grown out from a disastrous pixie cut, and I had also learned to actually smile when a boy talked to me. It was as good a time as any to ask Seth to collaborate with me on a song for the talent show at the end of the semester. I was obsessed with the Beatles that year,[2] so Seth suggested doing a duet of "The Night Before," with him also on guitar. I tried not to read too much into his choice of such a bittersweet song. And then, he handwrote the lyrics on a sheet of notebook paper and passed it to me. *Hand. Wrote.* That's like making someone a mixtape—it takes care and effort. Granted, the Internet wasn't around then, so you couldn't just do a web search for the lyrics and text them over. But still—how romantic! I was so pumped by our musical and intellectual synergy that I might have glossed over a few red flags.

First: Seth had a near-obsessive concern about the decorative sword mounted above our fireplace. Our rehearsal sessions took place in my parents' living room, presumably to dissuade the gentleman from making any untoward advances if we were by ourselves upstairs. As soon as he saw the

---

1 Totally not his real name, if you didn't already get the memo.

2 Which is super timely considering it was 1986 and the band had had their heyday about twenty years prior. Throughout my life, I've never been accused of having my finger on the pulse of a movement.

sword hanging from the mantle, he said, "Holy fuck! I'm scared." I tried to assuage his fear by telling him the sword was purely ornamental, like the Arabic home decor version of the American Gothic painting—you know, the one with the husband and wife holding a pitchfork . . . okay, maybe not a great example. The point is, it was art. The sword wasn't even sharp. But to a sixteen-year-old boy who had never been out of Kentucky, it looked like the weapon that the villain wielded in *Raiders of the Lost Ark*, before Indiana Jones shot him. Remember that scene? Do a web search.[3]

Second: our upcoming school trip to Washington, DC, was two weekends before the show. Seth was going; I was not. I knew it would take too much effort to convince my parents to let me go, so I didn't even bother asking. I should have guessed that *of course* Mindy Watson would have fallen asleep with her head on his shoulder on the long bus ride there. And I should have guessed that Seth would develop a crush on her and that they would start dating by the time they were on the bus ride back. But I certainly wasn't expecting that Seth would totally bail on our performance a week before the talent show—because "it didn't feel right anymore." *That* one threw me.

I was pissed. But even more than that, I was annoyed that the jerk had left me in a lurch by potentially making me miss out on my singing debut when I was *this* close to fulfilling my rock star aspirations. I scrambled to find a replacement guitarist, but no luck. Then I remembered there was a consumer recording booth in the mall where I'd gone with my cousin to record a kickass version of Hall & Oates's "Private Eyes." I went down and asked if I could get instrumental recordings. It turned out they had two of my favorite Beatles' songs, including "Let It Be." The significance of the lyrics was not lost on me, and I decided *this* would be my song.

There *will* be an answer, if you let it be. *Screw you, Seth!*

I spent three nights practicing in front of the mirror to nail down my stage presence. Then I selected my performance outfit—a mohair sweater with an image of a wildcat emblazoned with sequins. Stagy but classy (shut up, it was the eighties). I was ready for my stage debut. I imagined

3 Don't you hate that you need the Internet to read this book?

the look on Seth's face when the curtain rose and I nailed the song. It would be regret mixed with sadness, mixed with admiration, mixed with jealousy.

Eat your heart out, Seth.

I did fine during the *school* rehearsal, and I did fine during the *dress* rehearsal. Then came the day of the performance, and I was fine as I stood on stage *behind* the curtain. Then the curtain rose. I took a deep breath and . . . I WAS *NOT FINE.*

I completely froze.

The music began and I opened my mouth to sing—and nothing. I just stood, motionless and mute through the first verse. The only sensation I felt was the sweat trickling down my sides underneath my wildcat sweater—oh, and the sounds of snickering from several of the kids in the audience.

For what seemed like hours, I stood there, panicking inwardly but doing nothing outwardly. I watched the worried faces of my friends Lee, Chuck, and Charlie in the front row, their eyes and also their lips and hands pleading with me to get on with it. The music continued to play mercilessly, creeping into the chorus. I took a deep breath, praying that if ever a sinkhole would magically appear and swallow someone up, it would be now at this moment to save me from this horror.

Then I closed my eyes and just *belted* it out, figuring that if I was going down, I might as well give it my best shot. To hell with stage presence. I just wanted to get through the song.

I got through it. And I was decent. Actually, I was good.

I had done it. On my own.

My mother said she was proud of me for standing up for what I wanted. Chuck said he was relieved I didn't fuck it up. Even Mean Girl Katie approached me after and said she didn't know I had such a good voice. And when Seth approached, I pretended I had to run to the ladies' room and avoided him for the rest of the night *and* the following week.

It had all worked out in the end, and it was my first experience in being authentic. It was the first time I'd trusted my instincts and was rewarded for it. I had found my voice and used it to great effect.

16
The Almost Lunch Date

Remember Charlie, as in Charlie in the front row who cheered me on during my disastrous appearance on stage? Charlie, who had previously just been a buddy, saw my courage and later worked up his own to ask me out. He became my boyfriend . . . well, my *secret* boyfriend. A non-boyfriend boyfriend. Because, before I can tell you about Charlie (or James or anyone else), you need to know how it was in my family when it came to dating.

The concept of dating just didn't exist in my family. No negotiation, period. End of Story. I could never have told my parents that I was dating a boy. As a first-born, first-generation Iraqi Muslim teenage girl, telling that truth just might have been too much authenticity for them.[1]

You would of course remember that we came to the States to escape the fascist regime of Iraq. Well, my folks in turn instituted their own kind of fascism in our household when it came to how I could live my life. I cut them slack because they, too, were trying to balance two cultures. Look how picking up and leaving everything that was familiar to move to a new country affected me—and I only had three years to worry about. They had over twenty-five. You can imagine the compromises they had to make and their struggles to maintain their traditions and culture while living in a new time and place.

---

1 This became a long road that I would later spend many years working on crossing.

In all, my parents did their best to assimilate and give me the life of a normal American girl:

- I had ballet lessons.
- I went to sleepaway camp.
- I was a Girl Scout.
- I had piano lessons (which I quit because I wasn't able to play "Fur Elise" in a week, as Madame Gigi's posting on the Kroger community bulletin board had promised.)

As I got older, my freedoms expanded:

- I went to school dances (chaperoned).
- I went to parties (chaperoned . . . mostly).
- I went to rock concerts (surprisingly unchaperoned).
- I hung out with boys in a group.

I just couldn't hang out with boys alone. Anything that even resembled a one-on-one encounter with a member of the opposite sex wasn't allowed.

When I was sixteen, I was a lifeguard at the neighborhood pool. To this day, it was the best job I've ever had. I got to be out in the sun to get a tan, swim, and be paid for it.[2] My father wasn't too keen on the idea that I'd literally be up on a pedestal in a bathing suit so boys could ogle me, but the fact that I was potentially saving lives softened the blow.

Dad soon discovered he liked going to the pool. And because he was a pharmacologist who loved his work, the kinds of books he read poolside for leisure were books on the trade. Heavy, lumbering textbooks. Had the iPad been around, it would've been less embarrassing because

---

2 My mom wants me to add a disclaimer for all the young people reading this that you're not supposed to get a tan and that no amount of sun exposure is safe and that you should always wear sunscreen.

it would have at least *seemed* like he was reading *People* magazine. Dad would bring his tome of *Principles of Pharmacokinetics*, along with his purple beach towel, and stake his claim—close enough in case some boy gave me too much attention, yet far enough so he would have to shout in Arabic to me across the pool if he wanted to tell me anything. Kinda hard to be a cool and authoritative lifeguard when your Iraqi dad is sitting ten feet away, telling you that your crimping iron has been recalled for being a fire hazard.[3] Luckily, Dad's surveillance only lasted a couple of weeks—the sun had started bleaching out the pages of his book.[4] Anyway, that summer I met my biggest crush.[5]

James managed the concession stand at the pool. He looked like a young Timothy Hutton (that's Ryan Gosling to you millennials) and had the cutest mullet (which is the eighties version of today's man-bun). At first, he didn't seem to notice I existed. He was quiet and smart, always reading so many books on historical figures and espionage that I was convinced he was prepping to work in the CIA (I wonder if he ever made it). I spent most of my paycheck at the stand, ordering nachos and pizzas and popcorn, trying to make conversation and look cute—whatever it took to get him to find me interesting. But he didn't seem to care.

Until the last week of summer.

All the kids had started school, and the pool was relatively empty. We amused ourselves by hurling each other into the pool, the eighties summer version of sexting. Here's how it worked: you'd show up at the pool on your day off, in street clothes and cute hair. When the patrons left around closing time, you'd hang around casually but pointedly close to the pool's edge and wait. If you were lucky, the object of your affection would throw you in—and that's how you knew they liked you.

---

3 Dad also brought issues of *Consumer Reports* to the pool.

4 Dad would also like to reiterate the dangers of sun exposure. But he adds that humans need twenty minutes of sun every day, for the vitamin D benefits.

5 My biggest *teenage* crush, not counting Theodore from the second grade whom you already met.

That's exactly what happened on the day I came to the pool on my day off to pick up my paycheck. There I was, looking super cute in my new acid-wash jeans and my freshly spiral-permed hair,[6] just hanging out by the pool chatting with Teresa, a fellow lifeguard who was on duty. James walked over and—without saying anything—picked me up and threw me into the pool.

That's when I knew. He loved me!

I feigned horror at having my hair ruined while simultaneously pulling him into the pool. Then I dunked and splashed him and other things you do when you're in the pool with the person who loves you. Soon we were hanging out in the water, chatting about nothing and everything. He went to a private high school across town but was staying with his mom over the summer. His parents were divorced, he had a dog named Ollie North, blah blah blah. This stuff was interesting to me, but probably boring to you, so I'll skip it.

Eventually I came back to reality and caught a reflection of my hair, which was now a frizzy mess of poodle curls, causing me to leap out of the pool. The one thing they teach you in the Arab Girls' Manual is to never combine large noses with tiny poodle curls—which I was currently guilty of. The Manual also instructs that if you find yourself in such a predicament and a nearby rock is not available to crawl under, find the nearest kerchief or hat and cover your head immediately.[7] I grabbed a baseball cap and said I had to get home—but I wasn't ready to end my Dream Encounter yet.

Since I didn't have a car, I called Dad and told him I was going to get a ride from a friend—which he was happy about because he was listening to a soccer game on AM radio and didn't want to be interrupted. Then I asked James if he wouldn't mind dropping me off. He obliged, giving me fourteen more precious minutes alone with him until we

---

6 I figured I'd get it professionally done so I could get rid of my crimper; plus, it lasted longer.

7 I must clarify that there isn't such a manual. And if there were one, it wouldn't advocate crawling under rocks.

reached my house. I said good-bye and, as cutely as I could, got out of his car and walked on air up the path to my house, the Arab Manual–sanctioned soggy baseball cap still on my head.

An hour or so later, while I was taking a shower, I heard the doorbell ring. Dad answered it. I heard him exchange a few words with whoever it was, and then he shut the door. I didn't think anything of it until Dad gave me the details. It is less painful to remember if I present it like a movie scene. It went a little something like this:

DOORBELL RINGS. Dad opens it to reveal James standing on the porch.

JAMES: Hi, Mr. Salman. Is Ayser home?

DAD: *(peering over his glasses)* I am Dr. Salman.

JAMES: Oh . . . sorry! Dr. Salman.

DAD: Yes. Hello, son.

JAMES: . . . is Ay—your daughter home?

DAD: Yes. She is.

JAMES: Well, I was wondering if she wanted to get lunch or something.

DAD: No, she doesn't.

JAMES: . . . But . . . can you ask her?

DAD: No. Son, you go and enjoy your lunch, okay? She cannot join you.

Dad turns and shuts the door, leaving James standing, shaken, on the porch. Dejectedly, he walks away. Moments later, I, in sweatpants and wet poodle hair, fling open the door to try to catch him. But it's too late.

FADE OUT. ON MY LOVE LIFE. FOREVER.[8]

Dad told me later that he didn't like the idea of a boy assuming he could just come over, thinking I'd be ready for him. I saw James at the pool the next day and tried to explain, but his current book—a boy's struggle to survive World War II in China—seemed way easier to digest than the parental cockblock he'd suffered the day before.

The next summer, I was excited to find out that James was going to be working at the pool again, this time as a lifeguard. I could get my second chance! But sadly, he decided a week before he was to start to travel to Brazil with his dad. Eventually, I ended up seeing him again at the University of Kentucky a year later, but the moment had passed. I still think of him as (one of) the one(s) who got away.

Here's what I learned from that incident. First, when a guy drops you off at your house, wait twenty minutes to jump in the shower just in case he comes back . . .

Just kidding. That's so unfeminist. Girls and young ladies, don't do that.

No—the real lesson from this incident is that people with prominent noses should never get spiral perms.

8 Too dramatic? What? I was a teenager . . .

17

If Google Had Existed in My Teens, I Could've Had a Better Dating Life

My biggest regret about being a teenager in the eighties was living without the technology kids have today.

For one thing, I wish I had had a cell phone, which you can use to make calls to whomever you want without worrying that your parents or family members were going to pick up the line and listen in on your conversations.[1] In the mideighties, let's say you wanted to get on the phone with Paul to discuss your trigonometry homework. First you had to wait for the house phone to be free. Once that happened, and you were able to talk to Paul, you'd get three minutes into the call before the conversation would be sidetracked when your dad picked up the phone and immediately began punching in fifteen numbers to make a long-distance call, only to realize that his call would not connect to your Aunt Reema, which would then cause him to punch in more numbers. *Finally*, when the dialing stopped, you could interject with, "Dad,

1 The other perk about having a mobile phone was that it was a lifeline you could use to call for help if you were ever stuck on a deserted road with a flat tire. Of course, no one thought about poor cell service or dead phone batteries yet.

I'm on the phone," at which point he would grumble something and sigh heavily for twenty seconds before actually hanging up the phone so you could continue your conversation with Paul.

But perhaps the thing that I wished had been invented when I was in high school more than anything else was Google. It would have saved me so much angst and wasted time, and given me the alibis I needed in order to live life the way I wanted while still adhering (mostly) to the rules my parents had set. As you should know by now, I was the typical good girl, especially in high school. I didn't drink. I didn't sneak out late at night to toilet-paper people's homes (why is this even a thing, Suburbia?). I rarely went to wild parties—mainly because I wasn't invited. The point is I never had the occasion to lie to my parents. For the most part.

Being the oldest daughter, I had an incredible weight on my shoulders to do the right thing. My sister, the baby of the family, was the rebel and would do whatever she wanted and deal with the consequences later, which usually involved a loud screaming match. My brother, the middle child, couldn't really be bothered to rebel; he was too consumed by working at his computer and practicing his electric drum set. So, as the family's appointed role model, I was extremely duty-bound. I also was, and still am known as, the peacemaker in my family. But I was no angel, either. I just wanted to live my life. Especially after a year of being the "weird Arab lesbian girl" with the boy haircut.

So I got creative.

I discovered that I could often do what I wanted if I spun it in a clever way. Call it "creative marketing" or "knowing your audience" or "method ~~lying~~ acting." Whatever it was, it got me through that last tough year of being a Muslim Arab teenager in a small Catholic high school in suburban Kentucky. All the "lies" I told had a basic element of reality to them—half-truths, where I would emphasize the *truth* part and skim over the other details.[2]

2 Since then, this trait has allowed me to navigate many difficult relationship dynamics in my adult life, especially those in the film industry in Los Angeles, a climate known for "strong personalities."

Here are some examples of how I spun things to my advantage:

- My parents didn't allow me to ride in a car alone with a boy, which created a problem come time for the senior prom. So, I convinced my parents that prom was more of an academic thing. I also convinced two other couples to rent a limo with me. We all went together as one big group of buddies, safe and parent-sanctioned.
- As you know, I wanted to be a lifeguard because I could get a tan and get paid for it. Don't get me wrong; I took my duties very seriously, and no drownings ever happened on my watch. But my parents did not want me "gallivanting around in a bathing suit." So I convinced them that I would be helping to keep the waters of Lexington, Kentucky, safe. They acquiesced.
- If I wanted to hang out alone with a boy, I would say we had been assigned a school project together. Often, he'd come by my house to work on our "project," which meant my parents could appear downstairs at any moment. So we had to actually talk about schoolwork, which was a drag for the guy when he thought he was just coming over to watch *The Breakfast Club* on VHS until I kept pausing the tape to make non sequitur comments about European history. Also, there was that giant sword hanging above the fireplace, which was an inadvertent male deterrent . . . or maybe *not so inadvertent*. Well played, Dad.
- I wanted to go on the school ski trip, so I made up a story about how it was an educational outing that counted for pre-college credit. The karma came back to bite me when the trip was postponed. Then I saw *The Other Side of the Mountain*, the movie about a skier who becomes paralyzed, and I decided it was a sign that I, as an Arab, was probably not meant to be catapulting off an icy mountain on only two sticks.

Probably the biggest creative lie I ever told was that my new boyfriend was just a very good friend. Yes, after a year and a half of a multitude of unrequited crushes on almost every popular guy in school, I began dating Charlie, who was in my friend circle. Charlie was quiet, shy, and *so* cute. He looked like the guy in *Weird Science*—not Anthony Michael Hall or Robert Downey, Jr., or Bill Paxton. The dark-haired one.

I snuck out a lot to ~~make out~~ hang out with Charlie on his dad's farm. It wasn't as lascivious as it sounds. The farm was gorgeous, and his dad had an awesome stereo system with one of the first multidisc CD players. We would sit and listen to The Cure for hours, away from the countless pairs of Arab eyes in the community that might report back to my mother about the scandal of having seen me sitting alone with a boy. Lexington is a small town, and Arabs gossip. It was annoying, but I learned to work around it.

The degree of my ~~lie~~ half-truth depended on how long I wanted to be out. If I was fine with a short visit, I would say I was meeting Debbie at Rally's for milkshakes. Or that I was going to the mall with Lee, which meant I had to be home shortly after the mall closed at 9 p.m. But if I wanted to hang out longer, I would say I was going to see a movie with Lee or Debbie. The problem was, this was during a pre-Netflix age when movies played at set times that could easily be confirmed or denied by calling the theater or checking the newspaper. I'm not saying my parents would have gone to such great lengths to check on me, but if they had wanted to, the information was readily available.

Also, in an age before Google, you had to actually see the film if you wanted to know the plot. There was no moviespoilers.com where you could read the entire plot of a film in under a minute. My mother often wanted to know what the movie I had just "watched" was about—maybe because she was genuinely interested in the entertainment I consumed or because she knew exactly what I was doing and wanted to catch me in the lie.[3] So, if I ever watched a movie with Lee, for real, I'd

---

3 I'm keeping this lie intact until the book is published. Once my mom reads this chapter, she might be upset. But I'm hoping she'll be distracted by the fact that her daughter has since become a bestselling author, which might lessen the sting.

keep the news to myself and use it as an excuse the next time I visited Charlie's farm.

I was feeling pretty good about my ruse . . . until one weekend in June 1985 when I had a date with Charlie but had run out of movies I had already seen. This time, we were going to dinner at a fancy restaurant not too far from his dad's farm. I was on a short-lived oysters kick—and they had an all-you-can-eat raw bar. At this point, Lee had gotten tired of having to lie for me when on a couple of occasions Dad had called her looking for me.[4] I was out of alibis.

Finally, I worked something out. I told my mother I was going to see *The Goonies* at 7:40 at South Park Cinemas. It was opening weekend, and my friend Chuck was planning to see it. I figured by the time I got home from my date with Charlie, Mom would be asleep and I could surreptitiously call Chuck, get the plot, and be ready to give my casual review of it at breakfast the next morning. Off I went to dinner, and I had a lovely time. Mom was asleep when I came home—everything was going according to plan. I slipped into my room and called Chuck, who informed me that he had blown off the movie in favor of going to a party with some chick he'd met earlier that day at the bookstore. Fuck. I was screwed.

I called my friend Joey to see if he or anyone else had seen the movie. No one. What the fuck, people? Nowadays, *The Goonies* is often cited as a favorite movie by people my age. But for some reason on opening weekend in June of 1985, everyone had been too busy doing other things. Little did they know it would become such a classic . . .

I was struck with fear at the possibility of getting caught and of what would happen to me. It wasn't anything awful like getting beaten or

4 That was the other thing: I always had to give my parents the phone number of the friend I was hanging out with. Once, when Dad called Lee's house, Lee's mother informed him that Lee was out with her boyfriend and hadn't seen me all day. I was so distracted with how I would explain away my lie that, on my way home, I banged up Dad's car in an accident with an approaching pole. The good news was Dad forgot all about my Lee lie, though I *was* grounded.

locked in a closet. When Mom was upset with us, especially if we had betrayed her trust, she would unleash such a stone-cold silent treatment that we almost wished we *were* locked in a closet. Seeing her disapproving face could turn you into one of those victims from that horror movie *The Ring*.[5]

There was only one thing to do. I had to wake up early, slip out of the house before any contact with Mom, and go out into the world to locate someone who could tell me the plot of the movie. I wrote a note saying I had to return overdue library books and left, cursing my lot in life that had forced me down this rabbit hole of lies. I spoke to two clueless people in front of the library—yes, I had to physically put a book in the drop box so at least *that* part wouldn't be a lie—then I went to the cinema at the mall. I made a beeline for the guy at the box office; he would know. At first, he didn't want to say anything for fear of spoiling the movie, but perhaps the sight of a slightly crazed, unibrowed, awkward teenager scared him into submission. I had gotten what I needed.

Then, on the way home, I got into a car accident. I wasn't hurt, but Dad's eighties Cutlass Ciera was no match for the seventies Ford short bed truck I'd collided with. Once again, I had been saved by the ~~bell~~ car accident, which was of more interest to my parents than the movie I had "seen" the night before. They grounded me again from using the car for a month.[6]

To any young people reading this now who might be struggling with the same situation of how to creatively reveal information to your parents, all I'll say is: you kids have it easy! Consider yourselves lucky that you have cell phones so you can text your parents instead of having to give them your friend's house number, and that you have the Internet, which allows you to find the answer to any question that will make it

5 Spoiler alert for those who haven't seen it: the victims have heart attacks from fear and literally die.

6 After this second accident on a guilty trip home, I was beginning to think maybe I shouldn't *lie* and drive . . .

much easier to lie. For me, my dating lies were a pyrrhic victory. And it put me off oysters for the rest of my life.

And, to this day, I have not seen *The Goonies.*

18

"Much Making"

Have I shared with you the list of strict ~~commandments~~ rules in my parents' house that destroyed any opportunity for me to date? Here they are:

THOU SHALT NOT GO TO A MALE'S HOUSE
Which meant I couldn't go to 80 percent of the parties during high school.

THOU SHALT NOT BE THE SOLE PASSENGER IN A CAR DRIVEN BY A MALE
Which meant I had to do all the driving, or rent a limo for prom.

THOU SHALT NOT PARTICIPATE AS AN ACTOR IN THE SCHOOL MUSICAL IN SCENES IN WHICH A MALE CAST MEMBER RESTS HIS HEAD IN THY LAP
It was *Carousel*, and I was only an extra, but boy did my drama teacher, Mrs. Carmine, get an earful from my father.

THOU SHALT NOT WAIT TABLES IN ANY RESTAURANT WITH A BAR LEST DRUNKEN MALES MAKE PASSES
This one I was fine with—I'm clumsy and tend to drop dishes.

Dating was so taboo that, to my parents, there was no such thing as going out with several guys to discover what you want in a mate, or, more important, to discover yourself. My mother's favorite line was "I don't have a daughter who trolls around with men." She would say this in Arabic with such disdain that I would be too scared to tell her that Paul and I had planned to meet at the library to study for the SATs—and I would simply not show up though Paul was waiting for me. As you can imagine, that didn't do any favors for my social life.[1]

I went through my fair share of days avoiding being a daughter who trolled around with men. To my dutiful, eldest-child brain, it seemed like the worst and most shameful thing I could ever do. Looking back, I wonder what would have happened had I pushed back and said, "Actually, you do have a daughter who trolls. I trolled yesterday at the library. I trolled at the school cafeteria, and I trolled at the 7-Eleven across the street. In fact, I'm trolling right now in my mind! BWAHAHA!" In hindsight, it seems so silly that it was such a huge deal to me. That's the thing with fascist regimes: they use fear-based tactics to get you to fall in line.[2]

My mother was the strict disciplinarian in the family, which was not surprising. If you study a typical Arab family, you'll find that the mother often wears the pants, while the father is more laid-back and hands-off. Upon arriving in America, I was confused by the concept of sexism, ironically. Where I come from, Iraqi women are tough ball-busters—and the men let them be without considering it an attack on their masculinity.

On the other hand, it was weird for me to reconcile the gender double standard that was, and still is, very much alive in Middle Eastern

1 If you were ever in Lexington in 1987 and heard a rumor that Arab girls were jerks because they'd ask guys to help them study for their SATs and then not show up to the meeting, I take full responsibility. For at least five of these incidents. This was before cell phones, and there was no way I could text Paul—or Will or Rob or Mitchell or Shawn—to let him know I wouldn't be able to make it.

2 If you think I'm suggesting that my mother ran our family like a fascist regime, I can neither confirm nor deny that fact. . . . Never mind, I think I actually confirmed it in Chapter 16, "The Almost Lunch Date."

culture: boys need to sow their oats or they're considered sissies, while girls are expected to stay chaste and innocent. While I wasn't allowed to "troll with men," my male cousin was encouraged to go out with as many women as possible to get it all out of his system. And before anyone gets rightfully indignant at these archaic double standards, let me remind you that they still exist in American culture today, in parts of the country, usually among members of the older generations. Some people still say it's unacceptable for a woman to text the guy first if she is interested in a relationship. "Men need to pursue" is a line we still hear. To my parents' credit, they did not have different rules for my brother and me. But Zaid wasn't really a social butterfly, and he chose to spend weekends at home playing on his computer and honing his burgeoning graphic arts skills. He never wanted to go out—which meant I couldn't, either.

My dating embargo went on until I was nineteen. Then, suddenly the rules changed. *Now* it was time for me to start looking for—not a boyfriend—a *husband*. But this new phase came with a lot of restrictions. I couldn't just pick someone I wanted to marry. I'm not talking about an arranged marriage; it was more like a *suggested* marriage. There was a screening process—sort of a real-life dating app, like Tinder or Bumble, but without the ability to swipe left or right—that involved my parents' input. In its simplest form, I'd describe it as matchmaking . . . or, as my mother pronounces it, *much* making.

In "much making," the suitors had to fit certain criteria—good education, good family, no history of shenanigans involving goats.[3] So there I stood at the young age of nineteen, fresh into my college years, suddenly on the precipice of spinsterhood and presented with a list of bachelors deemed eligible by my parents.[4]

---

3 The latter happened to someone my mom knows back in Basra, so she always uses it as an example.

4 Bachelors in *America*, thankfully. If it had been up to my father, I would have been betrothed to the very nice barber in Basra who spoke only five words of English and whom my Aunt Reema was lobbying to send over to me. Mom put an end to that, reminding my father that he hadn't moved us halfway across the world only for me to marry a guy whose only words of English were "I take more off top."

Aunt Reema was very excited about this whole much making process. Even though her barber was vetoed, she continued to weigh in. She would send me photos of young men—very handsome men, actually. In fact, I soon discovered that most of them were models from a Lebanese clothing catalog (which explained why two of them were wearing nothing but underwear and carrying a briefcase). Aunt Reema, God bless her, loved me and thought I could have any man I wanted, even if they were underwear models. One time she actually sent over a picture of the actor Omar Sharif and commented that she thought he might be currently separated . . .

On some occasions, Aunt Reema actually had someone real she wanted to introduce me to. She would send pictures via the post office, and by the time the mail was delivered weeks later, that particular guy had either decided to go abroad for college or had found someone else to marry. Again, this was before the Internet, so my potential suitors presented themselves via tiny two-by-two-inch passport photos. My mother would sift through them, putting them through a screening process that focused on their careers, appearances, and maturity levels. One guy was twenty-eight years old, nine years older than I. Ancient! My mother would flick through all the photos, tossing them aside.[5] In reply, I would ignore her. The scenes played out pretty much like this:

> Mom holds up a two-by-two of a very severe- and somber-looking man with thick glasses. He's staring straight ahead from under a unibrow. She sizes it up with the scrutiny of a cartographer checking the accuracy of their work mapping a newly discovered land.
>
> "This one is studying to be a doctor. He is the brother of your cousin's podiatrist. Are you interested in meeting him?"

5 Come to think of it, not unlike the swiping left of today's dating apps. Mom was ahead of her time.

I'm very busy lounging comfortably on my bed, flipping through *YM* magazine and listening to Rick Astley[6] on my Walkman. I barely look up when Mom holds out the photo, picked out from her huge stack.

"No, he's out. Too serious," she says to herself before I can say anything.[7] She tosses the photo aside and continues flipping.

She stops. "This one is an engineer."

She holds the photo out to me. Again, I ignore it. And again, Mom yanks it back.

"No . . . not enough hair on his head but too much coming out of his shirt collar . . ."

Flip. Flip. Flip.

"Oh! How about this one?"

She shoves the photo on top of my magazine. I startle because I'm not expecting to see such a *huge*—

" . . . he could get that mole removed. Or at least trim the hair in it."

We both stare at the photo for a moment, mesmerized. Then Mom breaks the spell by tossing it aside.

"No, probably too much work."

Eventually, Mom crossed the line. I was sitting in the front row of my sociology class, listening intently to a lecture on third-wave feminism, when I turned a page in my textbook and an enlarged photocopy slipped out and fell at the feet of my instructor, Professor Ryan. It was a picture

6 Once big in the eighties for his music, Rick Astley today enjoys renewed popularity thanks to the Internet meme of "rickrolling."

7 Not that I was going to.

of a nondescript Arab guy. Plain. Bland. Generic. On his face was a yellow Post-It note, which read, “What do you think about this guy?”

Professor Ryan had been discussing the dangers of magazine beauty ads in objectifying women. Without missing a beat, she picked up the photo, held it up to the class, and asked everyone how the man in the photo would feel about his likeness being objectified. Then she handed the photo back while I prayed for a sinkhole to swallow me into the ground forever. I might have forgotten to mention that there was a guy in class I liked. After that incident, he suddenly stopped wanting to walk me to the school cafeteria for personal pan pizzas. And don’t tell me it was coincidental—the no-carb craze was at least two decades away. Later he confided to my friend, “I like Ayser, but I can’t date her. Her parents are too scary.”

Cockblocked by a culture I resented at the time, I’d had enough. I was in college, for fuck’s sake. In my anger, I shoved that photo under the visor of my mom’s car, after drawing devil’s horns on his head and writing in big, block letters across his face: “STOP RUINING MY LIFE!”

How would I have known that the picture would drop into Mom’s lap as she was backing out of the driveway, startling her so badly that she rammed into Dad’s parked car, causing a thousand dollars’ worth of damage? At least the much making attempts ended. For the time being . . .

19
It (Sorta) Gets Better after High School

I graduated high school with a promise to myself: when I got to college, I would have a fresh, new start. I was going to fit in. No longer was I going to sit on the sidelines and watch as my friends did X, Y, and Z. I was going to participate in X, Y, and Z, *and* probably A, B, and C, too!

. . . There was just the *tiny* technicality of me still living at home, which put a damper on the nonstop social life I'd expected to enjoy. I attended the University of Kentucky, which was a twenty-minute drive from home. With such a short commute, my parents saw no reason for me to live in the dorms when I could live at home rent-free.[1] I tried to reason with them that communal dorm living built character, but in their minds college dorms were about hedonism and debauchery—throngs of half-naked female coeds running around, being coerced to have sex or do drugs, while boys from nearby dorms snuck in through bathroom windows so you couldn't shower without being peeped on.[2]

---

1 Eventually, they did allow me to live in the dorms during my second semester—and only my second semester. The experience ended badly and led me to living in the janitor's quarters for the remainder of the year. But that's another story I'll get to shortly . . .

2 Apparently, Mom and Dad had learned about American college life from watching the movies *Animal House* and *Private School for Girls*.

But at the moment, I wasn't too concerned about parental rigidity. My schedule was packed with classes throughout the day and into the night, which meant I wouldn't be home much anyway. I'd say, "Mom, I have a lab in the evening so I probably won't be home until midnight." Both my parents bought it.

I was giddy with excitement over this new freedom. I was also elated that, for the first time since I could remember, I was starting a school cycle at the beginning of the school year. No more moving in the middle of the semester. No more transferring from somewhere else into a new environment and having to contend with being the new kid. Instead, we were *all* new kids. The playing field was leveled, and I was so ready.

During my first few days at college, I quickly noticed another interesting thing. For the first time in my life in America, I was *not* the most "exotic" or "foreign-looking" person in the room, or even on campus. I loved my new anonymity. No one cared who I was or looked twice in my direction—and it was bliss. For the first month or so, I relished literally disappearing into the crowd, a little fish in a big pond with a population of around 22,000. On my first day of school, I went up to someone to ask for directions. I recall feeling the need to let them know I was a freshman who was lost, as if my intrusion needed some sort of excuse or justification. I shouldn't have worried. They smiled politely, pointed me in the right direction, and kept on walking—as you'd expect one typically would. But I was pleasantly surprised by the seemingly mundane gesture. Simply put, it was weird to me that my identity was such a nonissue to this stranger when I was so used to being singled out. I didn't know what to do with my newfound normalness.

Unlike high school, college was an exercise in intellectual exploration and diversity. Being different was actually rewarded. The only problem was I had spent so much time in high school working on assimilating—becoming the perfect little preppy girl with smooth, bobbed hair, a loose white T-shirt tucked into perfectly rolled-up jeans, plaid sneakers, and a matching scarf tied around the waist as a belt. If I'd told people my name was Paige Sinclair instead of Ayser Salman, they wouldn't have batted an eye. So there she was, Paige Sinclair, just another Kentucky girl in college during a time when most young adults were starting to uncover their individuality and hone their uniqueness. Impeccable timing was never my thing.

For the most part, I was fine with being the least "different" person in the room. When I joined the college radio station, WRFL, as a DJ, I was happy to be considered among the small group of "mainstream pop softies," the ones who played R.E.M., Psychedelic Furs, and the poppier songs from the Smiths. The entire station was a diverse melting pot of students from all walks of life—punks, hippies, metal heads, Rastafarians, bluegrass lovers, experimental, Goth, and so on. We were a band of misfits in the best possible way. The irony was, if there ever was a time for me to dig deep and explore my truest self that was rooted in my Middle Easternness, it was now. Several students told me I was interesting and wanted to know what I was about.[3] I politely thanked them but continued to stubbornly cling to my girl-next-door exterior.

During college, I was still dipping my toe into the dating waters, having recently been broken up with by Charlie. He'd done it with a note—and not one written by him, mind you. After ghosting[4] me for a month, we finally met up to talk. When I asked how he was, he said, "Maybe this will explain how things are going," and handed me a note from his *new girlfriend.*

It said: "Hey cutie, I can't wait to see you tonight. Hope you're having a good trig class."

Who. Does. That?![5] How had my sweet Charlie turned into such an insensitive clod?

---

3 It wasn't lost on me that they tended to be men.

4 A term that, during the eighties, had not yet been invented but totally applied to my situation.

5 I guess that's what cowards did in those days. Today, they wouldn't even have the balls to break up with their partner face-to-face. After a month of silence, they'd probably send a screen grab of their new girlfriend's texts, prefacing it with: "This is what U need 2 Know."

I should have seen it coming after a month of noncommunication. But I was young and stupid. My naive self believed that he had been doing some heavy life thinking. Spurned and betrayed, I hoped he would fail that trig class and choke on a slide rule for good measure. When I asked him why, he replied, "People change." He wasn't wrong. He *had* changed. Into an asshole. I didn't trust guys for a long time after that.

As part of "Operation Get Over Charlie," my friend Jim and I drove around in his Chevy station wagon while I smoked a bong for the first time.[6] Jim thought a little pot might ease my heartbreak, and I was eager to try anything to stop my mind from obsessing.

That night, we were also on our way to our weekly Sunday evening WRFL radio station meetings with the rest of the staff. The room was a delightful mixture of patchouli, cigarette smoke, and weed—the latter mostly from my clothes. By the time Jim and I arrived, I was feeling sick and paranoid. I hadn't eaten anything before and had probably also inhaled the smoke wrongly and somehow gotten bong water into my lungs. As the meeting went on, everything felt surreal. I spent the next hour trying to keep myself from doing two things: a) throwing up, and b) talking.[7] I could not hear my friend Deb speaking, even though she was right next to me; however, somehow, a Joey Ramone–looking dude across the room who was whispering in his buddy's ear sounded like he was yelling in *mine*. I scrutinized him.

Another part of my heartbreak recovery plan was to go out with someone I would never have gone out with a year ago. In this case, he presented himself in the form of a tall, handsome, tattooed punk rocker whose name was Seraph.[8] At twenty-six, Seraph might have been too old for college *and* too old for my eighteen-year-old self. But in the interest of me breaking out of my comfort zone, I was ready for anything.

6 We drove because it would look suspicious if we were just parked.

7 I was convinced that if I opened my mouth, words would come out backward like that dwarf in *Twin Peaks*, and everyone would know I was stoned.

8 Formerly a clean-cut banker named Roger.

He was affable and funny, and so when he asked me out after the meeting, I agreed. Then, I quickly realized I was in no position to go out with anyone and called it off. In hindsight, it worked out for the best. There was the age difference, and there was also the fact that he wanted us to watch movies on VHS at his mother's house, where he still lived.[9] I may have been naive back then, but I knew when I was dodging a bullet!

It might have been the weed, but after that night, I also began to rethink my "nice, preppy girl" image. After years spent trying to fit into mainstream society, I had finally succeeded—which was now making me an outsider in *this* society of misfits. For the first time, I felt like the most vanilla person in the room. Everything about me was soft—my musical tastes, my clothing, my demeanor. I was just a nice girl, and while there's nothing wrong with that, I began to see the value of having some edge.

By the spring, my parents had agreed to let me move into the dorms—for just one semester. I planned to make the most of it. My new roommate, Pam, was an African American girl with a dry sense of humor. We got on like a house on fire, to use a phrase that's not typically in my lexicon. She quickly became like a sister, helping to ease the sting from my Charlie heartbreak. We were also inseparable and complemented each other wherever needed—if I was too quiet, she would snap me out of it; if she was obsessing about an exam that she was convinced she was going to fail, I would talk her through her anxiety until she was centered and calm.

It was one of the best friend dynamics I'd ever had since returning to the States from Saudi Arabia. I reflected on my good fortune—that I had only moved into the dorm during the second semester when Pam just so happened to need a roommate.[10] Once again, my philosophy that

---

9 My editor just pointed out that it's strange that a former banker still lived in his mom's house. I'd like to point out that after he changed his name from Roger to Seraph, any semblance of normalcy should have already gone out the window . . .

10 Her old roommate had gotten pregnant, and it's a drag having morning sickness in a dorm bathroom. She moved out.

life eventually works out if you're patient and let things be was being confirmed. There *will* be an answer, just like Lennon and McCartney had written.

But then one day, the switch in our dynamic was flipped.

I suppose it might have been building up for a while. There was that one time I failed to heed the apparently universal signal of a red tassel hung on the door—"Go away, I'm entertaining a male visitor"—and inadvertently cockblocked her. Worse, I'd barged in with my mother who'd made an impromptu stop on campus and wanted to see my room. In my defense, it was a Saturday afternoon, not the prime amorous hours of nightfall.[11] I later apologized, and things went back to normal . . . or so it seemed. Perhaps we weren't quite as sisterly as we once were. Gone were the depth, the jokes, the familiarity. When I tried to talk about it, she brushed it off, and my eighteen-year-old Arab pride caused me to not press further.

Then Pam's cousin came to visit from Detroit.

As soon as Carla walked into our room, she stopped cold, visibly upset by a photo I had tacked to the wall. It was a fashion magazine photo of the singer Prince. He was wearing a teeny-tiny minidress with fluffy tulle sleeves and neckline, showing off his hairy chest and hairy legs. He wore long yellow gloves and black stiletto heels, and he stood proudly, beaming into the camera. The photo was definitely intended to make a statement, and Prince knew how to deliver shock value. I don't remember what exactly appealed to me about that photo, except for the fact that Prince looked like he didn't give any fucks, and I was working on becoming that kind of person.[12]

But Carla didn't share my sentiment. She was shocked, and she didn't hold back.

"You have a *black* man in a *dress* up on your wall."

---

11 Plus, I was distracted by the prospect of my having left incriminating items lying around the room, which would cause my mom to insist I move back home.

12 A person who DGAF, not one who wears minidresses with unshaven legs. Though, I guess if I truly didn't care, I would wear whatever I wanted.

"Well," I said, "I just think it's cool."

"You think it's cool to ridicule him like that?"

" . . . What?!" I was taken aback. "No! I just like the photo!"

"Because it's a black man looking a fool!" she accused.

"No! Because he's expressing himself. This is—no!"

I was struck dumb. Back then, I wasn't skilled in the art of continuing a conversation in the face of potential conflict. I would get defensive and run away—and that's exactly what I did. I turned my back on Carla, walked over to my bed, and put up a big show of stuffing my books in my backpack and getting ready to leave the room.

Understandably, Carla was even more pissed.

"Yeah, walk away, white girl."

Shocked, I tried to tell her I wasn't white, but she snorted in outrage. "It's okay, Princess! Just go back to your sorority!"

I was momentarily transfixed by three words I'd never heard being used to describe myself: *white*, *princess*, and *sorority*. A year before, my aspirational inner preppy girl would have been thrilled at these designations. And in that moment, I was caught in those old feelings—for a minute. Then I came to my senses and realized it hadn't been meant as a compliment. For the very first time in my life, I'd experienced a taste of my privilege of being able to pass as white. It didn't matter that I'd felt like "the other" in America my whole life; I was capable of white passing, a privilege Carla did not have. It was a very strange reality to face.

If I had been sensitive enough at the time to the cultural baggage Carla was bringing up,[13] perhaps that incident would have changed me. Perhaps it would have been the tipping point that allowed me to finally let go of my perpetual need to fit in with the white majority. Perhaps I would have immediately recognized it as an important and sobering lesson in my path to self-discovery. But my eighteen-year-old self didn't see it this way. I had not yet learned about the concept of intersectionality. Let's just say I wasn't very graceful in the face of this attack. I shut

13 "Woke," in millennial speak.

down and mumbled, as I kept shoving books into my bag, "I don't have time to argue with someone who's pigheaded."

"Oh. Now I'm a pig?! The vilest animal to *your people*?" Carla spat.[14]

I didn't know what else to do, so I just walked out, my heart racing. It was my first antagonistic confrontation with a casual acquaintance. By the time I returned to my room that day, I found that all my furniture had been rearranged, pushed into the middle of the room, and my pictures removed from the wall. It was the first mean act I had ever experienced, and it freaked me out. I left again and quickly went to my friend Deb's dorm and used her payphone to call my mom. Thankfully, Mom refrained from saying anything to the effect of "I told you living in the dorm was a bad idea. Come home, immediately." Thank God for small mercies. But she did suggest I get myself out of that situation.

If I had been a stronger person, I might have dug my heels in and refused to leave. If I had been more open, I would have tried to discuss the issue and come to an understanding. But this was the first time I had experienced hate, and it hurt. Back then, I really, really, *really* needed to be liked. And I was used to being known as the "nerdy weird girl," not the "racist bitch."

I went to the housing office, only to be told it was too late to trade rooms since there was only one month of school left. And it felt like failure to move back home, so when the housing office told me there was a single room downstairs in the basement usually reserved for housekeeping, I jumped at it. It was actually a very nice room despite the fact that it didn't get any sunlight. But at least I could sleep without worry.

But before I moved, there was *another* thing I did that I'm not proud of . . .

The day of the move, I enlisted the help of my "fobby"[15] Iraqi cousin Omar and our family friend Delia, a tough-looking Saudi woman who was the complete opposite of what you'd expect a Saudi woman to

14 At least she was aware I was Muslim.

15 Slang for "fresh off the boat."

be—tall with stiletto heels, a spiky mowhawk, chain earrings, and tight miniskirt. She looked like a majorly badass Tina Turner.

I merely wanted their moral support while I got my stuff out and moved on with my life—but both Omar and Delia insisted that I "send a message." I was still pissed at Pam's cousin (who had already gone home by then) for touching my stuff, so I agreed it was not the time for me to turn the other cheek. Omar and Delia showed up with their heavy Arab accents, leather jackets, and dark sunglasses, which they kept on for the duration of the move. They acted cordially to Pam, asking how she was and so forth, but it's hard to appear cordial when you're wearing sunglasses indoors. Delia picked up a couple of Pam's textbooks and looked at them for a long while. Neither Omar nor Delia smiled. Every now and then, they would say something in Arabic to each other and then to me, while looking in Pam's direction. It must have been a disconcerting (and stereotype-perpetuating) experience for poor Pam to have two Arab heavies invade her space like this. It was over in twenty minutes, and I never spoke to Pam again—though she did tell a mutual friend of ours later that she was sorry about how things had gone down with her cousin.

So Pam, if you're reading this, I, too, am sorry. I'm sorry that your first experience with Arabs was so horribly unpleasant. I'm sorry I relied on stereotypical traits of my people during my move. I hope you've had happier and more enriching encounters involving Middle Easterners since then.

And I want you to know that I'm no longer scared of conflict. Nowadays, I take time to resolve issues and differences. I've learned to value meaningful conversations to clear the air.

And I've never had to use the Arab Family Thug method again.

20

I-raq Star

College was also the first time I experienced discrimination for being Iraqi.

It was August 1990, the day after Saddam Hussein invaded Kuwait. I was at London's Heathrow airport, coming back home to Lexington after a six-week study abroad program. Though I have an American passport, my birthplace of Iraq is stamped in its pages—which meant I was subjected to questioning and a thorough luggage search by the customs official.

HIM: *(as he rummaged through my suitcase)* Have you had contact with anyone from the country?

I'd just visited my uncle and his family in Cornwall, so, technically, yes. But I was sure he meant anyone who had more recent ties with Iraq.

ME: No.

HIM: (*finding an adaptor plug set I was bringing home*) What's this?

ME: An adaptor plug set.

HIM: What is the purpose?

ME: It's for a hairdryer.

HIM: Where is the hairdryer?

ME: It blew up . . . uh, died—uhhm! It stopped working, and I threw it away!

For the next several minutes, he combed through my suitcase with the skill of a parent checking their child for head lice. I stood still, trying not to fidget and praying that he wouldn't pay too much mind to the two hardcover books in Arabic that I'd wrapped up in a pair of very loudly striped jeans. The books were written by my uncle, a philosopher, and were gifts for Dad. And did I mention they were in Arabic? The last thing I needed was the customs guy to think I was bringing home pro-Iraqi propaganda.[1] I held my breath as he rummaged, and after what seemed like an eternity (but was only five minutes), he let me through.[2] It was nerve-racking, and the first time something like this had happened to me in my adult life. If only I'd known how many more detainments in airports there would be over the next two decades with the second Iraq war and post 9/11 . . .

The fact of my homeland didn't factor again into my life until the following year, during the air strikes of Operation Desert Storm. A girl in my Law of the Press class made an off-hand comment: "We should bomb *those* people." I remember thinking clearly: those people are *my* people. Sure, I hadn't been directly discriminated against, but the subtle microaggression hit hard. I wanted to punch her in the face,[3] but at the same time, I was too nervous to speak out lest I be targeted for a hate crime. It turned out her fiancé had just been sent to Iraq; she had been acting out of emotion and fear instead of hatred . . . but since fear

1 In fact, it was my uncle's poetry and musings on life as a youth in Iraq.

2 The jeans they'd been wrapped up in were probably so loud that they'd distracted the eye. I've never been so happy by an impulse buy.

3 I know, I know—playing right into the stereotype of the Angry Arab . . . *again.*

and hatred are just one notch away from each other on the dial, there's still no excuse for a comment like that.

I was sitting in broadcast journalism class when the United States announced we were invading Iraq during Operation Desert Storm. Someone had turned on CNN, and there was the news and the headline. I excused myself to the ladies' room, where I locked myself in a stall and burst into tears. I had never felt so isolated and fearful because of where I was from. Even though I was an American citizen and technically could not be kicked out of the country,[4] I hailed from a place we were at war with. I didn't want to hear any ignorant, racist diatribes from my classmates and the people I considered friends. Dammit, I had finally found my "place at the table" and felt comfortable being truly me. I wasn't thrilled about the possibility of losing it because of the inconvenient political climate in my former home.

Luckily, that war was contained, and the US got out quickly . . . which of course led to destabilization in the region, making the situation worse. Saddam renewed his efforts, and after the horrific attacks of 9/11, we invaded Iraq once more in 2003.

By our second war with Iraq, it was apparent that the Iraqi people weren't horrible coconspirators but, in fact, victims themselves. Once again, I was treated differently for my heritage—but this time with sympathy and much curiosity. Between the years of 2002 and 2005, whenever I was at a dinner party and the subject of my heritage came up, I would notice the expression change on the face of the person I was speaking to. They would instantly become deferential and sympathetic, as if they had just been informed I had a terminal illness. Sometimes they would even whisper the word, as if it were too taboo to say out loud, "This is Ayser. She's . . . Iraqi."

4 Our Iraqi friends who still lived in Saudi Arabia weren't so lucky. They were told their contracts would not be renewed effective immediately and had to return home, all because of an erratic and crazy Iraqi dictator to whom most Iraqis didn't have any allegiance.

During this apologetic phase, most of the people I talked to were saddened by what the US had done to my country and seemed almost ashamed to be Americans. I felt the need to tell them that most Iraqis had initially welcomed the invasion to get Saddam out, but that it was the resulting devastation and anarchy in the country that really upset us. Then, they would cluck sympathetically and suddenly announce, "I see someone I need to say good-bye to before they leave; be right back!"—and they'd never return. It was a fun game I enjoyed playing at dinner parties in the early 2000s—seeing who could leave the conversation quickest or least gracefully.

Which brings us to the political situation today. As I write this, it is 2018 and Donald Trump is president. Currently, a Muslim ban is being upheld by the laws of this country, disallowing immigrants from eight countries to enter US borders. At this writing, Iraq is not on the list, but, as many of us have found, the policies of Trump's administration change daily.[5] And it does make me think about my parents. My mother, who is part Iranian, has been wanting to visit Iran, where many of her relatives reside, and I would love for her to do that. But we have to consider if it is worth it when the target is on her back.

In 2011, we took Dad to Irbil, in Iraqi Kurdistan, to visit my uncle who was living there at the time. I found the local Iraqis to be some of the nicest people I know. The US had just pulled out and left them to their own devices. They were a country busy rebuilding after the ravages of Saddam's gassing of the fields in 1988[6] and then the two wars—Desert Storm in 1991 and Desert Shield from 2003 to 2011. It was surreal to be there. My uncle's villa stood on land that had previously been gassed by Saddam during the chemical attack targeting the Kurds. During construction of the property, it was apparently a regular occurrence to find human bones and remains on the site. For my parents to see a place that had once been green and vibrant and where they used

5 By the time you read this, who knows what will have happened.
6 The Halabja Massacre, in which five thousand people were killed.

to go for vacations as kids, but that had now become a beige wasteland, must have been a heavy emotional experience. It was even for me.

With all the pain, losses, and waste of time brought on by the war, the fact is Iraq is at least finally becoming recognized and normalized in the US. I no longer feel weird or apologetic about telling my fellow Americans that I'm from Iraq. Plus, one of the few good things about Iraq becoming a household name here is that people are no longer mispronouncing it.

It's "ee-rock" or "ee-rack," *not* "eye-rack." You take the little victories.

I'm proud to be an *ee-rocky* American.

PART 2:
TABLE MANNERS

21 California: Finally, I'm Home

After years of dreaming of moving to Southern California, I finally arrived in Los Angeles in August of 1994, three years after graduating from college and after a brief stint working as a local news producer in Lexington. As I drove in on the I-10 freeway on that dusty Sunday afternoon, I felt the final piece of my identity puzzle click in. The multiculturalism, the creative energy of LA . . . life was *finally* about to begin for me at the age of twenty-four.

Just two weeks earlier, I was sitting in my favorite Mexican restaurant in Lexington with my friend Marcy, who listened patiently as I agonized over whether I was making the right decision. I had just been accepted into the graduate film program at Loyola Marymount University, and though I was already committed and excited, I was experiencing major last-minute jitters and cold feet.

This was it! I'd been dreaming about this opportunity my whole life. What if I got to Los Angeles and it was nothing like I'd expected? Or worse—what if I couldn't make it there? I would certainly be safe in the cocoon of film school for the next four years, happily making films and escaping reality. But then what?

I mentioned a crazy dream I'd had the night before, in which I was being wheeled on a gurney and doctors were saying they needed to take my arm or I would die. Marcy slugged me lightly on the shoulder. "Don't you see the symbolism here? Your arm is your life here in Kentucky. If you don't cut it off and move to California, you will poison yourself with regret." Marcy had a slight flair for the dramatic, but she wasn't wrong. It was time for me to spread my wings and become who I was supposed to be.

Marcy made a valid argument, but still I was nervous. What if I didn't have any creative ideas as a writer and filmmaker? What if, after reaching California, I realized I had no talent and had to slink back home to Kentucky? How embarrassing.

"That's when you marry some rich Beverly Hills doctor and spend your days redoing his mansion and doing charity work on the side," Marcy said with a wink. Then she told me she just *knew* I would meet my husband at film school. She was trying to make me feel better, but I loved her for it. Her encouragement propelled me and my Mazda hatchback out on the 2,000-mile road trip.

Film school was the college experience I'd never had as an undergrad because this time I was finally living away from home. My parents and sister were relatively close by, a six-hour drive away in Las Vegas during a time when the city was experiencing a housing and economic expansion.[1] Whenever I needed a break from deadlines of film papers and editing, I spent the weekend at their place, dividing my time between their pool and hot tub while eating wonderful home-cooked meals, before returning to LA refreshed. For the first six months, my feet never touched the ground.

During this time, I met some of the best friends I'd make in my life—Lisa, Julie, JD, Jo-Ann, Mike, Michael, and Tony. The "LMU Crew." As the years went by, we drifted in and out of one another's lives, but each time we reconnected, it seemed like no time had passed. Back in grad school, we were simply having fun. No worldly pressures to face beyond making our films. I had taken out a large student loan

1 They had moved for work opportunities. My brother, who was living in the San Francisco Bay Area, was not too far, either.

so I wouldn't have to work (which in hindsight was not smart and *not* recommended). I was living in a lovely little protected bubble, discovering the endless creative possibilities of using my family as subjects and actors in my short films. As a result, the LMU Crew would often find themselves traveling back and forth to Las Vegas for shoots. They ended up getting to know my parents well.

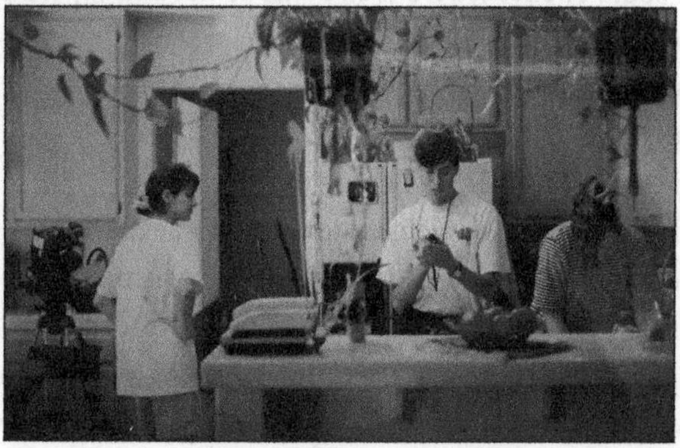

Me and part of my LMU Crew at my parents' home.

In return, Mom and Dad loved them, and to this day they consider them extended family. Dad taught Lisa how to make crispy rice, showed Michael how to make rosewater tea, and explained to Tony how boiling down an apple would release a type of cyanide that you could use to secretly murder someone. This last lesson was for research purposes—Tony was writing a crime film, and Dad was simply imparting pharmacological knowledge.[2]

This particular man, Tony, was also the man I thought I would marry. When we began dating, I called Marcy and told her that her prophecy was coming true—I had met a guy in film school, and it was very likely he would become my husband.

2 It might not be the best move for me to put here in writing that a Middle Eastern man showed a young Filipino man how to distill poison from a fruit, even if for the sake of art . . .

Tony had long hair and looked like a cross between Lou Diamond Phillips and a young Johnny Depp, with the most beautiful bone structure and complexion I'd ever seen. He was a romantic who would write poems and leave them on my car dashboard. He was spiritual and loved to set off for weekends in Death Valley on retreats—sans drugs, by the way; just himself and nature. He was our group's MacGyver. And he was a fantastic cook. I benefited from all of his dishes and experimentations.

Tony was the real deal.

The yang to my yin.

My soul mate.

Spoiler alert: . . . we did *not* get married.

With Tony came a new element to the dating experience that I'd not experienced previously. It was the first time my *partner's* parents disapproved of him dating me because of my religion, instead of the other way around. I mean, my mother wasn't thrilled initially—something about our future kids being confused because they wouldn't know which religion they belonged to—but I figured I just needed to wait and let her get used to the idea. I'd learned long ago with my family that the best way to introduce a guy was as a friend. Mom and Dad could then get to know him on his own merit without worrying prematurely about the implications of what their hypothetical grandkids would go through with mixed-race and mixed-religion parents.[3] Unfortunately, in this case, they were the easy hurdle. What I hadn't counted on was the amount of work I would have to do to get Tony's *mom* on my side, too.

Tony was very close to his mother, who raised him Catholic. She wasn't so thrilled that I wasn't of the faith. I felt prejudiced against from the other side, and let me tell you, it was stressful. But I was determined to do whatever it took to win her over. I mean, how hard could it be, when I had a lifetime of experience with my own parents?

---

3 Much later on, my parents just wished I could find someone—anyone—to settle down with no matter the race or religion. But back then, they still had the luxury of holding tight to their beliefs.

Whenever Pauline came into town, I would take her around while Tony was busy working. Pauline loved to shop, so I'd drive her to Rodeo Drive in Beverly Hills or Fashion Island in Newport Beach. On one particular shopping spree, we were joined by Sandy, the girlfriend of Tony's younger brother. We had a grand time, just us girls. In fact, Pauline was a very generous woman who loved to shower her sons' girlfriends with gifts. She bought Sandy a gorgeous buttery-red leather passport carrier, and she bought me a gorgeous but slightly ostentatious and ornate piece of jewelry—a Swarovski crystal pendant . . . in the shape of a cross.

A *Christian* cross.

Now, let me clarify that I wasn't offended by the fact that she had bought me a cross. It's not like I believed it would burn through my skin if I wore it.[4] I thanked her for the beautiful and completely unnecessary gift, leaving out the part about Muslims not typically wearing crosses around their necks. I started to put it in my purse. But Pauline blocked my hand and insisted I wear it—"To see how it looks." Reluctantly, I did so, watching her face the whole time. Did she look disappointed when the cross touched my bare skin and did not leave a fiery brand? She told me it looked beautiful and muttered something under her breath, which I'm pretty sure was "Too bad you're not a believer."

Whenever I saw her after that shopping trip, she would ask why I wasn't wearing the necklace. Once, I was wearing a chunky turtleneck sweater and told her I was wearing the lovely necklace underneath. When she asked to see it, I simply faked my death, and *that* changed the subject.

. . . I'm kidding about that last bit. I didn't fake my own death until Thanksgiving at Tony's parents' house in Louisiana. And it wasn't really a death I faked, but rather bad PMS and cramps, which allowed me to excuse myself from the dining table to the bathroom. Even though Tony had told his mom I didn't eat pork, Pauline had

---

4 I'd actually never worn one, so I didn't know if it would. I wonder if that was Pauline's intention of finding me out?

prepared as a main course her famous Filipino pork adobo. I guess I *could* have eaten and swallowed it, pretended it was chicken and choked it down. I was already sporting her Swarovski crystal cross pendant prominently around my neck—this time for real—and was the only person at the table wearing any sort of religious paraphernalia. So you know what? I wasn't feeling up to making any more conciliatory gestures.

So there at the long banquette-style table, in front of Tony's parents, his three brothers, their respective girlfriends, and two very Christian next-door neighbors in attendance, I did what any modern, liberated Muslim woman in my situation would do: I took two big bites of the pork and laughed heartily at Tony's dad's bad pun of the hour while simultaneously spitting the meat into my napkin. Then I surreptitiously put the napkin in my dress pocket. I felt pretty proud of myself and rubbed my crystal cross, silently thanking Jesus for getting me out of this predicament.

What I hadn't counted on was that Killer, the family Doberman, who was dozing nearby, immediately perked up and began sniffing around my leg. As he was usually very disciplined, no one in the family could understand why he was doing this. I muttered in mock embarrassment that perhaps he was attracted to me because it was "that time of the month." I excused myself and rushed to the bathroom, where I flushed my meat napkin down the toilet. Satisfied, I returned to the table only to find that Pauline had given me another serving of pork adobo because I had finished my first portion so quickly. Luckily, Tony intervened and told his mother to stop pushing food on me. But the campaign was not over.

Two months later, during her next trip to Los Angeles, Pauline asked me to take her to 5:15 p.m. Mass at church—and seemed annoyed when I couldn't readily identify which church had one at that time. I offered to take her the next morning to a church I knew had not one, but *two* masses, but she mentioned her routine of talking to God in the evening. Again, had Google been more accessible at the time, I could have simply looked up the information. But this was 1996, and the search engine was not to be invented for another three years.[5]

I loved Tony, but this seemed like an awful lot to put up with. To his credit, he tried to interfere, but his mother's mind was made up. She thought I was perfectly lovely and appreciated my style and poise—but ultimately I wasn't Catholic, and she didn't want him to marry a Muslim girl. And because getting our parents' approval was so important to both of us at the time, our relationship appeared to be doomed.

We were young, and everything seemed absolute and dramatic. I spent the first two years of our relationship angsting over the fact that he ate pork (he's vegetarian now) or went to church on Sundays (he's agnostic now) or made the sign of the cross whenever he got on the freeway (he's since thrown out any symbols, religious or otherwise). Every little ritual he did drove home how different Tony and I were. And yet we were so similar. He had grown up in a small town in Louisiana as one of the few Filipinos there, and he, too, felt like an outsider. Here was a person with whom I could be truly myself and who made me laugh and who knew what I was thinking before I even said it—and who fit in with my family. But because his beliefs conflicted with my own, we had an expiration date. It was a strange, weird time.

But we tried. With Tony, I made the effort to be present and enjoy our moments together instead of focusing on all the reasons we might not work out. However, this meant pretending that our differences didn't exist. We had another really nice year or so, and then an interesting thing happened. We outgrew each other. There was no big blowout fight. No one cheated on the other. No one pressured the other to get married. We were simply meant to go our separate ways. I'd always had a weird feeling while we were together that Tony and I had a "grad school" relationship. Sure enough, after being together for five years, we broke up six months after we graduated.

5 Young readers, count your blessings that you grew up when you did. It was so difficult for the rest of us.

Right before my thirtieth birthday.

My practical side appreciated the symmetry. I was thirty years old, newly single, the world at my feet. Where I went next was entirely up to me. The most exhilarating time of my life, right? But my emotional side wasn't buying it. I was feeling scared and rudderless and old. Looking back, at age thirty I was still an adolescent in terms of my maturity level and development, but at the time, I thought I was supposed to have it all figured out by then.

I forced myself to focus on the filmmaking career I'd come to Los Angeles to pursue, but I couldn't get a job—unless you count working at Video Services of Mattel Toys. I did some editing but primarily worked in the dub room, copying reels and doing general production assistant stuff to pay the bills while I waited for my big Hollywood break.[6]

Then it happened. Not my big break, but a very important first step toward it.[7] Ironically, Tony played an instrumental part. He'd forwarded me a job listing for an unnamed motion picture company that needed someone to edit simple reels together. I figured I was qualified enough (if not overqualified) and applied.

The company ended up being Miramax Films.

And that's how I ended up in my longest-lived business relationship, working for Harvey Weinstein, once considered one of the biggest power players in Hollywood.[8]

6 I also worked part-time at Banana Republic, mainly for the clothing discount.

7 As I've since discovered, there's no such thing as a big break (singular). At least for me, it's come in a series of small opportunities, as well as the ability to leverage each one into the next. It's taken me fifteen years to fully reap those benefits.

8 My experience of working for Harvey Weinstein occupies a weird realm that existed before our current #MeToo sociopolitical climate. In October 2017, of course, he would become embroiled in a sexual harassment scandal that would end his career.

22

The Weinstein Years: The Best of Times / The Worst of Times

My longest-running job was working as a freelance producer and editor for Bob and Harvey Weinstein. I was with the company for seventeen years, first with Miramax and then The Weinstein Company until I left in 2017 after Harvey was accused of sexual misconduct. It just felt too gross to work there anymore.

I should state right off: if you're looking for any personal gossip or insight to the Weinstein scandal, you won't find it here—mainly because I don't *have* any. Most employees did not know anything. The small in-house postproduction department I worked for was relatively insulated. I've never met Harvey and only ever met Bob, whom I found pleasant and respectful, during my last year when I worked closely with him on a short project. I never witnessed or experienced anything skeevy or illegal firsthand, and I learned about the scandal just like everyone else—from reading the news.

It was a big deal for me to be employed at Miramax at that point in my career. I was truly excited to be working for such a Hollywood heavyweight. Ask anyone who has worked for Miramax during the late nineties and into the early 2000s, and they'll tell you that something magical was happening. We were there for our love of movies, and it was like nothing I'd ever experienced. It seemed like the first time I'd lucked into anything.

It was the year 2000, during the start of the DVD boom. Every major film released in theaters went on to have a DVD release with accompanying bonus features that gave at-home audiences a look behind the curtain, revealing some of the movie magic. I was responsible for creating many of those features. The small, close-knit department I was part of worked on films after they were released, promoting and marketing titles like *Chicago* and *The Artist*. My boss would give me raw footage and tell me to put something together. Essentially, I was making little documentaries.[1] While I wasn't quite yet at the adults' table, making the deals and immersing in the glamour, at least I was *in* the room. You could say I was at the kids' table, which, at that point, was enough. I had succeeded in achieving my professional goal of working in the Hollywood industry.

Because of my news background, I also conducted interviews for our pieces, my favorite being the one I did with Hugh Grant for *Bridget Jones's Diary*. I had still been living in Kentucky when *Four Weddings and a Funeral* came out in 1994 and had such a crush on him in all his stammering, self-effacing glory. I never thought that I would meet him seven years later—not in a chance encounter like when you spot a celebrity at a restaurant and work up the courage to speak to them, but rather as a professional peer, working together to promote his film.

But while my professional life was buzzing with excitement, my personal life was quite the opposite.

I wasn't happy. In fact, I felt extremely heavy emotionally.

I was no stranger to depression, having suffered mild bouts throughout my early teens and into my twenties. They were usually hormone-related and only lasted a day or so. I would "grit my teeth and bear it," until the black cloud lifted. But now they were getting worse. I was suffering

1 Look, Ma! I've succeeded!

from an intense melancholia that could last for weeks. And nothing would help. Audrey Hepburn's character in *Breakfast at Tiffany's*, my favorite film, called it "The Mean Reds": "Suddenly you're afraid and you don't know what you're afraid of." I'd never experienced such a heavy emotional toll to this degree. As an Arab American firstborn female who was raised to be strong and authoritative, it made me feel weak.

And why was it happening now? I was thirty years young and properly independent for the first time in my adult life. I should have been celebrating my independence, freedom, and "Me Time," unencumbered by a partner, kids, pets . . . plants.[2] I was in my prime physically. I had a great job. I could pay my own bills easily. So why couldn't I appreciate what I had?

I had constant panic attacks, thinking that time was running out—for what, I'm not sure. I didn't have a biological imperative to have a baby like other friends my age. I believe I was simply feeling societal pressure to "get on with it" from both sides—all my Western friends were getting married and having babies, while my Arab friends had already done that back in their midtwenties; some were even already getting divorced.

Me? I had no life events to claim, unless you count working for a (then) respected mini-major film studio. I was completely out of sync, had no tribe to identify with, and felt rudderless, sad, and ashamed for not being able to feel gratitude for what I had. What did I have to be upset about? What if I was in the position of some of my distant relatives who had been left behind in Iraq? They had to fight for simple things like clean water. I was one of the "lucky ones"; I was living in America, land of the free.

Back then, because I didn't have a better understanding of depression as a mental illness, I simply felt like I couldn't *afford* to be depressed.

During those early times, I tried to will myself out of a mood and use the psychology my strong Arab mother might employ:

2 I couldn't even keep mint plants alive, and those grow like weeds.

"Do something productive and snap out of it."[3]

"Count your blessings. You could still be in Iraq fighting for uninterrupted electricity in your home."[4]

"Maybe Los Angeles is too much for you. Move back in with us in Austin."[5, 6]

I told no one about my emotional state, especially not Mom. Back then, it wasn't commonplace to talk openly about suffering from depression, especially not in Arab culture. Even my Western friends didn't quite understand why I was sad. Out-of-town friends lamented that they wished they could live a glamorous Los Angeles life, and one male friend even told me I was "too cute to be so upset." I wanted to punch him in the throat.

But I was frustrated because, deep down, I agreed with them. Again, I (erroneously) believed I had no real reason to be sad, which only served to worsen the sadness. I even tried turning my blues into a game to diminish its importance. I bought a small calendar and recorded my mood three times a day using a smiley face or a frowny face to denote happiness and sadness, respectively. If I felt neutral, I drew only eyes with no mouth to denote nothingness.

Most days began with a frowny face and ended with a neutral face.

When you suffer from depression, you're looking for anything to chase the sadness away. For me, that meant engaging in bad habits and bad decisions. I didn't turn to alcohol, but I developed a longstanding crush on a bad-boy director from work and picked up smoking to bond with him. Luckily, nothing horrible came out of this except for the sixteen months I wasted on someone for whom I constantly made excuses:

---

3 It goes without saying that telling a depressed person to "snap out of it" is the same as telling someone with a broken leg to "just get up and walk." It's not helpful.

4 This, too, is not helpful. It only makes a depressed person feel worse. Depression is an illness that can strike anyone—whether they live in a country under siege or in, well, America.

5 Yeah . . . my folks had moved yet again and were now living in Austin.

6 That last one was enough to send me into an *increased* depression. And it missed the point.

"He's just misunderstood"; "I can save him"; "He didn't mean to get his former girlfriend pregnant after telling me he wasn't seeing anyone else." You know, the lies women sometimes believe.[7]

I was so embarrassed about this chapter of my life that if you went through my stack of journals (which I still have, beginning from age eleven), you'll find this period conspicuously absent. Not because I didn't keep a journal, but because I burned all three and flushed the charred remains down the toilet. I wasn't keen on keeping a record of my days of smoking, being in love with an unavailable guy, battling depression, and bouncing among therapists (I would quit whenever they told me something I didn't want to hear—mostly that all problems stem from our mothers).[8]

My self-absorption caused me to lose friends. I had become a completely different person from the one I was one year prior. I remember thinking that if this was what Hollywood "success" looked like, fuck it, I'd go back to Kentucky. Or marry rich and become a housewife. Or chuck it all into the trash can and open a bakery in a small town. How do you go from having a near-perfect relationship with your soulmate[9] in your twenties to being an educated, professional thirty-something living for late-night work sessions because it meant more smoke breaks with Stuart and a chance that you could meet up later?? Aren't you supposed to do those things in reverse order?

Eventually, I did tell my mother (about the depression, not the *guy*; I wasn't that crazy). Being the consummate pharmacist that she is, Mom told me that perhaps the depression I had was the "newly discovered" PMDD (premenstrual dysphoric disorder),[10] which was basically PMS turned up thirteen notches. From my smiley-face calendar research, I

---

7 Ladies, you know what I mean; and if you don't, you're lucky . . . or lying.

8 In spite of their best intentions, moms can mess us up. But let's move on and take responsibility of our own adult lives, am I right?

9 I.e., Tony

10 PMDD was just a way for the pharma industry to rebrand what I had been experiencing since my teens.

discovered that the blues would hit me two weeks out of the month, usually around my period. It was an extreme sadness, the kind that made you apathetic and not want to get out of bed. During the other two weeks, I'd be fine.

But two weeks out of the month was basically half of my life. I didn't intend to spend half of my life in bed.

I took Mom's advice and got a prescription for Sarafem, a rebranded Prozac at the time. Though I was worried that my personality would change, I was ready to try anything. My doctor informed me that it would merely give me a platform until I got my land legs back, and I *really* needed my land legs. I was tired of going through the motions. I wanted to find joy in simple things again—like a cup of hot coffee in the morning. I filled the prescription, and slowly it got better. My daily calendar faces turned into mostly smileys with a few neutral no-mouth faces. The frowny faces decreased.

I was so grateful. I felt myself getting back to my center and finding joy in life again. I snapped out of my trance and left Stuart behind. I stopped smoking and took a trip to Europe with a gal pal, my first in years.

It was the spring of 2001, and I was the happiest I'd been in a long time. I'd learned to find joy again after that period of darkness, and it felt amazing. I was optimistic about what life would bring next.

Then, several months later, the unspeakable happened.

Two planes crashed into the World Trade Center, killing nearly three thousand people and changing everything as we knew it.

23

A Dark Pèriod

September 11, 2001.

I don't think I will ever *not* feel a shudder when I see this date in print.

I'll never forget that morning, waking up in my apartment to a call from Tony, who told me to turn on my TV. I had a fax machine in my bedroom, which also served as an office, and I used the attached phone as my landline. When I recall images from that day, I keep seeing the caller ID on that fax machine with Tony's name scrolling by . . .

A group of ten friends and I gathered at our buddy Mike's house and remained glued to the television until dinnertime, taking breaks to play board games to distract ourselves. No one wanted to go outside. It didn't matter that we lived in a quiet neighborhood in Pasadena, where we were quite safe from a terrorist attack. The rules had changed. If someone could commit such a horrific act, such as deliberately flying a plane into two skyscrapers, who was to say any of us were safe? I'm lucky in that no one close to me lost anyone in those attacks, but the fact remained that America, our America . . . *my* America, was permanently broken and would never be the same.

For weeks after, I avoided going to restaurants not out of fear for my safety, but because it seemed frivolous to have sushi in the aftermath of horrific tragedy. Same thing with Starbucks; I could get my caffeine fix at home. As the weeks went by, I gathered with friends and coworkers to attend group counseling sessions and interfaith prayer services in nearby churches, all to try to make sense of what had happened on US soil, and to allay feelings of vulnerability, powerlessness, and fear. Those sessions helped.

But then I began feeling something different—the isolation of being a Muslim.

Initially, I was reassured when leaders, Muslim and non-Muslim alike, condemned the actions of Al-Qaeda, the terrorist group that took responsibility for the attacks. President George W. Bush made it clear that the Western world was not at war with Muslims, but rather at those particular individuals. I waited for public figures and officials to continue the dialogue and actively engage in outreach and education in hopes that, somehow, some good could come from a horrific thing. I waited for more declarations that terrorism is not religion *nor should it ever* be considered religion. I heard a bit of this sentiment, but what I heard more of was "Don't judge an entire population by the actions of a few." It was an accurate and valuable statement, to be sure, but it didn't go far enough for me.

I began feeling paranoid and uneasy.

Would my coworkers and acquaintances suddenly start to suspect me? I thought back to the few folks at work who'd previously joked about me being a terrorist.[1] I wondered deep down if they really thought I might be one. I was too afraid to confront them. What if they said, "We weren't so sure about you a year ago—you seemed nice enough—but now we can't even look at your face because it makes us uneasy"? I wasn't emotionally ready to handle this kind of information.

So I overcompensated by being especially nice to the people around me. If someone complained that I'd rolled my eyes or looked at them in a negative way, I took their criticisms to heart. I didn't want anyone

1 This was before 9/11, when it wasn't as politically incorrect to say that . . . wait, what am I saying? Joking about Arabs as terrorists is at its least always politically incorrect and at its most racist.

thinking I was harsh, antagonistic, or swarthy-looking. I didn't want anyone thinking I was like *those people.* For the first time since high school, once again I longed to be blonde-haired, blue-eyed Paige who was mellow and even-keeled, instead of dark-haired Ayser who tended to be volatile. When during an argument my friend Scott asked why my people were so angry all the time, instead of calmly calling him out on his racism, I shut down and avoided him for a week. What if he was right about me?

I began pushing down anything that I thought was too "big" about myself. After a decade of embracing my uniqueness, I found myself swinging back to my prepubescent introversion. I toned down anything colorful—clothing, manner of speech, opinions. This time I was doing it not to be accepted into the cool-kid clique, but so that strangers wouldn't get that look of fear in their eyes when they saw me (accidentally) leaving and walking away from a large package of bourbon chocolate balls at the airport in Lexington. Calm down, blue-blazer-and-sneakers guy, I paid good money for those bourbon balls, and I'm not about to leave them behind on purpose!

It was a surreal time, and I tried adjusting to my new normal. And if I had a hard time as an Arab woman, you can imagine how it was for the male members in my family. My brother gave up on flying for the rest of that year because he was hassled so much during the first few months after the attacks. Luckily, I was living in Los Angeles, which was a bit more cosmopolitan than Austin, Texas, where my parents were now living. They were left alone for the most part, aside from some well-intentioned but ignorant questions:

"Why do Muslims hate us?"

"Do you know Osama Bin Laden?"

"Does it bum you out that you can't eat pulled pork?"

Seemingly innocent rituals like Halloween became opportunities for paranoia. When it came time for trick-or-treating, my parents' Iraqi friends in Austin darkened the lights and pretended not to be home. They refused to participate because what would happen if some kid accidentally ate bad candy and got sick? Would people immediately assume it was terrorism? Would the FBI come knocking on their door? So, they hid out of fear with the intention to protect themselves. But this had negative effects, causing even more isolation and alienation from the community.

The abominable terrorist act had also suddenly made me an unofficial spokesperson for my religion. I had two choices: to withdraw like those Iraqi families at Halloween and hide that part of me so no one knew I was Muslim, or to speak out and, in my own small way, bring awareness to my immediate circle. I chose the latter. I had an opportunity. I responded to every comment, no matter how stupid, like: "Do Muslim women wear the hijab to hide their horns?"

. . . Okay, maybe not *that* stupid. But I did have an open-door policy when it came to Q&A on what it meant to be Muslim. Go on, I invited the people around me. Ask me anything.

Was I unfairly shouldering the burden of proving that terrorists do not represent what the majority of Muslims stood for? Sure, I was. But I tried my best in this new, uncharted territory. I became actively involved with public advocacy groups such as The Muslim Public Affairs Council (MPAC) and did whatever I could to educate and enlighten the public. The silver lining was striking: for the first time in my life, I was actively reaching out to Muslims with the intent of becoming part of a community, something I'd conscientiously avoided in my younger years, which my parents had lamented. It's sad that it took such a heinous act to propel me to get involved in my community. But don't we all turn to our "tribe" when the world gets to be too much? Unfortunately, it takes bad shit happening to get the dialogue going.[2]

2 When people are busy being happy during times of peace, the only polarizing thing is whatever has last come out of Kanye West's mouth. Frankly, I would prefer to live in a world where people are polarized by only Kanye West.

Hanging around people who were like me kept me from isolation and going back into my depression. I made some really good friends during this period. Being involved with MPAC saved me.

I started believing that maybe things could be normal again. At least, I had hope.

24

#WhenWeSpeakUp

While we're on the subject, let's talk about prejudice against Muslims.

The same issues I had to contend with back in 2001 continue to come up today, such as during a night out with my best friend, Karen, fifteen years later. We were at dinner, discussing what had depressingly become the norm over the past few years—another attack on US soil where the perpetrator invoked religious fanaticism. This time it was the June 12, 2016, attack on the gay nightclub, Pulse, in Orlando, Florida. The perpetrator, Omar Mateen, was Muslim, and during his siege, he made a 911 call to pledge allegiance to the extremist terror group ISIS.

KAREN: Islam has enough problems without this asshole coming in and fucking things up.

ME: I don't think what this guy did can exactly be considered Islamic . . .

KAREN: I'm just saying the religion doesn't need him using it to further his agenda.

ME: He claimed allegiance to ISIS.

KAREN: Exactly.

ME: . . . which is *not* a religion. It's a militant cult.

KAREN: A cult that claims the teachings of Islam as a springboard.

ME: Sure . . . but I don't think people confuse cults with the beliefs of the average person of the faith, do they?

KAREN: . . . Damn that's hot.

ME: What?

KAREN: Her boots.

Karen jutted her chin, and I realized her attention was now on Charlize Theron, who was leaving our restaurant wearing badass black side-buckle boots.[1] The moment was gone.

As I was driving home, I started to wonder whether my good friend of eight years really could not make a distinction between a terrorist and a practicing believer of the Muslim faith. To be fair, my Muslim identity is not one that's traditionally visibly apparent—I don't wear a hijab,[2] I've acquired a taste for Woodford Reserve, and I can't claim the excuse of doing my Maghrib prayers[3] whenever I am late to dinner.[4] As one casual acquaintance pointed out, I don't "act Muslim." As subtly racist as that sounds, I try to give them the benefit of the doubt—when something is hard to put in a box, it might be easier to misunderstand. But as I told this particular individual, don't question my allegiance to my religion just because you can't see it.[5]

Still, in today's post-9/11 world, with all the awareness and dialogue going on, I prefer to hope that people are able to make the distinction between a believer of the faith and someone who subverts its teachings

---

1 If anything was going to take the focus away from a discussion about terrorism, it would have been Charlize Theron's badass black side-buckle boots.

2 I tend to favor sleeveless halter tops because they're cute.

3 Sunset prayers.

4 I am often late to dinner.

5 At its core, Islam literally means *submit to God*. So, to consider yourself a Muslim, you simply need the belief in God.

in order to carry out heinous acts of terrorism. After all, few would say that the Ku Klux Klan gives Christianity a bad reputation, despite the fact that KKK members pledge to uphold Protestant Christian morality. Almost every Christian denomination has denounced the KKK, just as Muslims have repeatedly denounced ISIS. Why was there a difference?

I'm hopeful that things are changing for the better. The world's gotten smaller, and thanks to old and new media, it's easier to receive information, which can lead to education and hopefully tolerance on both sides—Western and Middle Eastern. But unfortunately, the burden is still on me to advocate for my fellow Muslims in the wake of terrorist activity that is linked to Islam if I wish to fight against racism and xenophobia. Not every Muslim chooses to take on that burden, and indeed it is *not* our responsibility to defend ourselves against irrational bias. But I think my personal choice allows for more open discussion and improved awareness.

I've learned that everything bad comes from silence, such as isolation and alienation, while nothing bad can come from productive dialogue at the very least. My friend Rania is a well-respected doctor and hijabi-wearing Muslim who lives in Northern England. Sometimes she encounters patients who marvel at how well she speaks English—with the authentic regional Geordie accent. As Rania puts it, "People are just too caught up with themselves to bother learning that someone can appear visibly Muslim on the outside and be authentically British at the core."[6] When faced with such situations, do I choose to clam up and run away, yell expletives and accuse someone of racism, or do I call out the person's microaggression while providing access to education and awareness? I believe the latter can help stem the tide of fear and anger before it culminates in even more hate, prejudice, and violence.

After the Orlando attack, a statement was immediately released by prominent American Muslim scholars, leaders, and activists.[7] It

6 In my case, replace "British" with "American," and you have me.
7 http://orlandostatement.com

was a major first and crucial step forward. MPAC, which has worked tirelessly for over thirty years to promote what Islam really is, created social media outreach campaigns, featuring notable names. This is the type of action I hope to emulate in my own life.

As I write this, I'm getting ready to head out to finish my conversation with Karen. Only this time I'm going to her house, where we'll be free of any celebrity fashion distraction. We'll sit on her back porch and hash it out. And even if we continue to disagree, I take comfort in the fact that I'm doing my part to spread awareness, openness, and acceptance.

25
The World's Worst Muslim?

. . . So yeah, I'm proud to be Muslim.

But that hasn't always been the case. I haven't always waved my identity flag loud and proud, mainly because I wasn't sure how all the patchwork pieces fit together. Growing up without moderate Muslim role models to emulate, I struggled to find a balance between living a lifestyle authentic to me and staying true to the teachings of my faith. I do believe in all five pillars that make up the foundation of Islam, though I admit I waver in my diligence in observing practices 2 and 4:

1. Declaration of faith (Shahada)[1]
2. Prayer (five times a day)
3. Charity (Zakat)
4. Fasting the month of Ramadan
5. Pilgrimage to Mecca once in one's lifetime (Hajj)

It's only been recently that I've felt comfortable talking openly about the specifics or logistics of my Muslim practice. For one, I've always believed faith to be a personal thing. Second, I guess I harbored a tiny bit of insecurity at being perceived as "not Muslim enough."

1 The acknowledgment that there is no deity other than God and that Muhammed is his prophet.

Recently, I was invited to speak on a panel about being Muslim in Hollywood. The panel was tailored to the Muslim community and would be held at an Islamic center. My first thought was extreme pride to be able to represent my experience, since it would sharply contrast with most of the visibly Muslim people there.

But then I got really, really nervous.

What did I bring to the table as a Muslim? My parents were largely spiritual in their approach and taught me to believe in Islam's core principles—that people are equal in the eyes of God except by their deeds. From my five years living in Saudi Arabia learning the strict letter of the law, I only held onto the Islamic rituals that made sense to me. But was it accurate to now brand myself a Muslim when I was largely nonpracticing? I was in a small crisis.

I mentioned my concerns to Karen when I visited one day.[2] She had no shortage of advice and declared I should let the other panelists do most of the talking.

"You're the furthest thing from a practicing Muslim I've ever seen. You never mention praying. Every Ramadan you attempt to fast, but you don't do the whole month. Aaaand . . . you like your champagne."

She wasn't wrong. Muslims pray five times a day and fast during Ramadan, whether they feel like it or not. I don't kneel to pray that often. And though I don't eat pork because I never developed the taste, bacon-wrapped dates are another thing. Also, you're more likely to find me in the pub than in the mosque, probably because French fries are more delicious in pubs than they are in mosques.[3, 4] You don't get to pick and choose how you observe your religion. You just have to just do it . . . right?

---

2 Mainly to watch the red carpet arrivals for whatever awards show was going on at the time.

3 What I mean is pubs have access to food, and they also have better happy hours. (What I really mean is mosques *don't* have happy hours. But they do accommodate catering situations near the entrance.)

4 I apologize. I believe I've committed enough blasphemy for one chapter.

But as I listened to Karen's views about *my* relationship with *my* religion, I started getting angry. If she were a guy, I would have accused her of mansplaining.[5] What do you call it if she's female, white, and Buddhist? *Fem*splaining? *White*splaining? *Buddhi*splaining? . . . *Friend*splaining!

Karen wasn't being malicious. She was simply certain, based only on what she'd read, that I wasn't practicing the religion accurately or correctly. Therefore, she advised me to defer to my fellow panelists who appeared more devout.

Her reaction was the main reason why I often avoided discussing my religion, which always proved to be an especially touchy and polarizing subject. Even though the little voice in my head had similar doubts, I didn't like the implication that I was inauthentic when it came to my faith. It reminded me of something else my friend Joe[6] liked to say: "It's like being pregnant. You can't be kinda pregnant. You either are or you aren't."

As I weighed Karen's and Joe's concerns with my own, a light bulb went off and a thought came: religion shouldn't be an all-or-nothing deal-breaker.

The night before the panel, I crammed as if I were preparing for an exam the next day. I didn't want to be caught with my pants down (or, in this case, my veil off). What if my audience and fellow panelists thought I was being lazy in my interpretation of the faith? What if they declared I was a fraud? I couldn't handle the public humiliation. I brushed up on Islam basics and even downloaded *The Quran for Dummies*.[7] Then I said a prayer and left it to God.

The night of the panel, I walked into the room filled with eager people and noticed that many of the women were dressed in the hijab. I silently cursed myself for wearing skinny jeans, tall boots, and a relaxed

---

5 Fun sidenote: my last name being Salman means I am often guilty of "Salmansplaining."

6 A Wisconsin White Methodist male (hey, there's some fun alliteration in that!).

7 This happened, for real.

button-down shirt. I reached for my emergency Xanax and turned to the moderator of the event, my friend Sue Obeidi.

"What do I talk about?" I was suddenly panicked; the Xanax hadn't kicked in yet, dammit.

Sue patted me on the back with a laugh and said, "They'll probably just want to know how many times a day you pray." My eyes widened in horror as I tried to recall the last time I prayed (the night before, by the way), and Sue laughed. "Ayser, I'm joking! Just be yourself . . . and try not to say the word *fuck* too many times, *or at all*. This crowd is cool."

I shouldn't have worried. They *were* cool. Though I started off awkwardly, accidentally using words like *explosive* and *infiltrate* to describe how to get your foot through the Hollywood door (Karen and I laughed about my Freudian gaffe in private later), my fellow Muslims couldn't have been nicer, more supportive, and more willing to laugh with me. I relaxed, shared personal anecdotes, and spoke with the same authority about my experiences as a Muslim in Hollywood as my veiled sister next to me did.

That's when my mind blew up[8] with a realization—perhaps the biggest "splainer" of Islam to myself was *me*. Just because I wasn't a letter-of-the-law Muslim didn't mean I was any less a Muslim. Being Muslim is sewn into my fiber, just like being Iraqi is. I can't stop being Iraqi even though I'm now an American. And I won't stop being a Muslim even if ~~most~~ some years I do a lousy job of fasting during Ramadan.

Since the panel, I've met extremely diverse Muslims—queer, devout, modern, liberal, relaxed, lapsed, and even atheist.[9] Each of these individuals considers themselves as simply Muslim without any other qualifier; they're "Muslim enough." Finally, I feel like I'm giving myself conscious permission to do the same.

---

8 Just can't help myself with these awful puns.

9 Yes, I realize an atheist Muslim flies in the face of the definition of Islam as "submission to God," but certain Muslims consider their Islamic identity as more cultural than religious.

It's okay even if my Muslim behavior is different from the Muslim behavior you expect—all I know is it's real and authentically mine. And I hope that if any of you question your own authenticity or legitimacy, you'll give yourselves a break, too.

26

An Open Letter to President Trump

As a Muslim, the question I get asked the most post-2017 is "So . . . Trump."

Yes, I realize that's not a question, but it's as far as someone usually gets with me before we both resort to silent communication, including eye rolls and shrugged shoulders, unsure of where to begin. Where *do* you begin? We all have our own feelings and thoughts and opinions about his blatant disregard for and incompetence in . . . well, pretty much everything. I don't need to rehash the obvious.

But in January 2017, right after Trump's inauguration, I needed something to help me channel my anxiety.

So, I decided to write him a letter.

Mind you, I've never written a letter to an elected official in my life, let alone the president of the United States. As you can imagine, I was a tad intimidated and apprehensive, and it took me several drafts to crystallize my thoughts in an open and honest manner. In the end, I was too afraid to mail the letter, but in the interest of transparency with you, I'm including the whole unedited version below:

Dear President Trump,
WHAT. THE. ACTUAL. FUCK??
—Ayser Salman

. . . Not the best way to come out of the gate.

Dear President Trump,
How can you seriously impose a Muslim ban?!! Most of your wives have been immigrants. I know they are not from countries on the ban list, but still. Don't you think you're being a hypocrite?
—Ayser Salman

. . . Sounds like a letter to one of my film school buddies, instead of the man holding the highest office in America. I needed to be a bit more deferential. Maybe this?

Dear President Putin . . .

. . . Okay, that was a cheap shot. What can I say? I use comedy to deflect my discomfort.

I couldn't understand why writing this was so hard. I made some coffee, stress-ate twelve and a half Twizzlers, and took a moment to pet my cats (which is clinically proven to lower blood pressure). Then I ate the remaining half Twizzler and three more for good measure, and I sat down again to write an actual letter, from the heart:[1]

Dear Mr. President,
I came to this country with my family as a toddler. It was the 1970s, and we were escaping Saddam Hussein's fascist regime in Iraq. At the time we were attracted to this beautiful country

---

1 Disclaimer: this was written shortly after the inauguration in January 2017, and since then a gazillion things have changed.

because of the freedom to say what you want, do what you want, and be who you want. Now, I know it's taken America years to really get to the "be who you want part" (as my LGBTQ friends can attest). And as a Muslim, it's taken me a few years post-9/11 to really embrace my religion and do so publicly. Those are my own personal issues. But for the most part I've always felt at home in this glorious country. My father cries when he hears the National Anthem. And so do I—especially Faith Hill's beautiful rendition at the Super Bowl in 2000. Do you like Faith Hill? I'm a big fan. But I digress . . .

Mr. Trump, if you're trying to divide us, it's having the opposite effect. This is the first time in my life that I've felt such solidarity with my fellow Americans. People came out in the millions for the Women's March. And in tens of thousands at airports across the country to protest the Muslim Ban. I cried when I saw the photographs of lawyers working pro bono on their Saturday nights to free these detainees so they could return home, many of whom were elderly parents of American-citizen children who had only come to visit their relatives. Some of these were also sick and elderly parents of American-citizen children who had been granted entry to the US to receive medical care. Mr. Trump, doesn't that upset you? It should. What danger do these people pose to our national security?

Mr. Trump, I know you were born in America, but I also understand your mother came over from Scotland. Is that right? At least that's what Wikipedia told me. And chances are that when she sailed over, the first thing she saw welcoming her to the US was the Statue of Liberty with its inscription, "Give me your tired, your poor, your huddled masses yearning to breathe free. . . ." How does your Muslim ban reconcile with that sentiment?

And on the subject of the Muslim Registry—how would you even implement such a thing? Most of us are not visibly Muslim. With men you can't often tell, unless they wear a skullcap called a kufi *or* taqiyah, *but even then those are rarely worn outside the mosque except by the truly devout. And most Muslim women don't wear the* hijab *(head scarf) and can often be spotted in jeans or even (GASP!) shorts and tank tops!*

The point is, it can be difficult to tell who is Muslim and who isn't just by looking at them if they aren't wearing the "uniform." So what then? Will there be some sort of verbal test at the airport? "Have your bags left your possession since you packed them?" "Do you renounce Jesus?" Muslims believe in Jesus Christ, by the way. With Islam, you're just adding another guy to the mix, the prophet Muhammed (PBUH).[2]

You're afraid that Muslims equal terrorism. But that's . . . extreme to say the very least. Muslims are not terrorists. Sure, some terrorists claim Islam as their faith. But all *terrorists blame anything other than themselves for their horrific actions.*

So if your fear is that Muslims are terrorists, if that's really your concern, then the question at the airport that should be directed to everyone *could simply be, "Do you plan to blow anyone up in the near future?" followed by "Do you agree that humans should not blow each other up, especially in the name of religion?" And then if the answer to either question is anything other than NO for the first and YES for the second, then only at that point would you put these people in a room and question them further. I would support this sort of detainment because I, too, want to know what makes a person decide to blow someone up and I intend for them to be removed immediately. It's certainly not what a normal human being does and most certainly* not *what a Muslim does. It's the thinking of a fucked-up person—and that*

2 This means "Peace Be Upon Him" and is simply a show of respect.

title doesn't discriminate. It can be said of anyone in the world, at any time.

Mr. Trump, I'll admit I was one of the few people who didn't view your becoming president as signifying the end of civilization. I was surprised of course when the election results were announced, but I remember thinking, "This feels like Iraq." And like Iraq, we'll get through it.

But this is NOT Iraq. This is the country I fled Iraq FOR. A democratic country whose responsibility it is to not be fascist. And watching your first press secretary,[3] *Sean Spicer, speak at a press conference reminded me of "Baghdad Bob" back in the Second Gulf War. Remember that guy? He was the Iraqi information minister who would come out and rant about how America was losing the war, even as Iraqi soldiers were retreating and surrendering and it was clear America was making progress. I believe your administration refers to this as "alternative facts." Back then we called it "propaganda and spin."*

Mr. Trump, a lot of my parents' Iraqi peers supported you. I think it's because your rhetoric was familiar to them and what they've come to associate with a government. They've lived through several incarnations of Iraqi regimes, including the toppling of the monarchy only to gain Saddam Hussein in 1979, and then the toppling of Saddam in 2003 to gain the religious opportunistic chaotic mess, which is the country right now.

My friend Karen thinks I'm being too lenient on you. She wishes I took you to task more than I am. She wants me to suggest therapy, though she knows you won't go. She thinks you're a classic narcissist and mentally unstable. I told her that I'm not used to calling out the leader of my democratic country in such

3 Because there was a rapid rotation of multiple ones for a while after . . .

a manner. But then again, as I said above, your administration has whiffs of my dictatorial homeland.

Mr. Trump, if America becomes fascist, where will my family flee next? I suppose I could go to England. Bath is lovely—have you been? Oh, right, there's a petition now to keep you out of England because you'll embarrass the Queen or something. I'm sorry. It sucks to feel excluded. I know. I've spent my whole life feeling this way.

Look, I'm a just comedy writer who hails from Iraq and who grew up in Kentucky and who knows only a small bit about fascism. Maybe you'll read my upcoming book, The Wrong End of the Table. *Maybe you'll find it entertaining. But Mr. President, my father supported you in the very beginning. When I incredulously demanded why he would support a candidate who was going to deport him and build a wall at the Mexican border, Dad firmly said, "He won't do it. He doesn't mean any of it." To this day, he says that you're only doing this to appease your constituents and let them know you're working for them.*

My father and I don't talk about you anymore.[4] *I think he's still trying to be patriotic and "give you a chance." I think that's what being American means to him. I ask in return that you conduct your position as Commander in Chief with more respect than you have thus far. Treat the office with the honor it deserves. Maybe stop tweeting so much. Maybe don't undermine and ignore federal judges. Maybe stop commenting about the physical appearance of female anchors. With all due respect . . . maybe act more presidential?*

Mr. Trump, my father is an amazing man, teacher, human. He leads by kindness and example. He works at the US Department

4 It's now 2018, and I'm still working on finishing this letter.

of Veterans Affairs clinic, where he's a liaison of sorts. At eighty-eight years old, he inspires forty-eight-year-old veterans of the Gulf War. Full disclosure, first he freaks them out with his strong Iraqi accent. Many of these guys have PTSD, so when they hear his voice, it gives them flashbacks. But in his gentle, patient manner he soon draws them out. And they eventually share their stories with him. I'm so proud to be his daughter. If he has taught me anything, it's that I should lead by example. So I'm sorry for cursing your name. As an Arab, I was taught to respect my elders. And as an Iraqi I learned quickly not to criticize my government.

But as an American and a former journalist, as a woman, as a Muslim, as a hard-working member of Hollywood, I have to ask. What is your end game? I would like to think it's not to create chaos.

Dear Mr. President, please KEEP America great.

Please don't undo the greatness that already exists.

Please don't turn my beautiful country into the fascist homeland I left behind.

Best,
Ayser Salman

27
An Intersectional World, or: My Postelection Observations

Writing my letter to Trump was incredibly cathartic. It allowed me to process some of my feelings, which, up until then, alternated between the following two extremes: 1. "Holy Fuck, We're Doomed," and 2. "We've been through worse. Let's just get through these four years."

I suffered through a tumultuous bundle of mixed emotions; I was worried and scared, but also reflective and even gingerly hopeful. From these muddled thoughts came the following observations that I clung onto:

Election night reminded me of the 9/11 terrorist attacks.

It seems crazy to compare the election of a US president with the worst terrorist act on US soil, but that's how I felt the night of the election. I was worried that things were so bad to the voters who had pulled the lever for Trump that they were willing to overlook his racist, misogynistic, hateful behavior in order to bring in "new blood" because they believed the old way wasn't working. I was terrified that Trump's election meant that this same racism, misogyny, and hatefulness were winning. And as a Muslim, I was nervous. I knew I was pretty safe in my liberal city of Los Angeles, but what about my parents and sister, who were residing in Texas? What if I ventured back to Kentucky to visit friends? Once again, I did not feel safe in my country.

"America, the Middle East"

Then there was the part of me that remained stoic. As I watched the first press briefing after Trump's inauguration, I thought to myself that this was just like watching the news in the Middle East—Iraq in particular. We had a loose-cannon narcissist who said whatever he wanted and, when called on it later, denied he ever said it. The amount of conjecture and talking around a subject while not giving a straight answer was exactly what I was used to from watching Middle Eastern politicians on TV. I immediately called two of my immigrant friends for a reality check. Naz, who's from Iran, said, "I mean! Did we flee our oppressive homelands in the Middle East to come to the States just to trade in one fascist regime for another?" Marium from Egypt said, "Forget America, the Beautiful; now it's America, the Middle East."

My emotions were all over the place. Similarly, my friends also become more vocal and active. Karen was outraged about reproductive rights and got out and marched. [1] Mike marched for reproductive rights as well as LGBTQ rights. Karen insisted that Lena march for women's rights, which Lena was planning on doing anyway, but then she got pissed about Karen's sudden civic interest because as she said, "I didn't see her at any of our Black Lives Matter protests last year when our men were being shot by police!" And Naz was pissed at Stacy for being self-congratulatory about her participation in the Women's March—not because she bought the pussy hat, made the signs, and documented her experience on Instagram, but because a year ago she'd called Naz "a drama queen" when she tried to explain how dangerous a Trump presidency would be.

And that's how I learned about intersectionality.

1 On January 21, 2017, about 5 million people from all walks of life across all seven continents joined together for the Women's March, making it the largest coordinated protest in US history and one of the largest in world history.

Intersectionality is the theory I've been waiting for my whole life. The concept is defined by The Oxford Living Dictionary as:

> *The interconnected nature of social categorizations such as race, class, and gender as they apply to a given individual or group, regarded as creating overlapping and interdependent systems of discrimination or disadvantage.*

In its simplest form, it's the idea that people experience oppressions and life in general differently based on their culture, gender, sexual identity, etc. There's no way that Karen, the Jewish-turned-Buddhist Bostonian who spent most of her time in New York, would ever have the same experience as Lena, the Nigerian-Filipino from Atlanta. Lena's experience is nowhere near that of Kim's, our black friend from Chicago, even though they have the same skin color. And as an Iraqi Muslim female, I couldn't speak to the experience of Naz, my Iranian Muslim friend who identifies as an atheist and is also disabled.

Had I known about this concept when I was a teenager, it might have made me feel less ostracized from everyone who told me that I was "just being dramatic" whenever I was angry about X, Y, or Z—simply because my experience was not akin to theirs. Basically, I inhabited a different world they weren't privy to, which caused them to misjudge me and caused me to feel misunderstood.

This brings me to my last point, one that almost cost me my friendship with Karen.

Trump is a catalyst for change.[2]

You might find it bizarre that an immigrant like me is using the phrase *catalyst for change* to describe a man who proposed to ban my people from this country, who wants to repeal DACA (Deferred Action

2 By the way, Karen told me *not* to include this line, as it might make me lose readers. So . . . y'all still with me?

for Childhood Arrivals), who ordered air strikes against Syria,[3] who tweeted a video of himself hitting a golf ball into Hillary Clinton's back, who bragged about assaulting women, who called a football player a "son of a bitch" for kneeling during the national anthem, who went to hurricane-ravaged Puerto Rico and threw paper towel rolls into the crowd, and who signed the devastating tax bill that would make people like him richer and bury people like me further in debt . . .

Trust me when I say I spent a good deal of time trying to find the right words to describe Trump.[4] *Catalyst for change* might be an odd choice as it implies change for the better. But here's why I settled on it:

After the primary election in 2016, Americans from very different walks of life banded together in ways I hadn't seen in a long time. There was a huge surge in donations to groups and organizations that pledged to fight Trump's policies. People turned out in the millions for the first Women's March and in the hundreds of thousands for the second one. After the second march, at least two of my friends quit their jobs in Hollywood to work on political campaigns in advance of the 2018 midterms—something they both said they wouldn't have dreamed of doing before Trump.

Not all of my friends experienced radical shifts, but most of us felt like we couldn't continue comfortably the way we had. My friend Stacy told me that when Obama was in office, she sat back and wasn't as likely to get involved in rallies and protests, content that things were progressing the way they were supposed to. "We had the luxury of doing nothing since it seemed that our leaders had it all under control," she said. "Now? Not so much." We were motivated—forced—to take action in direct response to his presidency.

So when I say I think that Trump will ultimately make America *better*, I'm not talking about MAGA,[5] that divisive rhetoric that flows

3 And then tweeted, "Mission Accomplished."

4 Other word choices were *unifier*, which almost sent Karen into cardiac arrest, and *mobilizer*.

5 "Make America Great Again."

unendingly from a xenophobic and misogynistic society. That's not what America is about. I'm talking about the fact that many of us are angry about this explicit and implicit hate rhetoric—and that we are doing something about it, on a larger scale than I've seen in my lifetime.

Plus, on a personal level, the amount of calls I received from friends near and far asking about my well-being really touched my heart. People are combating Trump's recklessness with their own conscious effort to be mindful toward others.

It's a major silver lining, and change is happening.

I'm not afraid to say it: I'm so proud to be a part of this America, which is pretty damn great already.

28
Hookah Lounges Aren't Doing Arabs Any Favors

Enough about politics and religion, let's get to the fun stuff—sex and dating in my adulthood.

. . . Okay, maybe just dating.[1]

First, let me be candid. I don't typically date Arab men. Perhaps I was too soured on the idea from those "much making" attempts back in my early twenties. Or perhaps because the only kinds of Arab men I met in my early twenties were those who were always either in the mosque or at the bar. No in between. At the time, I desperately craved someone I could go to brunch with on Sundays, followed by a stroll through Pottery Barn and maybe an afternoon movie if we could find one playing that starred Hugh Grant . . .

Anyway, about two years ago, I decided I was tired of explaining to my mother's friends and friends of friends why I didn't date their Arab sons. I decided to give those Arab men a chance.[2] Also, I figured that because I and, hopefully, my intended paramour were both in our forties by now, we'd probably already have worked through enough of our issues to finally have a chance at being a compatible match.

1 In case some moms read this (mine), and also because it's the truth.

2 Also because I was having zero luck on the dating circuit with non-Arab men. More about that soon.

So, I went out with an Arab guy for the first time.

It was a setup: a friend of a friend of my mother's hairdresser or something loosely connective like that. His name was Ali, and we agreed to meet for coffee.

I confess, I went in preparing to be unimpressed. From stalking his Instagram and Facebook feeds, I knew the following about Ali:

- He was cute with a good sense of humor—the latter being key for me.
- As a software engineer, he designed apps and programs, which gave teachers better tools in their classrooms. So: smart and cares about the future. *Great.*
- He had a Siberian husky puppy named Priscilla who was featured in most of his photos. Check. Check. *TRIPLE* CHECK.

Our coffee date began promisingly. Ali lived up to all of his on-paper qualities and had a laid-back simplicity about him, which made him easy to talk to. We were both on the same page regarding how Arabs would be better served by the presence of more local food spots that served an authentic dolmah or good falafel. He also shared my disdain of stereotypically "Arab" things—such as hookah lounges in the United States. Turns out I'm not the only one who believes there is no point to hookah lounges other than to perpetuate some romanticized notion of Bedouin Arabs sitting in the desert smoking *shisha*. It's unsanitary, unhealthy, and, frankly, racist. When Ali said, "Hookah lounges aren't doing our people any favors," I almost fell out of my chair. I had just said the same thing to my sister two days before!

The conversation then naturally turned to our respective mothers. Both of us rolled our eyes in shared commiseration about how they always insisted on taking "souvenirs" from hotel rooms but would leave something behind out of fairness. Mom called it "exchanging goods." She might take a small bowl from the Hilton but leave behind a spoon she had acquired during an earlier stay at the Radisson. I'm not sure what rulebook she was following, but that's how she rolled.

And why do Arab moms insist on bargaining for everything? Is it so terrible to pay retail for something? Ali showed me a scar on his elbow that he sustained after being *bitten* by his mother while attempting to gently steer her away from Macy's when she spent twenty minutes bargaining down the price on an item that was already marked down three times on clearance. She didn't mean to bite him, he clarified. She was just in a trance. (But she drew blood.) The upshot was, he got a cool scar, and his mom purchased the Tahari Jumpsuit for five dollars.[3]

At this point in our coffee date, not only did I silently berate myself for my past anti-Arab-son sentiment, I was also beginning to think that maybe my entire life journey had led me here.

Maybe I just needed to meet all the guys (Arab and non-Arab) who were NOs in order to find one who was a YES.

Maybe this was the *universe* at work—holding me back for decades and now giving me a green light.

Maybe it was finally on!

I took a better look at Ali. His eyes were a gorgeous chocolate-brown, the type that pulled you in. He had these strong, craggy hands.[4] And the way he spoke about his dog, Priscilla . . . an animal lover, as well? *Come on*! I was hooked. When he got up to get us both some water, I practiced writing my first name and his last name on a napkin . . .

Okay, I didn't actually do that. For the record, I've never done that. Not even in junior high school. The point is, I was feeling a connection.

But then the conversation took a different turn. And the shoe did finally drop.

This is what happened, word for word:

---

3 Apparently, she still claimed it was an overcharge because the jumpsuit was missing one button.

4 I have a thing for hands, especially when the thumb kinda bends out.

HIM: You know, you're not what I expected.

ME: *(leaning in coquettishly)* What do you mean?

HIM: Well, my mother told me you were Iraqi.

ME: *(with a smile on my face)* Guilty as charged.

HIM: Iraqis are very proud.

ME: I suppose I am proud; I mean, I'm sure of it.

HIM: Yes, but you're easy-going and funny.

ME: *(still flirting)* Thank you for noticing.

HIM: . . . which is more of an Egyptian sensibility.

ME: . . . What, please?

HIM: Egyptians are happier. That's why there are so many of them on TV comedy shows and movies.

ME: Isn't that a stereotype?

HIM: Stereotypes exist for a reason.[5]

ME: So, are we talking about the whole "fleeing Saddam's regime" thing? We left Iraq when I was a baby. I wasn't really a *serious* baby. I mean, I always had this furrowed brow. Botox has helped . . .

HIM: Don't get me wrong. Serious is a good thing, especially for a woman.

ME: How so?

HIM: It means you're not frivolous and into shallow things.

---

5 Okay, he was not wrong about that. And hadn't I kinda done the same thing with Arab men up until now? So I let that one go.

ME: Such as . . . ?

HIM: Clothes and makeup.

ME: I love both those things.

HIM: Yes, but it's clear you're not ruled by them. Judging from . . . (*waves his hand, indicating my attire*).[6]

HIM: (*continuing*) Honestly, I was just happy you weren't Lebanese.

At this point, I wanted to flip the table over and bolt from this guy. But for some reason I stuck with it. I had to know . . .

HIM: (*still continuing*) Lebanese women—you can't tell if they have their real noses.

ME: (*What the fu—?*) . . . Oh?

HIM: I dated a girl once from Lebanon. She and her sisters all had nose jobs.

ME: So, you're generalizing a whole race based on one family?

HIM: Not just her. Several others from Lebanon. They like to get plastic surgery.

That was it. At this point, I wanted to flip the table *onto* the guy. But I didn't want to live up to any potential stereotype he had of Iraqi women being aggressive. So I took a deep breath, downed my water, and managed to make small talk with him for another thirty minutes until I excused myself.

---

6 A backhanded compliment if I ever heard one. I looked down at my snazzy white New Balance sneakers, which I'd deliberately paired with a fancy silk top and slouchy jeans. It's called fashion deconstruction, buddy. Look it up!

As soon as I got into my car, I checked my phone. There were six missed calls from Mom. I called her back. Might as well get it over with.

MOM: So???!!!

ME: He's racist.

MOM: What? You mean he hates black people?

ME: No, he's racist against *Arabs*.

MOM: How is that possible? He *is* an Arab.

ME: Exactly. But he had all these stereotypes and prejudices.

MOM: Like what?

ME: That Lebanese women can't live without plastic surgery.

MOM: Akh, what an idiot! But that's not terrible.

ME: That Egyptians are happy all the time.

MOM: That *is* actually true. It's because of the fava beans.

ME: What?

MOM: Egyptians eat a lot of fava beans, which is a natural serotonin booster. Ask your father.

DAD: (*jumps on the line, as if on cue*) Hi, Ayser!

MOM: Baba, talk to your daughter about why Egyptians are so happy.

DAD: The fava beans. They contain high amounts of levodopa, which helps regulate your mood. I found an article on this yesterday. I will read it to you.

ME: Dad, can you just send me the link? I can't talk long. I have to go to Pilates.

DAD: I can't talk long, either. We, too, have plans.

ME: Yeah? Where're you going?

MOM: Ayser, by the way, if you ever want a nose job, we would support you. (*Adding quickly*) I'm not saying you need one. Just that you have our blessing.

She hangs up, leaving me momentarily speechless, which is a common side effect of a phone call with my mother.

DAD: Your mother is very supportive. Is there anyone like her?

ME: "Supportive," yes. So, Dad, where are you going?

DAD: Cafe Darband.

I practically drop the phone.

ME: That's a hookah bar!

DAD: Yes, but they also serve a fantastic Turkish coffee that your mother loves, and I love their falafel. We are going to meet Abdul Qasim and his family.

I was stunned. With that comment, my dad had outed my prejudice and shut it down. Sure, hookah bars at first glance are ridiculous, but if they bring together families to socialize and foster a sense of community, why was I so cynical? I had to stop looking at the surface; I needed to go deeper.

As I drove home, I meditated on my encounter with Ali and the conversation with my parents. I realized I had been exclusionary. A total snob. And that itself is a form of racism: focusing on a small surface detail and blowing it up to become the bigger picture, however detrimental. I vowed, then and there, to do better. To be better. To work toward fostering community.

Yeah, maybe Ali wasn't my guy, but meeting him certainly opened me up to meeting a future Ali, or Juan, or Nigel. Who cares who he is? As long as he shares my values, I'm open.

29

Iraqis Take Forever to Say Good-Bye

After my date with Ali, I was more determined than ever to work toward breaking down any stereotypes I saw both within and outside of the Arab community. I wanted to foster inclusion and awareness. I was going to be the poster child for Arabs, debunking all of the stereotypes that existed about us, thus being a hero among my people. I went to bed dreaming of the accolades I would receive.

Finally, I had a purpose that didn't involve finding a husband.

I decided to enact my game plan the following week when I visited my parents for my dad's birthday. Mom had planned a party for their close friends, most of them Iraqi. Almost immediately, I failed to break down any stereotypes; if anything, the opposite happened. Because, as I discovered on this visit, there *is* one stereotype that is absolutely true about Iraqis:

Iraqi people take forever to say good-bye.

I'll spare you the details I had to go through to get to this observation and instead give you a primer, should you ever find yourself speaking to an Iraqi on the phone or standing next to one at a social gathering.

You can't just simply say "good-bye" to an Iraqi and leave.

Well, you can. But there are stages.

STAGE I is where you stand up, thus signifying the end of the gathering. Then, one by one, everyone else stands up.

In **STAGE II**, you go for a hug or handshake with the host or the most important person in the room. This is when you say how great it was to see everyone. How the dinner was the most delicious food you'd ever tasted. Where do you find the time to roll such perfectly tight dolmas? Etc. When you're finished with your compliments, the rest of the group will follow suit. When *everyone* has completed that activity, the group migrates slowly to the door.

You have now moved to **STAGE III**. This is where, if you're lucky, you're able to make your way out while smiling and waving, get into your car, and *drive away*.

If this is you: congratulations, mazel tov, mabrook, and good on ya! You have managed to say good-bye in less than ten minutes. You must be really skilled at this. Or, not actually Iraqi.

If, on the other hand, you're really Iraqi, you will linger with the group at the door and make small talk, things you didn't touch on during the gathering. Such as how your eldest son is doing at school, and does he really like the fencing club he belongs to? Or whether your cousin's youngest daughter will ever stop playing tennis on her roommate's Wii long enough to start looking for a husband?

This goes on for six more minutes. Then come the actual good-byes:

"Goodbye, sweetheart, we hope to see you very soon!"

"Yes, sweetheart, we must do this again very soon."

"Very soon. Give your mother my best!"

"I will give her your very best. And you do the same. Give your daughter a hug for me, and tell her to eat while she's at college. She doesn't need to lose weight from stress."

"I will give her a hug from you for sure! By the way, did you hear about Yasmeen's son's fiancée? She was getting too fat, so she had that operation where they put the band in your stomach . . ."

You get the idea. To deal with this, I've developed my own style of good-bye. When I'm ready to leave, I'm out in five seconds—"Bye" and

. . . gone. Some might accuse me of being abrupt and rude. I prefer to think of it as succinct and concise.

Also, it's much easier to say good-bye when you're face-to-face; you can drop a few visual clues, such as looking at your watch or slinging your purse over your shoulder. But on the phone, it's a bit more challenging. Usually, I do the "Sooo anyway . . ." business.[1]

As in, "Sooo anyway, I better get off the phone."

Or "Sooo anyway, I've got tons of ironing to do tonight."

Or "Sooo anyway . . . my cat seems to have started a small fire in my sock drawer."

That last one was made up. I don't have a sock drawer.

Dad's birthday party was a smashing success. Mom's dolmah received rave reviews. She even made her version of the traditional Iraqi fish dish *masgouf*, which is difficult when you don't have a *tanour*, an Iraqi brick oven. The guests talked about her culinary feat at length. I had to leave toward the end of the party to catch a cab and fly back to Los Angeles for a work meeting the next morning. When I left my house in LA the next day, I'm pretty sure Mom was still walking out the last two guests, saying good-bye on the porch.

1 Ellen DeGeneres did a great routine about it.

30
Grapes Are Eaten One by One

While we're on the subject, let's talk about Arabs and proverbs. Arabs love their proverbs, especially Arab men. An uncle once said there are four things dear to an Arab man—God, family, country, and proverbs. My father is no exception.

But where Dad differs from other Iraqi men is he doesn't recite Iraqi proverbs exclusively. My father is an equal opportunity proverb spouter.

If I call in the morning and ask him how his previous day was, Dad would draw on the Cherokee proverb "Don't let yesterday use up too much of today," meaning, "Today is a new day." It's great he isn't living in the past, but it doesn't really answer my question.

Proverbs are the perfect way for my dad to sum up his feelings. If you think about it, they are really the old school version of GIFs or memes. Take this Swedish saying: "Friendship doubles our joy and divides our grief." It has a nice message and gets to the point; I feel cozy just reading it. That's the sign of a good proverb—efficient with its words, communicates a good point, and easy to remember so it can be used during tough times.

But there are also many proverbs that *don't* get to the point. That aren't succinct. That don't make sense. And I'm sorry to say that many of these are Arabic proverbs.[1]

Before anyone accuses me, once again, of being a self-hating Arab, let me explain: Arabic is a language known for its flowery tendency to embellish simple statements. So when a statement is translated from Arabic to English, something is lost in translation. Similarly, English phrases that are translated to Arabic take on a whole new life.

For example, the simple American insult "drop dead" may be translated into Arabic as "May the fleas of a thousand angry camels infest your mother's nostrils."

. . . I embellish. I believe the correct expression in Arabic is "May the fleas of a thousand camels infest your armpits."[2]

Here are more examples.

The English proverb "easy come, easy go" is straightforward enough; the Arabic version is "What comes this way, goes this way."

. . . I'm sorry, which way? Does it come in from the left and go out from the right? Or does it go out the way it comes? Is it like "in one ear and out the other" or "things leave the way they come?" I'm so stressed trying to figure this out that I ultimately miss the message.

Some Arabic proverbs are deliberately vague, probably in order to be all-inclusive or noncommittal. Instead of the English "better luck next time," the Arabic version is "a better one in another one." This could mean anything! Why can't Arabic proverbs just be simple and direct?

And instead of the English "no such thing as a free lunch," the Arabic proverb takes a morbid turn way into left field: "Nothing is for free, not even blindness and deafness."[3]

1 Arabs like to draw stuff out, as we have learned from the previous chapter.

2 This is probably the reason why Arabs have a reputation of being so angry—I mean, passionate.

3 Look, I'll just pay for my lunch, thank you very much. Small cost to have all my faculties intact.

I asked my dad about that particular one, and even he couldn't give me a good explanation. In fact, he answered me using a proverb. He said that when attempting anything in life, such as learning proverbs, "grapes are eaten one by one."

I was surprised. This Arabic proverb was pretty decent. It was quick, it was true, and it got to the point. I chuckled with delight at this happy realization. Maybe there were Arabic proverbs out there that would resonate with me.

My father listed three more:

"The barber opened his shop; his first customer was bald."

Starting the day off on the wrong foot.

"A thousand curses do not tear a robe."

Sticks and stones may break my bones, but words will never hurt me.

"A fire in the heart, but no tear in the eye."

Keep a stiff upper lip.

I started to come around. Maybe there was something to Arabic proverbs, after all. They always paint nice images, and sometimes having a strong visual is better than brevity. Take what is now my favorite saying:

"We mentioned the cat; it came bounding."

Speak of the devil.[4, 5]

My little devil cats, Bug (foreground) and Cobby (background).

4 Some people consider cats to be evil. Sure, cats can be assholes . . . but just look how cute they are!

5 My mother cautions me against making arbitrary and forced references to my cats; otherwise, readers will think I'm a crazy cat lady.

31

Aloha Means "the Sign" in Arabic

About ten years ago, my sister and I took my parents to Hawaii. Before I get to my point, let me lay the background for you.

It had always been my mother's dream to visit Hawaii ever since she was a child in Iraq. She and her siblings grew up watching two types of films: Westerns and Elvis Presley musicals. Both pretty much informed her idea of the United States as a young girl. In her mind, America was one vast landscape where handsome, rugged cowboys fought bad guys, rescued beautiful but helpless women, and rode strong, white horses into bars, where suddenly they were treated to the hip-shaking music of rockabilly guys wearing leather jackets. And just outside the window, Elvis Presley sang to Ann-Margret on a beach blanket.

Once, when we went on a cross-country trip and stopped by Knott's Berry Farm in California, Mom went up to a performer dressed as a Native American and, with tears of empathy, spoke to him about how his land had been taken and how he was subsequently displaced—and how she understood his situation. Dad had to firmly but gently pull her away.

With her Old Western experience fulfilled, it was time for Mom's Hawaiian experience. She was in heaven. The sounds of the ocean, the sun, the fresh air . . . it was pure bliss.

Dad enjoyed the trip slightly differently. For him, it was more of a historical and etymological lesson. Memorably, Dad was convinced that the Hawaiian language had its roots in Arabic.

Yep.

As we drove around in our rental car, he would repeat out loud the names of every sign we passed, explaining how that word sounded *exactly* like its Arabic counterpart.[1]

Take for example the word *aloha*. A-LO-HA. According to Dad, it was the equivalent of the Arabic way of saying AL-LOW-HA (with a heavy H sound), which means *the sign*.

Okay, I thought, but *aloha* in Hawaiian means *hello*. Signs have nothing to do with hellos.

"Well," said Dad, "when you tell someone hello, you are giving them a sign."

"Oh yeah? Of what?"

"That you want to talk to them—that you want to greet them!" he said calmly, not understanding why I wasn't grasping this simple concept.

"Take also, for example, Makena Beach," he continued. "*Makena* comes from the Arabic word for *place*, which is MA-KAHN. See what I mean? When you say let us go to the beach, you are going to a place. Hence the name *Makena*."

At this point, I began to fear that Dad had had too much sun. We tried to bring him inside, but it only encouraged him. He found an atlas at the hotel sundries store and sat on the couch in the lobby clutching a frothy pineapple drink with an umbrella in it. He sipped away as he flipped through the pages, muttering to himself about this word and that.

"See, even *Maui*! MAH-WEE in Arabic also means the color blue, and look at all the blue ocean around us! It is so perfect!"

---

1 Just like the movie *My Big Fat Greek Wedding*, where Toula's father thinks the Greeks invented everything.

He paused, taking in the magnitude of this discovery. Then, he took another sip of his drink and resumed his flip, flip, flipping.

"Rand McNally! The maker of this map!"

"What about it? Don't tell me they are—"

"—Arabic. Yes!"

"Really, Dad? McNally? I think that might hail from a little further west, like Ireland."

"No, look here, it is plain as day. McNally is a shortened version of MA-KAHN ALI. Ali's Place! This fellow Rand must have gone to Ali's place to draw up these maps!"

Head spinning, I looked around for my sister, but she'd gone back to the room with Mom. I found them watching an old Western on television (which must have been some sort of head trip for Mom). I announced to Lameace that for next year's vacation we should go somewhere with less fodder for Dad's etymological Arab-ization.

. . . We ended up taking him to Istanbul, Turkey.

32

Christmastime in the Salman House

[This page intentionally left blank.][1]

1 What? You were expecting a huge chapter on culture clash? My parents hardly celebrated *any* holidays, let alone Christmas. They did give us presents, but we ended up wrapping them ourselves. What good is Christmas when you had to be your own Santa Claus? This chapter exists only because my publisher said I needed to address whether I felt ostracized by Christmas. I did—mainly because my birthday fell two weeks before Christmas, so I always received a combo birthday-and-Christmas gift, while I also had to buy everyone else gifts. On *my* birthday . . .

33

Too Much Hair to Manage

My family is anything but traditional, both by Arab and American standards. This is most evident in terms of how we celebrate the holidays. Arabs are known for being very social, often attending or throwing large parties that last into the wee hours of the morning.

Not so with us Salmans. As kids, we only celebrated Christmas so we wouldn't feel left out when we went back to school after winter break and were asked what Santa had brought us. Mom used to throw my brother and me combo birthday parties since our birthdays were two weeks apart, but once we got older, she got tired and gave up on the tradition.

Except for Thanksgiving. It's Mom's favorite holiday, and she's so excited about it every year that she adds her own Salman twist to the tradition. For instance, Mom hosts Thanksgiving one day later on a Friday to allow my relatives to fly in on Thursday when flights are cheaper and less packed. What does a different day matter anyway when it's about the whole family coming together?

Recently, my dad announced on Thanksgiving Thursday that he'd scheduled a haircut for Friday. This meant he would have to leave the house in the middle of dinner with the family. Well, this just wasn't acceptable to Mom.

"Why are you always cutting your hair? No one cuts their hair more than you. Not even Ayser!"

"I have too much hair to manage!" he bellowed back, mussing up his hair to make a point, creating a white mohawk on top of his head. "You have no idea how hard it is to handle my hair. I put so much mousse in it, and it is still unmanageable!"[1]

"Why didn't you take care of this yesterday?" Mom asked.

"Yesterday was Thanksgiving. Everything was closed," he countered, satisfied with himself. "And I'm going to the post office today to drop off some letters," he added.[2]

"You and your mail! Why don't I fix you a plate that you can enjoy at the mailbox by yourself?"

"Well, that would be nice, I'm sure the mailman has not eaten yet today."

"The mailman! You are worrying about the mailman?"

At this point, I jump in. "Dad, the mailman's fine. I'm sure he ate yesterday when it was Thanksgiving for him and the rest of the country."

Mom and Dad bicker back and forth a little more until he informs her that the barber only has limited hours due to the holiday and that he really has to go.

She simmers for a bit, then smiles and says, "Well, at least he still has hair to manage."[3, 4, 5, 6, 7]

---

1 Keep in mind that he is eighty-nine years old at this point.

2 That's another one of my dad's hobbies. Besides managing his hair, he *loves* mail. He loves going to the community mailbox at the end of the block. He loves buying stamps. He even loves getting bills!

3 My mother just called to let me know that this year she's considering having Thanksgiving at my place in Los Angeles. I remind her that I live not too far away from a Big Five sporting goods store, which stocks Dad's favorite slippers, and that he might get some ideas for taking advantage of their Black Friday deals and therefore still plan on slipping out of the house in the middle of her Thanksgiving dinner.

4 Mom says it won't happen because Dad doesn't like to drive in Los Angeles. I mention Dad's recent discovery of the delights of Lyft.

5 Mom has now decided to host Thanksgiving at my brother's house in San Jose because the only store nearby is Home Depot—and Dad's not a "fix-it-man," so he won't have any reason to rush off during dinner. She also wonders when it was that I became so argumentative, since I used to be such an agreeable child.

6 I would like to point out that I specifically held back from correcting her earlier—it's "fix-it *guy*."

7 My publisher would like me stop using this book as a platform to fight with my mother. I want to apologize to my mother and to all my readers.

34
My Father, International Man of Mystery

We don't know when my Dad's actual birthday is. The Iraqi village he was born in didn't have the best record-keeping practices. The story goes like this: Dad was told that he was born a few weeks after the spring floods of 1929, which occurred in April. He spent his youth with that general knowledge, blissfully unencumbered by any specific dates.

When he came to the United States as a young college student, the US told him to "be civilized, pick a numerical date, and represent your home country properly."[1] Going off what he knew, Dad chose April 20; he liked the number twenty and thought it sounded good. Once it became official, he realized it was also Hitler's birthday, but it was too late to back out. In his optimism, he figured he would own it.

I grew up thinking Dad was born in April. Each year I knew the order of my gift-giving: my brother's in January, my parents' anniversary in February, Dad's birthday in April, Mom's in May, my sister's in September, and mine in December. I took comfort in the stability of this knowledge and enjoyed the dependable order of these family celebrations, and I looked forward to each one of them. I especially appreciated the fact that birthdays and anniversaries would be celebrated on

1 Okay, they didn't actually use those words; they just asked when his birthday was.

the same date five or ten years down the road, unlike those free-floating Muslim holidays . . .

Let me explain. Since Islam follows the lunar calendar, the month of Ramadan and date of the subsequent Eid celebration are constantly shifting. I'm not talking about a variation of a few weeks like Easter and Passover, when you know you'll still be celebrating during the general springtime. I'm talking about how in the 1980s Ramadan was in the summer, then in the 1990s it moved to the winter, and now in the 2000s it's back to summer again. It's like we're on some kind of religious seismic fault line.[2]

Which brings me back to why I find beauty in fixed dates. Dad's April birthdate also accurately reflects his personality traits.[3] Dad's a typical Aries man with Aries traits—stubborn, intellectual, fiery at times. Along with the common wisdom that women tend to be attracted to men who are similar to our fathers, I also recognize that most of the men I've dated seriously—Tony and John[4]—are Aries.[5]

Anyway, all this to say I thought I had a solid handle on who my father was—until the plot thickened. When Dad was seventy-six, another "birth certificate" turned up, arguing that his birthdate was in *July 1930*! It turns out an uncle who was an architect recalled Dad's birth as coinciding with the completion of one of his buildings on July 7, 1930. Dad, being the quintessential diplomat, took into consideration his uncle's statement but finally deferred to his mother's story, which was probably more accurate since she had actually been present during the birth.

---

2 It reminds me of this road in Palos Verdes, California, called Portuguese Bend. The road sits on an active fault line and shifts so much that workers are constantly repaving it.

3 Yeah, I'm one of *those* who believes in astrology. Okay? No, I don't read daily horoscopes, but I do think certain traits are associated with astrological signs.

4 More about *him* later.

5 Both my cats were also born in Aries months . . . am I belaboring this? I'm not sure which makes me seem crazier—that I know my cats' birthdays or that I ascribe astrological traits to felines. They're totally stubborn Aries personalities (also known as "just being cats").

Dad and Zaid at my high school graduation, both looking like bodyguards.

Either way, for a brief, fun moment, I was able to view my reliable, straight-laced father with a dash of skepticism, as if he were a spy.

For years, I thought my family was the only one with a weird birth story. But recently, I've discovered that most of my Arab friends have similar stories about their fathers, too![6] It didn't matter if they were Sudanese or Syrian or Iraqi. The reasons sounded familiar—delays in the certificate-issuing office or the fact that no one kept records. This explains why many of my Arab friends' fathers have January 1 or December 31 birthdays.

Dad and Lameace, not too long ago.

This just confuses me. Wasn't Iraq the civilization credited with inventing algebra, and even writing?[7] How is it that our fathers were plagued with so many unrecorded birthdays? Did they just not care about birthdays, subscribing to the adage "Age is but a number"? I asked Dad, but he refused to indulge my questions, mysterious-spy-style.

6 For some reason, most of the stories pertain to the fathers, not mothers. This might be because the mothers usually tended to be younger than their husbands.

7 According to Wikipedia, one of the earliest systems of writing called "Cuneiform" was invented by the Sumerians.

Today, he's moved on from that lifestyle, apparently, now spending his time practicing calligraphy and sending me movie reviews via text. He and Mom have an evening ritual of watching one movie every night from their massive DIRECTV cable lineup—usually a Western or classic of some sort. He gauges the quality of the movie by whether or not he has managed to resist falling asleep during, and he'll send me little tidbits of trivia about the film that he finds on the online movie database IMDb.com. You know, typical spy-retirement stuff.

He's living a good life. And he deserves it.

Dad looking like he's straight out of an espionage film.

Me and my father looking like he's just gone into Spy Retirement. But did he *really* leave the spy life behind . . . ?

PART 3:

GUESS WHO'S COMING TO DINNER?

35

That Brief Moment I Was Mrs. Salman Rushdie

The following is a recent conversation between my mother and me.

ME: My agent wants me to make the book more edgy and less PG-rated.

MOM: That's easy. Put more cursing words in there.

ME: I might have to delve into dating and things that Arabs aren't used to talking about openly.

MOM: Why don't you just make up a fake cousin and give her all the sex stories?

ME: Because that would be lying. And this book is supposed to be about me, not some random cousin.

MOM: *(covers the phone and yells to my father)* Baba! Talk to your daughter. She wants to spill all of our family secrets to sell this book.

I hear the muffled grumblings of my father in the background. A beat later, I hear the beep of my call-waiting.

ME: Hold on Mom, someone's calling me.

MOM: It's your father. I told him to talk to you.

ME: But I'm on the phone with you.

MOM: You know your father. He does what he likes. *(Covers the phone and yells.)* Baba! I'm on the phone with her right now. Try later.

The beeping of the call-waiting stops.

ME: . . . Okay, anyway, it's not just about sex. I need to get into current events.

MOM: Finally, you listen to me! I always wanted you to follow in the footsteps of Christiane Amanpour.

ME: Well, it won't exactly be that important. But I want to write about what it's like for me as a Muslim living in this country right now.

MOM: Good. Not everyone likes a funny Muslim. You need to talk about deep things that are important to people.

ME: But I can do it with humor.

MOM: Try not to . . .

ME: I'm a little nervous . . . about pissing off the Muslim fanatics.

MOM: Just don't attack the Prophet.

ME: I don't plan to. But what about terrorist groups like [redacted]?[1] They hate moderate Muslims.

---

1 Name redacted because my mother is concerned that if this book ends up online, I will forever be associated with [redacted].

MOM: I'm sure terrorists have bigger concerns than whether or not you pray five times a day.

ME: But [redacted] hates people like me who aren't religious. They hate us even more than they hate "infidel" non-Muslims.

MOM: First of all, stop talking about [redacted]. Don't even mention that name.

ME: See?! You're worried, too!

MOM: I'm not worried.

ME: But you just said don't say the name of . . . that group . . . who "Shall Not Be Named."

MOM: *(getting impatient)* I'm saying it's not productive to mention them. Why even talk about them? Just stay away from it. And stop being so paranoid. Are you still taking your Lexapro?

ME: Stuff like this is all over the news! Look what happened to Salman Rushdie.

MOM: You're comparing yourself to Salman Rushdie now?!

ME: I'm just saying Salman Rushdie has a lifelong fatwa[2] on his head and he has to go into hiding.

MOM: That didn't prevent him from getting married. To that beautiful lady from Top Chef.

ME: Padma Lakshmi?

MOM: Your father likes her. But not as much as he likes Catherine Zeta-Jones.

---

2 This is a ruling on a point of Islamic law given by a recognized authority. In this case, it sentenced Salman Rushdie to death (though fatwas are more than that).

ME: Well, he's not married anymore. Salman Rushdie. To Padma at least.

MOM: What?

I hear Mom tapping on a keyboard.

ME: What are you doing?

MOM: Googling Salman Rushdie . . . . He's been married four times! Four marriages! Wow.

I brace myself for what I know is about to come.

MOM: So Salman Rushdie has a fatwa on his head and has been married four times. You have no fatwa on your head.

ME: *(resigned)* Mom . . .

MOM: I'm just saying. If you're going to compare yourself to Salman Rushdie, you have to do it fully. When are you going to be married? *(A beat.)* Ayser, can I ask you something?

ME: (*deep inhale*) . . . Mom. I'm not a lesbian.

MOM: I'm just saying it's okay. Your father and I have discussed it and have decided we will accept you.

ME: Thanks, Mom. But I'm not gay. Though now I really wish I were.

MOM: It doesn't make sense that you're still single. What went wrong? I think it's because you have cats.

ME: Seriously, Mom!?

MOM: I'm not saying get rid of them. Just get a dog, too. You can meet so many men while walking your dog in the park.

ME: Great, another thing to piss off [redacted] . . . !

MOM: Why would your dog piss off [redacted]??

ME: Because strict Muslims think dogs are dirty.

MOM: Ayser, [redacted] aren't considered Muslim. They're terrorists. And can we please stop talking about them?

ME: Good point. Okay, Mom. I'll consider a dog.

MOM: You're just being polite. Anyway, if you have a fatwa on your head, then you will have something in common with Salman Rushdie. *(She taps on the computer.)* Oh, he has been knighted; he's a Sir now. Well, if he's single . . .

ME: Mom! I'm not gonna marry Salman Rushdie.

She suddenly starts laughing.

MOM: Yeah. You would be Mrs. Ayser Salman Rushdie. That would be too confusing!

This sends us both into peals of laughter.

And that's how I realized I will never have a future with Salman Rushdie.

36

Broken Engagement, a.k.a. Muslim Divorce

A few[1] years ago, with my fortieth birthday approaching faster than I wanted it to, I got engaged. I was engaged for a couple of years more—and then I wasn't. It was a civil breakup, and I'm still friends with my once-betrothed.

Okay, I'm sorry. When I say *engaged*, I'm leaving out part of the story. John and I actually performed a ceremony known in the Muslim faith as the *Katb-Al-Kitab*, which essentially means you're married in the faith but not in the eyes of the law. So, to an Arab, I'm considered to have actually been married; but to a Westerner, I was only ever engaged. For the purposes of this book, let's say I was engaged.

Okay, *okay*; I'm sorry. I've also just left out a whole entire chunk of story. The main premise of this book has been how I found myself caught between two cultures and how I flailed around trying to navigate life and ultimately settle down with a guy. So now that I finally (sort of) did, I can't gloss over the details, can I?

John was unlike anyone I'd ever met before. He was smart, sensitive, and searingly funny—to this day, I still laugh heartily remembering things he'd said more than ten years ago.

1 . . . fine, "Many."

He introduced me to interests I thought I hated—baseball, golf, and cats. I still can't grasp the first one, but I've come to appreciate it as an intellectual numbers game of sorts. While I'd previously thought of golf as a boring and pedantic sport, once John took me out on the driving range, I realized how wrong I was. I discovered I had good form, and hitting balls was a great way to relieve stress. I felt a zen feeling of calm on the range. I was hooked. I took lessons, and John bought me golf clubs.

And cats? This last one I never saw coming. I was a lifelong dog person with scant regard for any feline creature, especially kittens—until I wasn't. I fell in love immediately.[2]

These characteristics and a multitude of others made me fall for John. Unfortunately, after a while, we found we were better off as friends. There really wasn't any drama . . . okay, I mean obviously there was just enough drama for our relationship to not work out, but not too much that would cause future animosity. Miraculously, we're still friends, and John still plays a part in my life, sharing custody of our two cats, whom he visits when I'm out of town. You might say the true testament of a friendship is whether you can get engaged, then dis-engaged, and *still like each other.*

Ironically, our breakup was the calm before the storm. Two months after we split, the drama really began in my brain. I dove headfirst into a black hole of analyzing and categorizing every single mistake I'd made previously in my life, according to severity.

My failed engagement is not number one on the list. It's more like the tenth. It ranks behind the time I was thirteen and gave myself a home perm. I ended up looking like John Oates of Hall & Oates, minus the mustache (. . . barely).

Or the time I was eighteen and got pulled over by an unmarked cop car. He made me get into his car, and I, idiotically, complied. After studying my license and inquiring whether I really was 120 pounds, he let me off with a warning. This was shortly after the movie *The Silence*

2 With the cats. But also with John, way before that.

of the Lambs was released, and, according to my friend, the only reason this "cop" set me free was because I wasn't his body type.

My failed engagement even ranks behind the time not too long ago when I chopped a watermelon while running the disposal and the knife slipped into the drain, breaking in half and popping back out, narrowly missing my face.

There's not much to talk about regarding my broken engagement, a.k.a. my Muslim divorce. But there is much to talk about *dating* after said broken engagement, a.k.a. my Muslim divorce. Especially since I'm an Arab woman.

First, let me say that at least the concept of dating, if you're newly divorced, is finally acceptable (ironically). Your family won't worry about your reputation anymore because, heck, you've already been married. As far as they're concerned, you've become an adult who can make your own choices.[3]

Not only is dating now acceptable, but your family also doesn't get in your business about it. There's no pressure to date because you've already "been there." According to Middle Eastern moms, at least someone wanted you *once*. It's a weird badge of honor. And when you find yourself back in the dating scene and coming home from a bad night out, nothing pulls you out of your blues more than getting out your wedding album and seeing how happy you once were, right?[4, 5] One woman I know still has her wedding picture up on her wall; she cropped out the groom and hung it up because her "makeup was so good that day; why waste it?"[6]

---

3 I know, it sounds very provincial. But it makes perfect sense if you use the cultural psychology I grew up with.

4 In my case, I have to be careful not to look past page three because the rest of the album is blank, and this will remind me that I never even *had* a wedding. Come to think of it, I should just get rid of that album . . .

5 And also, the answer to this question is "Of course not."

6 She even went so far as to Photoshop her wedding face onto future photos, and now all the photos of her on Facebook show that same dreamy expression, even the ones of her at her brother's graduation from law school.

But that's about where the benefits stop. Postengagement and post-marriage dating come with their own set of problems. First, no matter whose decision it was to leave the relationship, Middle Eastern moms always say it was the woman's. Some even throw "divorce parties" for their daughters, which are similar to engagement parties but different in that instead of lingerie, guests are asked to gift power tools so as not to encourage promiscuity in newly single women. The sentiment is: "now that these women no longer have a man around, they'll need to learn how to operate a drill."

Second, after you've decided to force yourself to get back out there, you tend to take more chances and select people who don't normally fit your type. The reasoning? You've already selected your type once, and that didn't work. Or, in my case, you've already selected your best friend whom you shouldn't have married in the first place, and so now you're going to choose that guy with the full-sleeve tattoo commemorating his defection from Jehovah's Witnesses.[7]

My full account with most of these men—and men in general—may not fit in this chapter. So, I'll save it for the next one.

7 And what a glorious tattoo that was! It was abstract and colorful, spanning from his shoulder to his forearm, and ending with an inspirational quote in Sanskrit. Ladies. Is there anything sexier than reading Sanskrit off a well-muscled forearm?

37

A Bunch of Lines about a Bunch of Guys

There I was, in my forties, staring down the next phase of my life. I realized I needed to put myself out there if I wanted to meet someone.

The thing is, I *hated* the concept of dating. All my past relationships had been with guys I'd either met in college or through work friends—you know, organically. Now, I was out of college, and all my work friends were coupled up and socialized as couples. Sure, I was proactive and signed myself up for classes to do things that interested me while attempting to meet guys, but the people I encountered in those situations were a mixed bag.[1] Really, the only option left was to "get out there and date" *(blech)*.

I hated everything about dating: the mindless small talk, the awkward hug vs. handshake issue at the end (and if you chose to hug whether you should do it with or without making boob contact), not to mention the preplanning: high-necked and sleeveless vs. low-cut, long-sleeved tops; hair up or worn down for flirtatious twirling; etc. It was too much to keep track of and excruciatingly stressful.

---

1 I did meet some very nice septuagenarians when I took a painting class at the community center, and none of them mentioned grandkids . . .

In fact, you might ask, "Does *anyone* really enjoy dating?" Well, many women I know do love the process of meeting new people and discovering shared interests. They love the thrill of finding out whether Joe the radiologist and kids' basketball coach could be *the one* or just another in a string of workshop relationships.[2] They enjoy dressing up and ordering a beet margarita with jalapeño foam[3] at the latest medical-supply-closet-turned-trendy-bar venue. And some are particularly skilled in the art of flirting, choosing the perfect moment to bend down and pick up a fallen pencil.[4] I wish I had that aptitude, but dating casually just isn't my thing. I prefer to get to know someone as a friend before I decide, from a safe distance, if feelings should get involved.[5]

My aversion to dating made me wonder. What was my problem with dating? What was I so afraid of? That I'd be on a first date and suddenly realize I didn't like the guy, and that I'd be forced to do something rude like flip the table over and run screaming out of the restaurant? Or was it that I'd fall for a guy who wouldn't like me back? If I'm being perfectly honest, it was pretty much the latter. Ultimately, if two people aren't right for each other, then they're not right for each other. But Arabs value pride and dignity above all else, especially the women. It is hard for us to accept rejection; *we* have to do the rejecting first.[6,7]

But there was another part of the equation for me. Even if it was clear to both of us that we were not a good match and we mutually

---

2 The relationships that don't last but that help you learn more about yourself.

3 A very LA thing.

4 My own career of flirtatiously picking up a pencil was cut short back in college after I ended up busting my forehead on the edge of a table on the way back up.

5 This also has a lot to do with my upbringing as a Muslim Arab woman. You'll remember that since I couldn't introduce Jason to my parents as my "date" or "boyfriend," I said instead, "Here's Jason, my *friend* from sociology class who has two master's degrees and is interested in learning more about the Holy Quran."

6 When my friend Hoda's husband turned to her in the delivery room after the birth of their first child and said he'd never loved her and didn't want to be married to her anymore, it was *she* who filed for divorce as soon as the staples were removed.

7 And now you're probably beginning to realize why there will likely never be peace in the Middle East . . .

called it quits, I still abandoned my tough veneer of the proud Arab woman and ended up pining—a lot. Arab girls aren't supposed to pine; they're the heartbreakers. But not so for me, and this is where I experienced a culture clash with my personality.

I've been in three committed, monogamous relationships in my life, each lasting at least five years. Well, four relationships if you count Charlie in high school. We had a lovely six months where we went to the Sadie Hawkins dance and senior prom and spent countless clandestine hours together on his dad's farm. But eventually, the secrecy got to be too much for Charlie, who realized he wanted a girlfriend he could actually drive around with in public.[8] After our breakup, my love for him lingered, and the dramatic teenager in me told myself I would never love again. But I counterbalanced my emotions with the image of the strong Arab woman my mother had raised me to be, and I vowed that I would be fine with being single *for the rest of my life.*[9]

Then I met Jeff. Jeff was the teaching assistant for my debate class at the University of Kentucky. He looked like Wolfgang Amadeus Mozart, or rather, the actor who played him in the movie *Amadeus*, Tom Hulce. We kept it professional until the semester ended. When he asked me out, I was intrigued, especially since my father had been my mother's professor in college. The symmetry appealed to me. But as this was essentially my first relationship, and I had no idea how to be in a relationship at the time, we broke up.[10, 11]

When I moved to California for film school, I fell in love for the first time.

I believed I would marry Tony. How could anyone not fall for a long-haired, ponytailed, sensitive guy who used e. e. cummings quotes in casual conversation or left poetry on your car windshield? We dated for five

---

8 And do more with than just kiss.

9 Just like my Aunt Reema, who happens to be a very important pediatrician in Dubai. She's single and totally happy.

10 It didn't help that my mother grilled him for hours on end about how he would measure up as my husband, even though marriage was nowhere near being a possibility.

11 It took me five years to "break up" with Jeff. It really only solidified when I moved away to California. I'm not proud of this.

years, navigating pressures from both sets of parents until the relationship ran its course and we mutually decided it was best not to continue.[12]

That breakup stung. I lost a lot of weight. You know that pit in your stomach that makes you not want to eat or drink anything—except for peppermint tea? It's a crappy feeling, though what takes the sting off is when you successfully manage to wear and pull off an old item of clothing you'd been holding onto just in case it ever fit again. With this breakup, I also began what would become a ritual of selecting my heartbreak anthem, the one song I'd play on an endless loop. Tony's was "Something's Always Wrong" by Toad the Wet Sprocket. I also took long walks on the beach, contemplating how sad it was that I would never love again . . . *AGAIN*.

Eventually, I healed, left behind the bad feelings and Toad the Wet Sprocket, and was able to look at ponytails again without feeling that despondent twinge in my gut. I moved on—and gained weight.

My third relationship ended in an engagement and Muslim marriage—and then a broken-off engagement and a Muslim divorce. As I've mentioned, John was unlike anyone I'd met before. We were best friends. He was wonderful with our beloved family dog, Lulu, who stayed by his side "off leash" during hikes, something she wouldn't do when she was with my mother or me. Dad loved talking to John, and Mom also thought he was very intelligent and a "nice boy."[13] And so we decided to make plans for the future.[14]

---

12 This may be off-topic, but right before we broke up, Tony pulled his hair into his trademark ponytail and cut it off. I wasn't sure if this was his way of starting anew or if he was mirroring Samson from the bible, who derived power from his hair. Tony saved his ponytail in a plastic bag and safekept it—for its power source, I assume. I'd like to point out that when Los Angeles experienced a big earthquake one day, Tony didn't even feel it, despite being located near the epicenter.

13 Especially because of how neatly he made his bed and folded his clothes instead of just crumpling and shoving them into a drawer or suitcase.

14 It's good to get married—at least once—if you're Arab, as I've mentioned. You could be pushing sixty, the ruler of a prominent democratic country, or the winner of a Nobel prize—but if you've *never* married, your Arab elders would congratulate you on your professional achievements, offer you some tea, and then ask, "When will you be married?" For Arab mothers, it's far better to have loved and lost love rather than to never have loved at all.

Soon, John and I realized we weren't happy and didn't want to be together just because it looked good.[15] We split, remaining friends and maintaining joint custody of Bug and Cobby, our two cats. Because this breakup was so lacking in drama, I actually *gained* weight immediately instead of losing it. WTF? And there was no corresponding soundtrack.

Shortly after this breakup, my friends came forward with advice. It was like they had been hiding behind furniture in a dark room before jumping out and startling the guest of honor at her surprise party. I received a lot of opinions. Some solicited. Some not. Stuff like:

"You need to get back out there."

"You're amazing, and the right guy will find you."

"Maybe if you showed more cleavage. Men like breasts. I'm gay, and even I like boobies."

And after months of "window shopping" on Shopbop while watching *The Voice*, I slowly put myself back out there, allowing myself to be set up through friends, flirting at parties, and hanging out with my gay best friend, hoping he would realize how irresistible I was and fall in love with me . . . at least temporarily.[16]

Despite my dislike for casual dating, I found there were some things I appreciated about it. I realized it was more than searching for and finding your soul mate. It was also about your own personal growth and enrichment. Whereas previously I'd played it safe, I now began trying new things, such as:

- Riding on the back of a motorcycle several times (the last time was on the freeway; don't tell my mother)
- Developing a love for grilled seitan I never knew I possessed
- Discovering that tattoos are beautiful works of art, especially when they cover a long, sinewy bicep

15 Today it's called *conscious uncoupling*, but back then it was called *we fucked up*.
16 Spoiler alert: it never happened.

- Realizing that a guy could look you in the eye and tell you you're the most captivating woman he's ever met but *still* never call you again
- Acknowledging that sometimes guys are noncommittal idiots (because there are also a lot of asshole women in Los Angeles)

Under the excuse of trying something new, I decided I was going to *not* worry about protecting my heart, and instead go for the experience. I'd already gone through the whole process of getting to know a guy slowly and dating with the goal of marriage in mind—not once, not twice, but *three* times. And none of them had worked. Things had to change.

So this time, because I was too free-spirited, naive, or arrogant to guard my heart, I fell hard—not once, not twice, but a whopping three times.[17]

The first one, Dylan, I had no business being with.

Dylan was my friend and also ten years younger than I. He was a producer with a penchant for hot sauce. He would put it on everything, even ice cream.[18] Dylan liked to work out, loved musical theater, and was well groomed, which made a lot of people think he was gay. My gay friends always hit me up about him, and I'd tell them to back off because he was mine. Until one day, when he wasn't.

Dylan's actually a good guy, and really the only rotten thing he's done was tell me he absolutely didn't want to be in a relationship, only to announce three months later that he was engaged to a pretty redhead Pilates instructor named Taylor. But forget Dylan. This is actually about *me*, and about how I dealt with the end of the relationship. Here's an interesting thing that happens when you're no longer in your twenties or early thirties or even late thirties—life becomes less dramatic. Though I was sad about Dylan, I'm not sure I was really heartbroken. Can you be heartbroken when you know it was an experiment that

---

17 Gotta say, I dig the symmetry.

18 Which is actually quite delicious, as it turns out. Hurrah to trying new things!

didn't work out? Isn't heartbreak reserved for love? I patted myself on the back for reaching emotional maturity but grimaced at my waistline, which wasn't shrinking in spite of the fact that I was going through a breakup.

After Dylan, I spent nights alone posting photos of sunsets on Instagram and listening to a lot of melancholy music, stuff like Air Supply, The National, and the theme from *Schindler's List*.[19] And once again, my friends came forward with sage opinions:

"It happens when you're not looking."

"Maybe you should take a break for a while and work on yourself."

"Maybe you're showing too much cleavage. Try a halter top to show off your shoulders."

I knew my friends were concerned about me, but I also knew I was dug in and the only way *out* was to keep digging. If I took a break from dating now, I might never get back out there. So I pressed on, and I met Travis.

Travis was a setup by a friend. I had transitioned from dating a friend to dating a friend of a friend. Progress! Travis was a good ol' boy from Kentucky with the best manners I've seen outside of an episode of *Gunsmoke*. Of course, we bonded over our shared hometown—technically my third hometown, since the first one was a little further east. Technically it was his second one, too; his family actually hailed from Oklahoma and even had a road named after them that was featured in a lot of old Westerns.

Travis was muscular and buff, the opposite of what I usually go for—lean and lanky and often with that pale British look I loved.[20] We dated for three months before he chose to end it via text message. So much for Southern politeness. What's more annoying is I didn't get the message for twelve hours because I had gone to the Apple store to get

19 I hope I don't offend anyone with that last one, but I can't help that it's such an emotionally affecting score.

20 Karen says it's my subconscious desire to be occupied by the Brits, just as Iraq was occupied by them in the 1920s.

a new phone. The first text I received was: "Um we need to talk . . . ," followed by how he thought of me as a "dear friend" but wasn't "feeling it" in the romance department. A *DEAR FRIEND*!?!? I went back to the Apple store and asked for a different phone. There was clearly something wrong with this one because it was sending me weird messages from a guy whom I thought I was dating but who had just friendzoned me.

This heartbreak was less melancholy and a little more energetic—read: I was fucking pissed, mainly at myself. Had I misread the signs? Seen only what I wanted to see?

I felt like a failure and mentioned nothing to my mother. My confidence began to slip. I was 0-for-2. What was wrong with me? I had incredible insomnia and would be up before the sun. That meant sunrise pictures on Instagram. My musical choices got a little angrier, too—Nine Inch Nails, AC/DC . . . Taylor Swift.

When the anger subsided, I took the opposite extreme. No more friends or friends of friends. I was going to meet a complete stranger. I signed up for a couple of online dating sites and met a few guys. I googled each of them, and if we had even one friend in common on Facebook, they were off the list. I couldn't take any more chances of things not working out and having to have some reminder of them in my life.

Once again, the Greek chorus of my friends' advice rang in my ears:

"You're really brave to keep going out there like that."

"Thank God I'm not out there right now. Sounds like it sucks."

"Honey, let's take you shopping. That beige sweater makes you look like a lesbian."

Next, I met Christopher, a commercial photographer. He was of Italian and Native American descent, with a shaved head and the most beautiful nose I'd ever seen—a perfect ski slope. He wrote poetry but had a biting sarcasm about him that kept me on my toes. Christopher shot print ads for fancy car companies and expensive industrial sinks, and whenever we went anywhere, he liked to point out if he spotted one of the sinks he'd shot. One time at Griffith Park Observatory, we spent fifteen minutes analyzing a sink outside of the public restrooms. I guess that's longer than the preferred lingering time, because a security guard approached us. I look especially swarthy in fluorescent light. The guard was just doing his job.

This relationship ended after I accidentally caught Christopher with his tongue in another guy's mouth. In fairness, it was at a gay dance club, and how was he supposed to know that I would be there for "80s One-Hit-Wonder Night," too? It was pretty close to a mutual breakup. While I'm pretty confident I can compete with some of the hot young ladies in LA, I'm definitely not confident enough to compete with the hot young men.

We parted ways, and this time I had a healthier, more philosophical attitude about it. "Guess he wasn't fated to be my guy," I told my mother. To cope, I listened to Beck while hiking and posted those obligatory photos to Instagram. At least my relationship to music and the sun seemed to be evolving appropriately and healthily.

Then, a few months later, the circus came to town.

Actually, it didn't, but I've always wanted to use that phrase.[21] No, it was the band The Replacements that had come to town for a concert. There, I ran into my old friend Todd who had brought his friend along. I know I'd sworn off the friend circle, but look, it couldn't be helped.

At first glance, Alex seemed like an average nice guy. During the concert, he performed lovely gestures like gently steering me into an unobstructed view of the band and away from the idiot in front of me whose sole purpose seemed to be watching the show through the screen on his phone and alternating between that and checking Facebook, presumably for other camera phone–filtered views of Paul Westerberg singing. As I listened to the stories Todd told of growing up together with Alex and how Alex used to defend him when they got into fights, I'm not saying I fell in love right then and there, but . . . Oh! Alex had

21 Though it wouldn't be out of the realm of reality for me to run away with a guy from the circus at this point.

shoulder-length hair that smelled like Clairol Herbal Essences shampoo, one of my favorite shampoo scents. At one point during the show, it got hot, so he pulled his hair up and out of his face into a ponytail, which then became a *MAN. BUN.*

Would you blame me for my absolute aversion to man buns, the accessory of so many (hipster) men? Whenever I see one, my reaction is akin to when a dog sees another dog threatening his master. First, the low growl; and then if the other dog gets too close, it becomes a full-blown bark. My reaction is visceral. The only people allowed to have man buns are the singers Gavin Rossdale and Hozier, as well as people of the Sikh faith.

But right then, as I watched Alex put his hair up, I felt something. Not aversion. Not disgust. Not even mild tolerance. I actually liked the look on him. This is when you'll say I accepted the bun because I liked the guy.

Fine, I liked the guy enough to like the man bun, okay?![22]

Since I'd met Alex "when I wasn't looking," I took it as a sign from the universe that he could be The One. I even professed my love to Alex, so sure was I that it was meant to be. The complication was that Alex was in the off-again part of the relationship at the time that, eventually, would soon become fully on-again. Big. Fat. Drag. Once again, I lamented my luck. Seriously, universe? Why did you send this guy my way if it wasn't meant to be?

After pouting about it for ~~days, weeks, months,~~ a year, I finally accepted the relationship for what it was, a deep connection with someone else when I'd needed it most. I decided that falling in love can take on different forms. I could say I truly loved Alex in a way that transcended romantic love. It was a real friendship with someone who I knew had my back.

---

22 I have a confession to make. Alex didn't actually pull his hair into a man bun the night of the concert; I wrote it that way for dramatic effect. But he does wear it that way when he works out, which is actually the only acceptable way for a man to wear one.

Throughout my dating adventures, I discovered a pattern: the more guys I met, the less quickly I fell in love with each one. And the easier it was to let go. You know how they say baby rattlesnakes are more lethal because they can't control their venom? Well, maybe I was finally growing up to be an adult rattlesnake in control of its heart and emotions.

Soon, I decided it was time to get out of the dating world for a while. I was running out of interesting angles from which to capture a sunset from my rooftop, my iPod selection needed updating, and I got tired of buying extra toothbrushes.

I was just glad for the friends I'd made.

38

None of My Exes Live in Texas

Sometimes your Significant Other loses that title but still remains an important person in your life. I've always believed that just because one aspect of a relationship with someone ends, it doesn't mean you should cut that person out completely. After all, most likely you were attracted by aspects of their personality that could continue to fuel a friendship even if the romantic dynamic is gone.

I'm a minority in having this perspective. Many friends assume I'm still carrying a torch for my exes or keeping them around in case I want to get back together in the future. The truth is, they are just friends who *happen* to be exes.

But of course, in order for our new dynamic to work, there are rules:

1. There must be at least one year of no contact between you to avoid any crossover feelings.
2. It helps if your ex is coupled up with someone else so that even if you have crossover feelings, you won't be able to do anything about it.
3. It's best to not attempt any of this while you're in your twenties because, if you're anything like me, you may still be too emotionally immature to handle the complexity of an

ex-turned-friend relationship, i.e., assuming he is just being nice to you because he's like a brother when really he's lonely and wants to get back together.

4. You have to be very transparent with your current partner and make sure they are comfortable with you being in contact with your ex.

When Tony and I broke up, we immediately shifted into being friends. I blame it on that young arrogance that makes you think you can conquer anything—and also on my misdirected rebellious Arab streak[1] that often manifests at the wrong time. If something is off-limits, I become overly fascinated with it, which has caused me much heartbreak. So even though I knew I had to keep some distance between us for a while, arrogantly I decided to throw rule number one into the trash. "I can't get hurt by him again. It's not possible."

Ha-frickin'-ha!

It took me being in a relationship with John to realize that my friendship with Tony was wrong because we hadn't carved out the necessary distance and boundaries. It caused confusion, and eventually I had to cut him out of my life, even though that meant I was basically cutting off a part of myself. Tony and I didn't speak for about ten years. The first few years, I nursed feelings of guilt and often felt the need to call him and apologize for something. But I forced myself to let it go. Tony left town, which is honestly my favorite way to fully get over an ex and heal. When we reconnected three years ago through mutual LMU friends, so much time and distance had been put between us that none of it mattered and we revived a healthy friendship.[2] And it was much easier to stay friends with John—we abided by the rules and shared our cats, keeping up a system of vet visits, pickups and drop-offs, and sharing cat stories.

---

1 Okay, fine, it's not specific just to Arabs. Maybe it's just an "Ayser streak."

2 Signs of a healthy friendship: letting him crash on my couch when his house was being flea-bombed.

My mother didn't understand all this at the time. She still nursed a lot of anger over the breakup—anger at John for walking away from our relationship, anger at me for not being angrier at him, and anger at our cats because maybe if they had gone outside and walked on a leash like dogs, none of this would have happened.[3] Dad, a very emotional soul, told me he didn't even want to hear his name. Their concern was extremely sweet but also slightly annoying, as *I* was the one who had just gone through a relationship—and I was fine with being out of it.

Yes, I was fine. Fine with the breakup, fine when John got remarried. I had gone through enough analysis, self- and therapist-aided, to conclude that I was okay. Gradually, the people close to me came around and began to understand. Soon after, when I was buying my first home, John, having gone through the same process with his wife, was instrumental to my purchase, more so than my realtor or my parents. Whenever I brought up my realtor's advice with my parents, Mom would nod and say distractedly, "That's fine, but what does *John* think?" Which was most comforting to me.

I've got to say, as a woman in my forties, I still seek my mom's approval. It's the Arab in me.

---

3 This one I don't quite understand, but *you* try reasoning with an angry Arab mother.

39

"You Can't Blame Everything on Your Period; Sometimes You're Going to Be a Crazy Bitch" and Other Advice from Mom

My mom is a bit of a badass.[1] She is direct, vocal, and strangely specific about her rules—like when we lived in Saudi Arabia and I wasn't allowed to visit my friends who lived in stand-alone villas out in the desert but was allowed to visit those in large apartment buildings. Her reasoning was that if a fire broke out, it would presumably be harder for the fire department to reach the remote villa than it would the apartment building in the city. This made no sense to me back then, but if you've learned anything from this book, it's to never to cross my mother's inner Medusa lest you be turned to stone.[2]

1 Don't let me grousing and complaining about her in the earlier chapters of this book convince you otherwise.

2 It was Medusa's frightful appearance that turned the men who looked at her to stone; but my mother was, and still is, a beautiful woman.

Whether my mother likes it or not, she's the expert in our household on all things medical, despite the fact that Dad was her professor in college and has a slightly higher degree. Mom took a break after her master's when my brother was born but returned to school and got her PhD in Pharmacy (PharmD) in the early nineties. In fact, we were both at the University of Kentucky at the same time, which was very cool. I'm really proud of her for doing that.

If I ever want a clear and concise answer about a medical issue, I go to Mom instead of Dad, mainly because he meanders when he explains anything.[3] If I call and ask Dad whether he enjoyed the dolma I made and left in the oven, he'll extol the benefits of eating said dolma with yogurt because it aids digestion, and I'll have to ask several follow-up questions in order to find out whether he in fact enjoyed the dolma. On the other hand, Mom gets to the point quickly and stands by her opinions with conviction. Which means she is the best person to call for advice, especially during a recent life transition when I had a question about wonky menstrual cycles.

I called her just before I was preparing to visit my parents in Austin.

ME: Mom, I have to tell you something.

MOM: (*in Arabic*) Oh Lord, hopefully something good.

ME: Yeah, it's not bad—I have been having more mood swings than usual.

MOM: Is it about time for your cycle? If you're on your period, don't come. I can't handle the stress of fighting with you.

ME: (*fighting the urge to say "Love you too, Mom"*) . . . no, I just had it last week.

MOM: Good! Your skin will be looking dewy and healthy. It's good because Qasim's wife is having a dinner party for all the Iraqis. And they want to meet you.

3 Not unlike me, as it turns out.

ME: Okay, Mom. But listen, I'm having mood swings—and also hot flashes.

MOM: You're taking too much thyroid medication. When was the last time you had your blood levels checked?

ME: My thyroid is fine. It's my estrogen, and my cycles are—

MOM: You know, sometimes it's not our periods. Sometimes we just act crazy. Like me, sometimes I can be a real bitch . . . I think it's when I take too much Benadryl. I'm so glad you didn't inherit bad allergies from me. You took after your father in that regard, though you got his deviated septum—

ME: MOM, IT'S NOT MY THYROID!

MOM: Stop yelling, Ayser. You're definitely taking too much thyroid medication. It's making you aggressive.

ME: Mom! Listen to me!

MOM: (*exasperated*) Spit it out then!

ME: *(deep exhale)* I went to the doctor, and she told me I'm in perimenopause.

MOM: No.

ME: What do you mean, "No"?

MOM: I'm too young to have a daughter in menopause.

ME: I didn't say menopause, I said "peri," which is even before premenopause. I guess it's like a warning that menopause is near.

MOM: Okay, stop saying menopause. If you keep saying menopause, it's going to happen![4]

---

4 Maybe like an evil Beetlejuice or something.

ME: What's the big deal anyway? The only thing I'm worried about is becoming a dried-up prune, and they have lasers for that as it turns out, both top *and* bottom.

MOM: (*in Arabic*) Ayser, for shame! And I hope you don't post this stuff on Facebook; you'll scare everyone away who wants to meet you.

ME: If they can't handle the real me, then they're not worth it.

MOM: I wish I taught you how to attract a man. I was so focused on making you a strong-minded individual. I went too far. It's my fault.

ME: *(talking over her)* Mom. Mom. Mom!

MOM: It's true! I made you too independent. Now you'll spend the rest of your life alone.

ME: Stop, Mom. We're not going through this again.

MOM: *(heavy sigh)* Okay, Ayser. I'm tired. What is it you want to tell me? That you're in menopause? You're too young. I was fifty when my first symptoms began. And usually daughters take after the mother in that regard—oh, you know what? It might be because you don't have kids.

ME: Really, Mom?! This again?

MOM: It's true. Anyway, you don't have any of this—check your thyroid levels, I'm sure you need to adjust your medication. You gained a bit of weight when I last saw you.

At this point, I've muted the phone and am screaming at the top of my lungs. It's a coping mechanism I've developed so I don't have to yell at my mother.

ME: (*Much calmer, but hoarse*) Mom, I checked the levels. Everything is fine.

MOM: They probably didn't do the in-depth testing. It has to be your thyroid.

ME: So, you're saying you'd rather I have a disease than the natural course of life, which is meno—

MOM: Stop saying it! Of course I don't want you to have a disease; what kind of monster would that make me? I am just saying if it's thyroid, it can be fixed.

ME: Well, medicine and technology can also help with this. Maybe we need to start talking about . . . the *M* word more to demystify it. Times have changed, and there's new technology. Look at all those beautiful actresses who have already gone through it—Julia Louis-Dreyfuss, even Angelina Jolie.

MOM: How about Julia Roberts? Do you think she's going through it?

ME: I don't know, but she looks pretty amazing.

MOM: *Pretty Lady* was on cable last week.

ME: You mean *Pretty Woman*?

MOM: That movie always reminds me of you when you were in college. How many times did you watch that over and over?

ME: I wanted hair like hers.

MOM: Okay, Habeebty, I have to go to Zumba now. Remember to bring layers when you come, the weather has been unpredictable this spring.

We hung up, with me feeling annoyed not to have an answer to my question.

But then I paused for a moment to reflect. Mom's reaction wasn't far from how many of us view the dreaded *M* word—women and men alike. I, too, am personally a little freaked out when I hear the horror stories of women going nuts, sweating their faces off, gaining a million pounds, and become raging bitches. But who's to say those horror stories will come true for me when I get there? Science and our lifestyles have changed. And we know more about menopause than ever before. Why couldn't I expect to take control of my own journey? Did I have to rely heavily on my mother for medical expertise? Why couldn't I be my own advocate?

So, I decided to do just that. As badass as my mother is and as crucial as her medical advice is to our family, I have to chart my own course, too. And I do it with love and in the hopes that phone calls with her will become much more rewarding.

What a wonderful evolution that would be.[5]

---

5 And, like any evolution, it will take a while . . .

40

Neurosis Is the Mother of Invention

People tell me I'd make a great mom. My own mother, especially—which is why she harps on me constantly to have a child. Mind you, I'm not one of those people who never wanted kids; in fact, I always thought I'd adopt.[1] One of my heroes, Diane Keaton, first adopted when she was fifty years old, and both mother and children are doing fine.[2] Though, as my friend Leslie is quick to point out, "If you had Diane's money, I'm sure it wouldn't be a problem. But in your current financial state, you might want to have a plan B."[3]

The point is, I have many of the traits commonly associated with motherhood—patience, compassion, leading by example, and, perhaps most important, always carrying a large bag that contains anything you could ever need in any situation. Need a Band-Aid? What size? I have it. Popped a button on your blouse? I got double-sided tape *and* safety pins. Sinus pressure? I have Sudafed—the real stuff you have to give

1 I have a recurring dream where I'm visiting a foreign country and I witness an explosion. The sole survivor is a young child of about five years old, and when we lock eyes, we know it's meant to be. . . . Okay, I admit I watch too many movies.

2 From what I've read. I don't know them personally.

3 Don't you just love my friends?

your driver's license for, not that silly stuff your six-year-old can pick up in the aisle by herself.[4]

But don't think for a minute that I'm bragging about my maternal instincts. It's only because I've had so many issues that I've had to figure out how to work around or overcome them with these life hacks. In short—I'm a neurotic. And as any neurotic knows, we spend time thinking about the stuff nonneurotics don't.

I'm not talking about large-scale things like the zombie apocalypse or a structure fire or how the universe will expand and one day break apart.[5] My worries are usually inwardly focused, such as "How career-damaging is it when on my first day at a job a guy walked by my office to introduce himself and I asked, 'And what do *you* do here?' only to find out he owned the company?"

These issues accumulate and leave me little time to worry about "realer" things, like watching the safety demonstration on a plane (I promptly fall asleep). But when it comes to the tiny minutiae of *me*, or anything about my person, you can bet I've spent time analyzing them to death and figuring out a way to solve them.

Forget the phrase "Necessity is the mother of invention." My motto is "*Neurosis* is the mother of invention."

Because of all the time I've spent trying to fix what's wrong instead of just letting it be, I feel I'm well equipped to offer some how-to advice, Dear Reader.

Disclaimer: this chapter contains issues of a sensitive nature that Arab girls aren't supposed to talk about, such as pit stains, nip slips, and alternate uses for tampons.

"Headlights."

Not actually a nip slip since no actual skin is exposed, a headlight is still embarrassing and attracts unwanted attention, especially when you're

4 Unless they're placed high up on the shelves.

5 See: *Annie Hall*.

in eighth grade. I'm talking about the problem most young women had before padded T-shirt bras were invented—it resulted from the combination of a too-thin bra under a cotton shirt in a cold classroom. And even though you might be in an all-girls school in Saudi Arabia, an educational institution is still no place for "Wet T-Shirt Night" at Bobo's Tavern.[6]

Here's how you can take matters into your own hands, so to speak: soft double-ply toilet paper folded into small squares should take care of any headlights in the case of a padded bra malfunction. Just be careful that they don't look like you've got lumpy beanbags in your shirt.

Perspiration.

If you grew up in the seventies and eighties, you may remember the deodorant commercial that warned, "Never let 'em see you sweat." It stressed me out. I desperately wanted to *never let them see me sweat.* Up until I turned thirty-two and discovered clinical-strength deodorant, I couldn't figure out how not to sweat. As an Arab, I often use my hands to talk, producing large, sweeping gestures that may reveal a giant circle of sweat pooling under my armpits. If you're like me, you might find this so embarrassing that you stop engaging in philosophical debates in college—because you literally can't communicate without using your hands to talk. During the winters, I kept my coat on indoors to mask any dampness, but the problem was I got overheated, which caused sweat to bead up above my brow and frizz out my hair—another major issue among Middle Eastern girls.

I can tell you that I missed out on some fantastic college conversations with affable young men. Stupid sweat glands. I tried using dress shields, but I was always sweating through the adhesive, and the shields would end up migrating. For a while, I had the bright idea of folding a paper towel in half lengthwise and tucking it under my arm, held in place by my sleeve. As long as I didn't gesture too much, I was high and

6 A fictional place. Any comparison to a real venue is coincidental.

dry! I congratulated myself on being a genius . . . until the one time I wore loose-fitting sleeves. I'd found myself engaging one-on-one with the hottest guy in the poli-sci circle on campus. We were so in sync and connecting so well that I swear I heard wedding bells. But then I made a gesture and felt something slip. I looked down and didn't notice anything awry, so I continued, gesturing animatedly. That's when Hot Guy started chuckling. I looked down and discovered the paper towel rising from my cleavage like some great white shark's fin. My almost-future husband commented on my great comic timing, which in hindsight was a compliment, but at the time I wanted nothing more than to be taken seriously. I excused myself and never saw him again.

More "in a pinch" ideas you can thank my neurosis for:

- Tampons placed in shoes can relieve the pain of pointy or tight shoes—just please make sure you use dry, unused ones.
- Sanitary pads are good clothes defuzzers. See above caveat.
- Sharpies are not advised to be used to cover gray hairs, mainly for the carcinogenic aspects. Hats are better.
- If you need to quickly polish your black shoes while you're rushing out the door and accidentally stain your beige carpet, then try to remove the stain with bleach, thus causing a big white blotch—don't fret! Black coffee poured directly on the white blotch will camouflage it enough that you get your deposit back when it's time to move out of your apartment.
- It's never a good idea to give your shirt a "quick press with the iron" while you're wearing it—even if you turn the iron on the lowest setting. Take off your shirt instead.
- The third time will *not* be the charm when you attempt this same thing thinking you've got it down this time.
- If you find a roach in your floor fan, there's no reason to throw the entire fan in the garbage, since "cockroach juju" is probably not a real thing.

- A tiny lemon rind makes an excellent earring back—and you also have garnish for salad. (Just kidding about that last part; that's gross.)
- Used coffee grounds work as an amazing and invigorating (albeit messy) body scrub.

On second thought, with the exception of the last item, consider this a how-*not*-to list, courtesy of my previous mistakes.

Happy to do a public service.

41

A Conversation with God (When You're Sick as Hell)

We've all done it. Woken up in the middle of the night sick with the worst headache or stomachache or hangover and made desperate bargains with God about how we'll promise to change our ways if He just takes the pain away.

Typically, I'm not like the people who prefer to find God during a crisis. In fact, I spent a lot of time talking to Him when I was younger, usually during my prayers: "Dear God, protect Mom, Dad, Brother, and Sister. Let me do well on my history test, and let Robbie like me and want to do paint-by-numbers together."

When my family moved to Saudi Arabia, I learned to do proper Muslim prayers, complete with the ceremonial ablutions,[1] and I enjoyed my daily talks with God. As I got older, and particularly after we left Saudi Arabia and moved back to Kentucky, it became harder to pray five times a day, and I tried at least to do it in the morning. I'm not proud of how lax I got, but the truth is, life got busy. And like any relationship, if you don't work at it, it slips away.

I still continue to have my chats with God; it's just that the platform has evolved, becoming more spiritual and less ritualistic. I've often

1 The ceremonial act of washing parts of the body before prayer.

found my connection to Him when I've been out in nature, for example, witnessing a gorgeous sunset over the bluffs of Palos Verdes, California. Other times, it's been in an amazing piece of music.[2] Sometimes I'd get both together and *kapow!* It would be sublime.

But of course, I've also had my fair share of moments of pleading with Him when I've been so sick I felt as if I were about to die.

So, there I was one night, kneeling over the toilet. I had been jolted out of a deep sleep an hour earlier by the most hellish migraine of my life. Nausea. Vertigo. All forms of hell. And now, forty-five minutes into that tortuously slow descent to death, I realized the bittersweet hilarity of the situation:

"I'm holding my own hair out of my face as I'm throwing up."

I said this out loud to no one and laughed and cried hysterically from the absurdity. Then I started laughing and crying about the fact that I'd had enough composure to find the situation hilarious in spite of the fact that I was clearly dying. Then one of my cats wandered in—possibly having heard me talking out loud—and I started thinking about how cats were terrible in situations like these because they didn't have thumbs to help me hold back my hair. And then I got scared and thought, *Maybe I'm already dead.* If these weren't afterlife thoughts, they were clearly ones of delirium, which is often the stage before you flatline.

Either way, I needed to consume something quick. I dragged myself to the kitchen to look for some cola and crackers to calm my queasy stomach but quickly discovered I had neither in my pantry because I'd recently adopted a no-sugar, no-carb diet. I cursed myself and my idiotic California lifestyle and shook some sea salt into my hand and swallowed it. It helped.

As the high of my purge wore off, I started feeling crappy again, so I drank some water and got back in bed. As I lay there, I realized I hadn't

---

2 To any young Muslims reading this, don't let anyone tell you that it's blasphemous to find God in music. The Holy Quran is often recited in a melodious voice, resembling singing. Just make sure you don't find yourself dancing to this.

properly prayed in a long time. I figured it was the right time to reconnect with the Guy Upstairs. It had been a while, and I had a lot on my mind.

1. Dear God, it's been a while, and I have a lot on my mind. I hadn't intended on this being our first encounter back. I'm sorry for my current state.
2. Please, God, don't let me die alone.
3. If you let me live, I won't mess around with ironic Halloween costumes (like Male Hipster Douchebag, especially when the mustache makes me look like Saddam Hussein).
4. I won't leave the house in a baseball cap, yoga pants, or shapeless jeans.
5. God, if you let me live, I will start actively looking for someone to settle down with.
6. I will make eye contact with the businessman at the gas station.
7. I will go where the men are.
8. Where do the men hang out these days?
9. Should I start going to the Mosque?
10. I'm going to start going to the Mosque.
11. What am I thinking? You can't meet men in the Mosque. Sorry, God, it's this migraine.
12. Should I join a softball league?
13. . . . I don't like playing softball.
14. Maybe a pottery-making class.
15. Do straight men make pottery?
16. My girlfriends are great about connecting me with dudes. Perhaps my lazy male friends need to step it up. They're the ones with more dudes as friends.
17. Or my gay friends. Do they have straight male friends?
18. Am I hanging out with my gay friends too much?
19. Karen says I should stop hanging out with my gay friends. I'm going to listen to her.
20. But my gay friends are awesome.

21. God, I'm worried I won't find anyone anytime soon.
22. How the fuck have I not met anyone yet?
23. Am I putting out a vibe that says, "I don't want to meet anyone"?
24. I will ask Karen for a reality check about the vibe I've been putting out.
25. Maybe I should call Mom and ask her.
26. Scratch that. That's a horrible idea.
27. However, I will listen to her and stop wearing gray and black.
28. I will also wear more blush, like she wants me to.
29. Maybe even get my eyebrows done.
30. I'll get back on the online dating sites.
31. This time, I won't be funny in my profile. I will be serious and mysterious.
32. I won't click on anyone whose profile picture features a bicep tattoo.
33. I won't click on anyone whose profile picture shows him playing guitar on stage or holding a microphone (unless he's doing a TED talk).

By the time I got to this point, I was feeling relaxed, mainly because my migraine meds were finally kicking in. And I realized the crux of it—I needed someone in my life to hold my hair as I threw up.[3]

I had stepped out of the dating scene about a year prior, aware I needed a break to take care of myself. Clearly, now it seemed my priorities had reorganized. It was time to refocus my attention.

I fell asleep, happy in the knowledge that, beginning tomorrow, my life was about to change.

---

3 Okay, I'm not being completely literal. But what you *do* want is to have a guy in the other room, located a safe distance away, waiting for you to emerge so he can present you with a bowl of soup. Like that scene in *Sex and the City* when the strong, independent Samantha gets sick with the flu and realizes how nice it would be to have a man around to bring her liquids.

42
Love & the Search for Meaning in the Universe, Pt. 1 (The Wrong Kind of Saddle)

When I woke up the next morning, I was still loopy from the drugs but also psyched that I knew exactly what I had to do: not only to jump-start my love life, but also to steer it into that two-car garage next to a white-picket-fenced-in home. The previous night's conversation with God was justification enough; it'd brought about the sudden realization that I was ready—to be coupled up, to find a nice guy, to find *THE ONE*.

There were just too many benefits to being coupled up. In addition to having someone hold your hair up while you puked, you also had someone to make you food, buy you tissues, and scoop out the cat litter box. Other benefits of having a boyfriend/husband/domestic partner:

- You have a standing date for holidays, as well as any revival Loverboy concerts.
- You have a built-in excuse for when someone asks you to do something or make a commitment: you can use the whole "I have to check with my other half" thing.[1]

1 Note to single people: using your kids/parents/job works just as well.

- You can take advantage of two-for-one deals on plane tickets and sushi bars.

I made coffee, reloaded the dating apps on my phone, and sat down to update my information, thus launching "Dating Ayser 2.0: Back in the Saddle." It was a new, formidable me: smart, serious, ready for a long-term relationship. I was out of my experimental phase of dating and now looking for something real. I repeated my mantra for swiping right:

No tattoos. No microphones. No guitars.

While we're at it, no photos of anyone in front of Machu Picchu.[2]

I swiped right several times, and if there was a match, I let them contact me. Sometimes, I would simply write, "hello."

While I made my move online, several more well-intentioned friends also set me up with guys they knew. And thus began Round Two.

TIM: Writer friend of a writer friend. Nice guy. Wanted to talk about writing and only writing, including the process of writing, such as where I best got my inspiration and what I ate to reward myself and . . . *snooooze.* Needless to say, this relationship wasn't going anywhere outside the writing room.

Because of Tim, my friends coined the name *boardroom* to refer to a guy who carries on ad nauseam about work.

CARL: Friend of a friend. Another setup. On paper, hilarious and adorable and charming; in person, he reminded me of that singing, dancing frog from the old Merrie Melodies cartoon who refused to perform once brought in front of the talent agent. Actually, to be perfectly honest, we *both* became that frog when we met face-to-face. Neither of us had anything to talk about. On one of our dates, we went to see a movie, so we only had forty-five minutes to engage with each other—and still, we couldn't do it!

2 The travel equivalent of "I like long walks on the beach."

Once, after a trip to Brazil, Carl gifted me with a fuzzy empanada coin purse.[3] It was such a sweet gesture that I gave him a third chance, but again there was no chemistry.

So, my friends coined the name *fuzzy empanada* for a guy who is great on paper, but not so in real life. I moved on.

BRAD: Met online. Direct and blunt, which was refreshing as I was tired of the wishy-washy dudes I'd encountered as of late. I should have known not to proceed when, after giving him my phone number and chatting with him for the first time, I asked him for his last name and he responded, "Do you want my social security number, too!?" This was a clear sign to not go through with meeting this individual, but I'm the queen of giving someone the benefit of the doubt. I sucked it up and went out with him.

At dinner, as I eagerly dug into the roasted brussels sprouts appetizer the restaurant was famous for, Brad announced he liked submissive women. Not thinking twice that this might refer to a sexual preference, I carried on with the date.[4] The restaurant was very loud, so I kept needing to lean in,[5] literally, in order to hear him. And I'm sorry to say he was not gifted in the sweet breath department. I held my spicy drink under my nostrils like a nosegay, which had the unfortunate effect of making me sneeze. I developed a sort of dance, swaying back out of range to avoid his breath whenever he said something,[6] and swinging forward when it was my turn to speak.

Once the date was over, we clapped hands in a half-shake-half-fist-bump sort of way and said good-bye. A small part of me still considered seeing him again—perhaps he'd had a bad night. Then I googled dom/sub relationships and froze in horror as I realized what I would be

3 That's not a euphemism.

4 Even if he meant *submissive* in terms of demeanor or personality, I should still have left. In fact, if that's what he'd meant, I should have run away, screaming.

5 Not in the Sheryl Sandberg way.

6 Mostly his opinions on how the movie *Fifty Shades of Grey* ruined dom/sub relationships forever.

getting into. Just as I was about to delete his phone number from my contacts, my phone pinged with a photo text. It was from him, showing a photo of a weird-looking leather strapped contraption and the message, "You're back IN the saddle, I HAVE a saddle . . ."

Suffice to say that was the end of that.

In honor of Brad, my friends coined the terms *nosegay* to refer to a guy who has unfortunate physical (or physiological) attributes that make him an unsuitable partner.[7]

MAX: Another online connection. The first time in my life I've been stood up on a date. Ever. I took it as a sign that I was finally taking chances in life and not playing it safe. Look, Ma, I got stood up! . . . And, not to play into stereotypes, but he was German,[8] and so I never saw *that* coming.[9]

I thereby declared Round Two of dating in my forties over. By now, I'd done it enough to know it wasn't for me. If it happened, it happened. I no longer wanted to go looking for it. As I drifted off to sleep, I noted how wonderful it was to be older, when you had the luxury of just not caring anymore.[10]

---

7 Before I continue, let me qualify that I realize my girlfriends and I might seem like assholes for objectifying these poor men who, I'm sure, are good catches for someone else out there. I guess it's one of the (few) perks of being a member of the weaker gender that lives in a systemic patriarchy—that we are allowed to engage in a little light bashing from time to time. Kids, don't do this at home.

8 Germans are often stereotyped as being punctual.

9 When my mother found out that her oldest, first-born baby was stood up, she called to tearfully tell me she couldn't sleep at the horrible thought. I told her that I'd made it so long in life without being stood up that it was practically a badge of honor.

10 Okay, the truth is I was later jolted awake by a horrible nightmare in which I wore a shapeless beige sweater and orthopedic shoes, and I had three inches of gray hair growing from the roots and four long chin hairs that literally popped up before my eyes. I woke up screaming and, even though it was one in the morning, got into my car and drove to the nearest all-night CVS to purchase two boxes of Clairol Nice 'N Easy, new tweezers, and Nair crème bleach for any stubborn mustache hairs. At home, I dyed my grays and plucked and bleached my facial hair to oblivion before falling back asleep.

43

Love & the Search for Meaning in the Universe, Pt. 2 (The Cockblock, or My Life as a Rom-Com[1])

The next morning, Alex, my almost-future-husband-turned-friend,[2] called me on my way to work. It was our morning tradition, as my drive usually occurred during the time he took his break at work. At this point, we had been friends for about a year and had settled into an easy-going buddyship. I recounted my dream and subsequent self-makeover as he listened empathetically.

The good thing about my friendship with Alex was that I could talk at length (and often did) while he listened without interrupting. This could have been attributed to his condition—he had a mild form of Asperger's that resulted in him not getting offended by many of the things I said. That morning, I was so sleep-deprived and grumpy I blurted out something that had been on my mind and on the lips of most of my well-intentioned friends:

---

1 I apologize for the excessive number of chapter titles. I would like to thank my publisher for allowing me this creative freedom.

2 See the earlier chapter, "A Bunch of Lines about a Bunch of Guys."

"I think you're cockblocking me."

Understandably, he was slightly taken aback. But, as usual, he took it in his stride.

"Ayser, no."

"But maybe me always engaging with you is preventing me from meeting the guy I'm supposed to be with."

"No."

"Don't you think we should at least consider it?"

"No."

Some quick context and history: I've always believed, as my friend Cristina once said, that you meet The One when you least expect it and that nothing will stand in the way of your meeting (so you might as well relax and enjoy the ride). I'd met Alex when I least expected it, at a concert when I hadn't made a fuss with my appearance, simply showed up with my hair pulled up askew, wearing jeans and boots, and exuding an air of contentment and relaxation. Alex told me he thought I was the most beautiful woman he'd ever seen, and I believed him, even though he decided to get back together with an old fling. But Alex and I found a way to stay in contact, finding our own way toward a genuine friendship. For my part, I liked coming up with my own rules—which often meant no rules. It stemmed from my experience with living in a dictatorship and straddling two worlds, often being forced to modify the traditions of one culture to fit another.

My relationship with Alex defied all labels. We had an undeniable connection, which began as an attraction but then transcended it. We were able to look past the romantic implications—I because of my cultural background of constantly being forced to reframe things from a moral perspective (i.e., *not being in love with a guy who had a girlfriend*), and he because of his being on the spectrum, which allowed him to see past societal norms (i.e., *seeing things purely and without subtext*).

Alex's condition meant he was able to keep his relationship with me in a box while he continued with his other life, and at first I was pissed off—but also hopeful. I'd seen enough screwball comedies to wonder if

I was the "quirky but adorable hurricane of a girl" who would bulldoze her way into his heart and make him realize he'd been wrong all this time. I'd seen enough romantic comedies to wonder, "Is Alex the one I've been waiting for?"[3]

Inevitably, people started asking how long Alex and I had been together. And I wondered why we weren't. To further confuse things, Alex was responsible for one of the most romantic gestures I've ever experienced from anyone.[4] I call it "The License Plate Thing." Two weeks after we met, Alex was at a toy store looking through vanity license plates, and he texted me to say he was sad that there were no AYSER plates. I texted back, "Haha, welcome to my life!" A few minutes later, he texted: "I fixed it!" followed by a photo of three license plates laid out together in a haphazard patch to spell out A Y-SER.

Alex's romantic gesture.

Come on! I was bowled over. Who wouldn't find that incredibly romantic? What was more magical was that a few months prior, I'd watched a romantic scene on a network show where the main guy did the exact same thing for a girl with an unusual name. I remember actually thinking, *What a sweet scene. I wish I'd written that, and I wish that it would happen to me.*

Well, *it was happening now.* I was living in a romantic comedy!

It didn't matter that he wasn't *my* guy. He was *a* guy who had made a lovely gesture, and I ate it up.

My friend Karen was less enthused—and also less direct.

It took her seven missed calls, five voicemails "just calling to check in," three picture texts involving a pit bull snuggling a panda bear, and

---

3 I'd also seen enough psychological thrillers to worry that I'd come home and find a boiled rabbit on my stovetop, the work of a jealous girlfriend.

4 Besides John's shiny new quarter as dowry—see Chapter 2, "My Trouble with Men."

one large, loud birthday gathering at a restaurant to finally tell me what was on her mind: "PLEASE DON'T FALL IN LOVE WITH A GUY WITH A GIRLFRIEND!"

At first, I chose to ignore her. In my mind, it wasn't about what would happen in the future; it was about *being in the moment*. For the first time in my life, I, Ayser Salman, daughter of an anxious, tradition-born Iraqi mother, was capable of living in the moment. It was something to be celebrated.

Or so I thought. When I was finally able to remove the fears and noise and—let's be honest—the love goggles, I uncovered the next layer: my inherent desire to live a rom-com life and my need for male attention, be it straight or gay.[5] I was so keen on redefining my romantic life that I put on blinders to anything or anyone who told me otherwise. Once I realized that Alex was merely giving me an outlet in which to put my feelings, that he was giving me the male attention I craved, I was finally able to demystify him. I stopped seeing him as a mysterious, long-haired musician and began seeing him as a regular guy—one with many faults. All at once, it was like a light switch going off, and the question of "Is he the one I've been waiting for but who just doesn't know it yet?"—which had long plagued me—disappeared and became moot.

I left the rom-com, the screwball comedy, and the thriller behind. I stopped turning to Alex as much as I had before. And even though I'd previously decided I was done with dating, I felt I had to put myself back out there again. This time, it was different. I wasn't so much running *toward* something; instead, I was running *from* something, mainly Alex.

And thus, I entered my third phase of dating.

5 I feel the need to emphasize how embarrassed I am to have ever felt this way.

44

Love & the Search for Meaning in the Universe, Pt. 3 (The Nice Guy in the Haystack)

When Dating, Round Three, began, Alex tried to coach me from the sidelines. By this point, I had become more careful and guarded regarding the things he had to say, and I listened to his theories on dating in Los Angeles with a grain of salt.

Alex believed that it was just hard to find love in Los Angeles. He firmly subscribed to the notion that anyone who came to this town had a degree of instability and was therefore unsuitable as a partner. I assume he didn't include himself among this group, because whenever I made a point to this effect, he changed the subject and talked about my tendency to view Los Angeles with overly rosy glasses.

Alex was not wrong about my love for Los Angeles. I've been here for twenty-five years, and I love this town, unabashedly. LA offers the right amount of diversity to this Kentucky-raised immigrant girl. There's also the near-constant sunshine and the fact that you can go for a hike in the Hollywood Hills at 2 p.m. and then drive down an hour south and catch a gorgeous sunset on the Palos Verdes cliff. Add to that the film industry, which attracts a certain kind of person: nonconservative, creative, offbeat—*my* people. To anyone who complains that this town is full of assholes, I tell them it's possible to live a douchebag-free (and traffic-free)[1] existence.

It's a different story when it comes to finding love in Los Angeles. There's a ton of noise around the topic, and I've never seen so many people have so many opinions about one subject as locals do about dating in Los Angeles. Even people who have never dated in LA have thoughts about it—usually negative. I can't say I agree. I had two of my most important and formidable relationships while living in LA, to which Karen points out, "Well, you're no longer with them." I respond, "Yeah, because I grew. And outgrew them. But that doesn't make me any less grateful that they came into my life."

Still, I was having a harder time meeting someone now than I did when I'd met both Tony and John. I attribute it to age. I'd had those relationships in my twenties, and by the time you reach your thirties and forties, you acquire baggage. With women, this can manifest in the "LA men are assholes" argument. It's not totally inaccurate, but it's also, in my opinion, an archaic way of thinking.

While I used to be more closed-off when I was younger, age has made me more of an open book. I care less about mores and social standards and generally feel it's easier to give someone the benefit of the doubt. Naive? I prefer to think of it as optimism or a desire to learn what makes people tick. I think it's easier to keep your guard down with new people than to put the walls up.[2] I come from a culture where meaning is sewn into everything; there is no meaninglessness. As a result, I'm

---

1 To avoid traffic in LA, make sure you don't go anywhere between the hours of 7:12 a.m. and 8:17 p.m., except for Sundays when you can safely wait until 10:16 a.m., but no longer if you don't want to lose your mind.

2 I do inquire whether someone is an ax-murderer when I first meet them, because, as a rule of thumb, ax murderers should divulge their intentions. It's part of their code of ethics.

constantly looking for the reasons behind my meeting someone and what that means to me.

In response to these thoughts, Alex sent me a couple of articles that basically detailed the fact that it's nearly impossible to find love in Los Angeles. One particular underlying theme in all the articles pissed me off. They seemed to give a pass to assholes by saying, "It's Los Angeles, what do you expect?"

I angrily called Alex. When he picked up, all he heard was my long, exasperated sigh.

"Let me guess, you didn't like the articles?" he ventured.

"OHBUTLETMETELLYOUWHY!" I sputtered.

I launched into a long rant. To me, this kind of mentality was no better than saying, "Boys will be boys," as a way to excuse inevitable douchebag behavior. The subtext behind this statement was that women were supposed to just deal with it and let it go. It was old-fashioned, sexist, and lazy. Further, for me, it called to mind a lot of the negative stereotypes that exist in my native culture. "It's different for girls" was always the rule of thumb, which I hated. Translation: the boys could do whatever they wanted, but the girls had to behave. The boys could screw around because it was in their DNA to do so, while the girls had to be ladies, because if they messed around they would be considered damaged goods and lose respect. Men had a stronger sex drive and should not be expected to "keep it in their pants," but apparently women did not have this same compelling need and so were expected to "keep their legs closed."

This kind of thinking is responsible for an individual's loss of standing within the community at its best, and honor killings at its worst. It's wrong, wrong, *wrong*. And I thought I'd left it behind when I left Saudi Arabia. You can imagine how annoying it was for me to come to Los Angeles, a city I consider the Mecca[3] of progressiveness, and hear this provincial view on dating.

3 See what I did there?

Alex listened patiently as I ranted for a good ~~ten minutes~~ hour—then he pointed out that his best buddy once worked at a gym where the personal trainers would bring condoms to work.

"Alex," I said, "are you trying to get me to admit that this city is shallow and shitty? Sure, there are aspects to it that are like that because of the industry. But from my point of view as an immigrant, it's the first place in America where I truly feel I belong. I want to believe in it."

I wasn't advocating that we chase after assholes to reprimand and teach them a lesson; I value my sanity and free time. I was just saying that we should *say* something if we witness unacceptable behavior. Instead of dismissing it, we should engage. Was that naive? I decided to embark on an investigation. I was already using dating as a distraction from Alex, but now I had a new mission: dating would be my experiment.

From the start, it seemed like the universe was testing me in light of my conversation with Alex.

PARKER: a quiet guy who invited me to camp out in his living room.[4] I thought we'd had a lovely time and so found it rather odd when he informed me he needed a few days to decide whether he would choose to continue dating me. Had I finally had my first asshole encounter?

I wasn't ready to hear Alex's monosyllabic judgmental response, so I didn't tell him about Parker until weeks later. And I certainly didn't tell Karen, who by now had taken to bringing up all her past mistakes as cautionary tales anytime I even mentioned a new guy.[5] I made peace with the fact that Parker filled my one-asshole-guy quota—I was only going to allow myself one—and I forgot him and moved on.

So when a few days later he texted "hello," presumably to announce the decision that he had "chosen" me, I told him with no emotion that

4 Not a euphemism—we actually sat in a tent and ate s'mores and drank hot cocoa and listened to Bad Company by nightlight.

5 If I have to hear about Joey Swintosky and his commitment issues one more time, I'm going to scream.

what he'd said was rude but that there were no hard feelings on my part and . . . "See ya." He texted again the next day to invite me to a rock concert. I didn't go. By the time he texted again to invite me to an art show, I figured the universe was trying to tell me something. At this point, a regular person might have slowly inched away or cut off all contact, but I didn't see it that way. All my life I've always felt I was missing out (you know, being at the wrong end of the table and all that), and I needed to find out for myself if I had merely misinterpreted the situation.[6]

At this point, Karen had unleashed such an avalanche of texts on me that I had to set her number to "Do Not Disturb." She told me to cut my losses, that nothing good could come out of this and that maybe he was a sociopath and that my head would wind up in his freezer. Whereas before I'd get a couple of panda videos before she launched into the blunt truth, now she began her texts with images of a skull and crossbones, a GIF of Jack Nicholson from *The Shining*, and a visual interpretation of an STD (they look like angry raspberries).

I wish I had some horrific story to tell you about Parker on our final date—but I don't. The biggest crime he committed was not talking. He went into a bit of a trance while we checked out the art. I thought the date was over, but when I bade him good-bye, he came out of his trance long enough to suggest dinner. I ended up sitting across from him at the table, watching him stare into his seafood risotto. When he suggested drinks afterward, I couldn't handle it; God forbid we would spend the hour studying the shrub in our craft cocktail. I was *out*.

At the end of the day, at least Parker had proved himself *not* to be the asshole I thought he was . . . just missing a key social filter. It's true that I love finding out what makes people tick—but they have to actually *tick*. I returned into the vast, murky waters of the dating ocean, this time with candidates my mother would approve of.

---

6 You'd think this restless trait of mine would have been better used if I had become a scientist or statistician to solve important social problems.

GARRETT: the divorced MBA from Pasadena with two teen kids, who owned his own company (and a boat!) and who actually picked up the phone and called me instead of sending emojis of wine glasses to announce his desire to have a glass of wine with me. And despite my well-intentioned friend Matt questioning whether I really should be dating a guy whose wardrobe seemed to be made up of only Tommy Bahama clothing (judging from his profile pictures), I found Garrett interesting.[7]

Unfortunately, he invited me out for a drink on a night when I'd already made plans with a girlfriend. I certainly wasn't going to bail on her for some guy I barely knew. He was gracious and said we'd meet up the following week when he got back into town . . . and I never heard from him again.

I'm pretty sure he drowned at sea. I observed a respectful moment of silence for him and then moved on to:

ARASH: an electrical engineer with a penchant for coffee and coffeemakers. Arash, who was Indian, was cultured and well traveled, and he had strong beautiful hands and a gorgeous head of long, wavy hair. In my humble opinion, he should have been a model, not spending his time nose-deep in circuits. Our budding relationship ended when, after the first date, I gave him a ride home but declined his offer to come inside for coffee. Suddenly, he desperately needed to get out of my car.[8]

I observed a respectful moment of silence for the cosmopolitan, cultured son-in-law my mother would never have and moved on.

EDDIE: a talented B-list actor ten years my senior who apologized profusely for the United States' part in fucking up my country as soon as he learned I was from Iraq. What appealed to me about him was he actually picked up the phone and called, but there was no spark, and

---

7 He had his own company, for goodness' sake.

8 Most likely to kick-start that modeling career I inspired him to pursue.

that was that. Still, he was super nice and respectful, and I'm glad to have met him. I still catch him on TV sometimes and have a newfound appreciation for his "gruff police chief" or "stern-but-kind high school teacher" roles.

DEV: a very nice Indian guy who got my sense of humor and made plans two weeks in advance, which was a rarity in a town where no one could commit to meeting even two hours in advance.

I observed a respectful moment of silence for our lack of chemistry; a cool guy otherwise.

TOM JONES: Yep, that's his real name. I liked to use his full name whenever I called or texted. We bonded over the fact that both of us are writers. An overall good egg. But, again, no spark.

MARK: a contractor who lived in Orange County and who had worked in Iraq. He disappeared after I told him that Orange County might as well be called Mosul for the amount of Iraqis who live there.

JIMMY: a very nice hypnotherapist-slash-actor-slash-bartender who thought the country of Kuwait was part of Iraq. And he didn't understand the difference between Afghanistan and Iran.

And those were just the guys who stood out.

Round Three was getting exhausting. My time was becoming too valuable to be wasted on experiments. I decided, again, to just stop. I had yet to settle into a new home I'd purchased two months prior. And more important, I had to finish this book.

I'd say that writing this book has been the most rewarding period of my life in a long time.

If not ever.

45

Tattoos and Other National Security Risks

In my early forties, I decided to get a tattoo to commemorate my life and what I've learned so far. Yes, I'm aware of the fact that this could be considered a midlife crisis desperation move, but let me remind you that I'm a late bloomer. I prefer to think of it more as finally being grounded enough in what I want that I'm ready to have something permanently marked up on my body.[1]

I knew I wanted my tat to be small and on the inside of my left wrist so I could refer to it readily. One option was the image of a small cute octopus, my spirit animal. Octopuses are intelligent and clever, and some would even call them shifty because they don't give a shit what you think; they just do their thing. Google that video where the octopus gets put into a jar, unscrews it from the inside, and then refuses to get out, and then tell me you don't agree. The other, perhaps more meaningful tattoo I considered was an Arabic inscription that would be written in my dad's handwriting. I considered using one of the short proverbs he's fond of or any other piece of work from his newfound calligraphy hobby.

1 Okay, I see how that sounds midlifey.

Dad recently retired (shortly before he turned eighty-nine) and spends his free time honing a few of the multitude of styles that exist in Arabic calligraphy, much to Mom's consternation. She wants him to go out and get some sunlight, but all he wants to do is sit and work. And he's really skilled.

So, I thought that tattoo idea would be a nice tribute to Dad . . . but my parents completely disagreed.

By now, you know that my parents have their own firm ideas and beliefs about the world that I can't do much to change. I had hoped they would outgrow some of their concerns and fears as they got into their senior years; as the saying goes, age mellows people out. Supposedly.[2]

Well, my folks are fond of saying, "It doesn't matter how old we get or how old you get; we are always going to worry about you because we're the parents and you are the child." Endearing, if not completely annoying. So, unsurprisingly, they were not on board with the tattoo idea when I brought it up during one of my visits. Specifically, they thought that inscribing Arabic words on my wrist would be a surefire way for me to be stopped by the TSA at the airport.

MOM: Why does it have to be Arabic writing? Why not a heart or a flower?

DAD: But make sure it's a distinctive heart or flower or they will think it's a buried message.

ME: Because hearts and flowers are generic and don't mean anything to me. I want one of Dad's quotes in calligraphy.

DAD: I can write something and put it on a glass plate. Remember how your brother made your mother one with her name on it for Mother's Day last year?

---

2 My hope was that they would buy a porch swing and sit and watch the neighbors go by, or maybe travel in an RV across the United States.

ME: Yes, it was lovely. But I don't want it on a plate. I want something I can carry around.

DAD: Why don't I inscribe it on a bracelet that you can wear on your left wrist and look at whenever you want?

ME: That would be lovely, Dad.

DAD: Okay, great. I will tell your Aunt Reema to pick a nice gold bracelet from Dubai.

ME: But I'm also getting a tattoo on my wrist.

DAD: *(peers at me over his glasses)* You're still on this subject?

ME: It's the *only* subject. You guys keep pushing the bracelet. Anyway, what's the difference between having Arabic on a bracelet or on my bare wrist? It's still Arabic writing, which, according to you guys, can be misconstrued as terrorist talk.

MOM: *(in Arabic)* Ayser, be practical. Terrorists wouldn't put their manifesto on jewelry. People could steal it.

ME: *(Unable to argue with that Mom logic)* Oh . . .

MOM: Also, no terrorist would put anything secret on a shiny gold bracelet. It's too obvious.

ME: What if it's a locket that you can't see unless you open it up?

DAD: Stop being difficult.

ME: I'm just saying, you want to put Arabic writing on a metal object that likely would set off the X-ray machine, instead of on my wrist, which doesn't set off the machine and which I can hide.

MOM: Ayser, do you think we are peasants? We'll get you an twenty-four-karat bracelet; there's no higher gold material. And gold doesn't set off the alarms.

ME: You didn't answer why TSA would be so interested in what I have on my wrist.

MOM: They might consider it a national security risk.

ME: What?

DAD: We hear stories.

ME: You guys have to stop watching Al-Jazeera.

MOM: It was BBC actually. They stopped a woman who had pages of Al-Qaeda manifestos in her suitcase. When they searched her, they also found a tattoo on her inside thigh with suspicious instructions.

ME: *(deep inhale)* Mom . . . what does that have to do with me?

MOM: You're the one who wants a tattoo. I'm telling you a story that happened to someone like you.

ME: *(trying hard not to hyperventilate)* She was nothing like me! Sounds like she was a legitimate threat with those written manifestos.

MOM: What if they think you are like her when they see Arabic writing on your hand? TSA officials are trained to Taser you first and ask questions later.

ME: I don't think that's true.

MOM: *(getting an idea)* Unless you wear a Band-Aid on your wrist! If they ask you to remove it, you can tell them you can't because you have an infection.

DAD: No, then they will quarantine her because of the health risk. No, it's too risky. You can't get a tattoo.

I'd had enough.

ME: Guys, this is crazy! I'm a grown adult in her forties! I can make my own decisions, and I'm doing this! I'm sorry if you don't like it!

They both look at me in momentary stunned silence.

And that's how I came to own this gold beauty, pictured below.

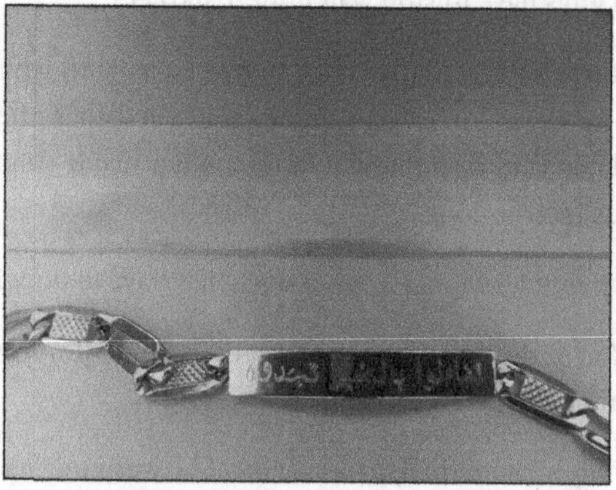

Arabic Inscription that translates to "Hope for Good, and You Shall Find It."

46
The (First) Penultimate Chapter (A Rebel without Approval)

I wanted this chapter, the second to last chapter, to be named literally. But to be honest, this is technically *not* the penultimate chapter if you count the very last chapter, an acknowledgments section where I thank everyone who has helped me to get to this point in my life. When I think about how far I've come, I think about the people I could not have done without. Essentially, I think about my parents and how, as a grown woman, my opinions, hopes, and dreams for them continue to evolve.

I previously said I hoped they would become more mellow with age—which didn't happen. They are an Old World couple from the old country, and I can't fault them for holding onto (what I consider are) outdated beliefs. My parents had made enough sacrifices bringing my siblings to this country and giving us a better life than we could have ever had in Iraq. Compassionately, they fought their own cross-cultural battles in the way they chose to bring us up, remaining true to their traditions while also providing us with a good American childhood. Now that I was grown up, it was up to me to do my part—finding myself and where I stood in the mix of it all.

Once again, Karen was the catalyst to a self-revelation. After *another* argument. This time it was because I'd told her I wanted less of her opinion and more of her support as a friend. She got defensive and said she was trying to save me from making the mistakes she'd made. That sounded strangely like something my mother would say. Then Karen asked me why I kept coming to her for advice when I always ultimately decided to do whatever I wanted anyway. Did I just want a sounding board?

A sounding board!? That really pissed me off. After all those years of friendship?

I'd like to say I was so upset I knocked off the glasses and dishes from the table with a sweep of my arm, sending them crashing to the floor, and stomped angrily into the street. But that's actually a scene from the movie *The Silver Linings Playbook*. Instead, I didn't say anything. We changed the subject and finished dinner like civilized humans. The next several days, I fell quiet. I called in sick and shut myself away for a long three-day weekend, talking to no one,[1] like one of those women in the villages during their "moon time." I went into my tent and stayed there (except for one grocery store run to buy lemons for my bourbon cocktails—because self-imposed isolations are better with bourbon cocktails).

I spent that weekend pacing around my apartment, alternating between organizing my shoe closet and sipping on homemade bourbon cocktails, angrily berating myself for constantly attracting people who were opinionated, overbearing assholes.

Was I seeking my mother in all of my relationships?

. . . Had I become *my own* fascist regime?!

I'd hit the nail on the head. I had escaped Iraq for America, only to live within a fascist household of rules and restrictions; and when I was finally old enough to throw off that oppressive regime, I'd escaped to LA and inherited a whole new one, a bubble that consisted not only of

---

1 Except my mother, who worries if we don't talk every day.

the friends I'd chosen, but also of the pressures I'd put on myself. This realization took me by such surprise that I reacted by throwing my red suede heel across the room.[2]

The more I thought about it, the more it made sense. I'd grown up seeking Mom's approval. Once I stopped needing approval from her, I created a surrogate from which to seek approval—by surrounding myself with many well-intentioned but opinionated friends. Then, in the orbit of my own minidictatorship, I'd felt the need to bring them around to my way of thinking and couldn't let it go when they disagreed. Never mind that I knew, logically, that everyone has different perspectives of the world. I did it anyway. Every single time. I couldn't stop myself. And each time, I did my own thing in the end. If that was the case, why did I still put myself through these machinations? Why was I so damn stubborn?

I, Ayser Salman, was a grownass woman who wanted to do her own thing—*but who also wanted everyone to accept her.* A rebel who needed approval. I had appointed myself as both dictator and oppressed people. The famous game changers in history I used to idolize—Isadora Duncan, Frida Kahlo, and other rebel spirits—would turn over in their graves if they saw me now.

And as quickly as that realization emerged, my need for acceptance vanished instantly. It felt like a huge weight had been lifted off my shoulders. And like many epiphanies, once you have them, you can't fathom going back to your old ways. I was ready to forge ahead, confidently and without hesitation.

And so, to Karen, I want to apologize for my enabling behavior. Thank you for bringing it to my attention and helping me topple my own regime. I look forward to the better days of rebuilding and reconstructing . . . reinstating a new Ayser . . .

---

2 And thus I became the second Iraqi to throw a shoe out of anger—at least my shoe wasn't aimed at the president of the United States.

47
Moving Over to the Right End of the Table

My realization was like a light switch going on. All at once, I relaxed and stopped working so hard. I began to let things go. I stopped analyzing the littlest things in search of some hidden meaning. I began to take life as it was. Things clicked into place. My interactions with my family got easier and less dramatic. My work relationships improved. I stopped taking things so personally and stopped trying to prove something. As I looked around, I realized I was happy where I was. It certainly wasn't where I'd expected to be when I envisioned my adult life as a younger woman, but that's beside the point. I'm *here* now. It's taken me a lifetime and tons of experiences with friends, family, journal entries, and ill-advised romantic dalliances to realize that I'm right where I should be. My journey in life has brought me here.

The following event is incidental—and not central—to my self-awakening. But I feel I owe you the story. As often happens when you're just happily doing your thing without pressure or expectation, I met someone.

Actually, I reconnected with him.

You might remember Michael from my LMU crew. I've always been fond of him as a human being—his laid-back vibe; his lanky, lean look. He'd never been anything more than a friend back in film school when I was with Tony, and after graduation Michael got married and had a kid.

Recently, we connected and met for dinner to catch up. He was no longer married. We rekindled a spark, something that might have always been there all along. For the first time in a long time, things felt right. No games. No pretenses. It felt real.

During that dinner, I'd asked Michael what he would tell his twenty-three-year-old self if he could go back in time. Michael thought for a moment and said, "Probably to not have been so timid—and to have asked you out."

That got me thinking. What would I say to my twenty-three-year-old self? Heck, what would I say to my twelve-year-old self? Or the six-year-old who stood there at St. John's Court in Columbus, Ohio, waiting for the yellow school bus to take her to an alien place for the first time where she couldn't communicate with anyone?

I would tell her it would all work out. And to relax and have more fun along the way.

I'd say, "Sometimes you're at the wrong end of the table, and sometimes you're in the middle of the action. But it's never permanent. We all wind up at the wrong end at some point in our lives." I would also tell her not to discount her time spent at the wrong end of the table, because sometimes you have to spend time at the *wrong* end in order to appreciate being at the *right* end. And in my case, perhaps you'd realize that, sometimes, you were at the right end all along—either it took everyone else this long to realize they needed to be on your side, or no one showed up but you're too busy eating the truffle fries and jalapeño mac-n-cheese to care. You were right where you needed to be.

I would tell Past Ayser to remember that awkward teenager who, even after freezing on stage in front of a packed auditorium and forgetting the lyrics, didn't run away but silently reset herself and jumped in on the second verse of the Beatles' "Let it Be," always believing that "there will be an answer." I would tell Past Ayser that, buried in the noise of insecurities, other people's opinions, and life in general, she had a fountain of inner strength.

I'm not sure why Michael has come back into my life. And for the first time, I'm not letting my neurotic Iraqi immigrant brain try to control the outcome or analyze our every encounter for some deeper meaning. I'm content to just let it be and enjoy the moment.

. . . *Except* for a brief moment the other day when I flipped over to the Dark Side and was engulfed by thoughts.[1]

Was I lying to myself? What if nostalgia and my tendency to seek out symmetry in life was causing me to put on those same rose-colored glasses? Was I still buying into a happily-ever-after rom-com finale? Or what if I had become a hardened, jaded, bitter self-sabotager from all my past dating encounters? What if I ended up hating him and ruined the past memories of our friendship?

What if?

Well, what if *not* . . . ?

Earlier tonight, I stood in the outdoor quad of the Walt Disney Concert Hall, where I was meeting Michael for an orchestra performance. I watched as he emerged from the elevator. Before he saw me, he raked his hand through his hair in a gesture of part-confidence, part-uncertainty, and I was struck by how sexy that was. Had he really become cuter over the years? Or was he more attractive simply because I saw him as a human who was comfortable in his own skin after he'd sloughed off years of built-up baggage?

Michael told me he often felt like he was at the wrong end of the table, too. Whether an Iraq-born, Kentucky-raised Muslim Arab woman or a half-Mexican man from Northern California or someone else, I've realized that we're all unified in our differences. We've all felt like an outsider at some point or other, and we have always worked to fit in. As I mulled this over, I thought, *This is what it feels to be at the right end of the table.*

I've probably always known this deep down, but I've had to travel a lifetime to let it emerge.

---

1 Old habits die hard.

Epilogue

It Takes a Village

How did I get here? I owe it to a multitude of people, in both personal and professional spheres of my life. This chapter is a shout-out to everyone who mentored me, was in my corner, and helped me get this book out into the world.

Beginning with Lowell Mate. This book is your doing, sir. The minute we sat down to dinner at Ca' Del Sol restaurant a few Decembers ago and you asked, "Ever thought of putting your vignettes into a book of essays?" I had, but it was way down on my list, so I reprioritized. I'm pretty sure my life changed at that moment. Thank you also for connecting me with Amy Schiffman.

Amy, I remember sitting in your office having just begun writing the book, and you declaring that this would be the year. Literally an hour later, you found me my book agent. Thank you!

To said book agent, Murray Weiss at Catalyst, who has been a tireless advocate not just of this book, but of me in general: you are a genius, a gentleman, and a true mensch. Side note, my sister loves your name and gets a kick out of saying it often . . .

To my brilliant editor at Skyhorse Publishing, Kim Lim: you took my words and made them better than I could have imagined. It's been a dream collaborating with you. I never knew this part of the process would be so fun!

And to the other individuals I'm grateful to consider part of my team:

To Ann-Marie Nieves, who might be the reason you're reading this book right now. Jamie Mandelbaum: you've been with me since I was a teeny fish. Thanks for sticking with me and introducing me to the newest member of my team, Shadi Bakhtiari, who is awesome beyond words. And to Jeff Portnoy, thank you for believing in me. You are a tireless rock star, and I look forward to our future creative journey together.

To Reza Aslan for inspiring me by being a "relaxed and hip" Muslim back in a time when there were no such role models out there: thank you for your grace and generosity to me through the process of writing this book. And especially for connecting me with Safa Samiezadé-Yazd, who has become a great friend.

To Safa, your own story inspires me so much, and I can't wait to see it in book form. You've helped me come out of my shell and "own my Islam," and you've emphasized that no one can tell me how to practice my faith, which is why it's called *faith*.

To my other Muslim sisters who helped pave my way and supported me, telling me to write whatever I want—and if it offends people then all the better, since that gets people talking, and dialogue is always good: Edina Lekovic, Marium Mohiuddin, Sue Obeidi. You are my heroes!

To Lydia Wahlke, who is the kind of friend who you know always has your back even when you don't speak for years. Thank you for your support throughout the writing of this book and beyond, especially that time you were sick with a hundred-degree fever.

To Lance Still for putting me in touch with Judy McGuire, who helped me navigate the choppy waters of first-time publishing, tirelessly answering my endless questions and putting me in touch with the awesome Binders community of writers on Facebook.

To Debra Rogers for also helping me navigate these waters and who's number one in the "I got your back, babe" category.

To Jude Roth, my friend for over a decade and sister from another mister who's read and heard the stories in this book so many times. You pushed me to keep going when time and time again I faced rejection or crisis of faith. You have figuratively saved my life on so many occasions during our friendship—though I would not doubt that I could add the word *literally* in there should it one day come to that.

To Mike Daley, the perennial Will to my Grace. You are the best Irish Catholic brother I could ever ask for—and yes, fine, at times you can be a real "ONE."

To my tribe who's had my back for years: Nancy Cox, Nicole DeMasi, Suzanne Farmer, Matt Hamill, Lisa Kors, Camile O'Briant, Michelle Friedman, Chris Kanchananon, Shea Sinclair, and Gavyn Michaels—all of whom I'd happily move to a desert island with.

To the magical fairies in my life: Sara Jane Colgin, Femi Corazon, Julie DeSavia, Karen Evans, Emily Barclay Ford, Lisa Gould (Gouldie), Hansy, Corina Maritescu, Julie Harris Walker, and Cindy Yantis. You have performed miracles for my soul so many times just by being your lovely selves. And especially Lisa Davidson, who has an amazing talent for being down-to-earth and not of this world, all at the same time.

To Andrea Quinn for not only teaching me to receive and then let go, but also for your support over the past decade. I'm lucky to call you my friend—and "Fairy Godmother" seems more fitting than *mentor.*

To my mentors and teachers: Scoobie Ryan, Raymond Betts, Mrs. Roser (my third grade teacher), Marilyn Beker, and mostly Jeffrey Davis for teaching me that, when writing, always "come from character" and write from the inside out. I hope I've done you proud.

To my gals from Riyadh: Nuha Amara, Shahira Ahmed, Kindah Atassi, Dima Fares, Amina Khan, Rehana Khan, Rasha Mukhtar, Rula Omar, Sara Rahman, Howayda Sharabash, and Naushin Zulqarnain—I miss you girls and those surreal, formative years.

To everyone who opened the doors that led me to write this book: Karyn Benkendorfer, Deb Calla, Jen Grisanti, Alan Kirschenbaum (RIP), Charles Howard, Cathy Ladman, George Sunga, Ron Taylor, and Cathleen Young.

To Pilar Alesandra, who's been a champion from day one, in spite of the fact that I tanked her ladies' writing group with the "Great Ralph's Sanitary Napkin Debacle of '09" or that I later ruined both of her white couches by sitting down on an uncapped ink pen (not once, but twice). Thank you for smiling through both those incidents with your inherent grace and poise—and that lipstick! It never smears! And for continuing to be my friend despite these foibles.

To Lee Jessup, who began as my writing coach and very quickly became my friend. Like a champ, you effortlessly kept me disciplined even when I desperately wanted to meander or give up. For that, you're a true hero.

To the boys who inspired the chapters on men and dating: AW, GO, JF, JW, KT, MC, TM, and Theodore—thanks for the inspiration (and memories). Even if we're not in touch now, know that I think you're good guys (though I probably hated you at the time when things were bad). Except for Theodore—I never even got a chance to get close to you. I hope you're well.

To Francisco for giving me heart, John for unlocking its truth, Micah for freeing my soul, and Michael for giving it wings.

To the residents of Columbus, Ohio, I thank you in advance for being good-natured about the fact that I mentioned some less-than-stellar Columbus stories that colored my memories of early immigrant life in America. Thank you for understanding that it was only one lonely girl's subjective experience and not at all indicative of any objective reality.

To Zaid, for being my conscience and rational brain in times when my family got to be too much. Also for still speaking to me even though I tried to decapitate you with a *The Jungle Book* record when we were kids.

To Lameace, for giving me the opportunity to make you laugh and whose distinctive giggle is therapy for anything that ails me.

To Jehayer Al-Johar for your big, open heart and believing in me always.

For my late maternal grandmother, Sadiqa, who, when I was born, declared that I would be someone to be reckoned with.

To my parents, not just for giving me these delicious stories, but for imbuing me with the strength of character to find humor in life.

To Dad, who gave me my love of books and thirst for knowledge and taught me the importance of having a childlike wonder no matter how old you are, because: "Many things are possible," and "Anything is possible."

And above all, to Mom, who always knew I could and would. Everything I am is because of you.

About The Author

Ayser Salman was born in Iraq back before it became a curiosity and moved to the United States when she was a toddler. She spent much of her childhood in the 1970s trying to fit in among her blond-haired, blue-eyed counterparts and telling everyone to call her Lisa because it was "just easier that way."

After shunning her parents' dream of her becoming a doctor in favor of journalism school, Ayser worked as a news producer in Kentucky before moving to Los Angeles, where she is an award-winning producer and editor for promos and original content for clients such as Miramax Films, Disney, Universal Pictures, and FX. Ayser also teaches writing at LMU School of Film and Television. In her free time, she writes and speaks about her experience of being the "Other" in America.

Ayser lives in Los Angeles, where you'll probably find her skating on the beach (with old-school roller skates, thankyouverymuch).

You can find her on:
Instagram: @aysersalman
Twitter: @aysersalman
Facebook: www.facebook.com/aysersalman
Website: www.aysersalman.com